PASTA

PASTA

Italian, Asian, American . . . and More

Food&Wine
BOOKS

American Express Publishing Corporation
New York

Editorial Director: Judith Hill
Assistant Editors: Jackie Bobrow and Susan Lantzius
Wine Specialist: Richard A. Marmet
Designer: Nina Scerbo
Photographer: Dennis Gottlieb
Food Stylist: Deborah Mintcheff
Prop Stylist: Randi Barritt
Illustrator: Karen Scerbo

Cover Photo: Pappardelle with Veal and Mushroom Ragù, page 223

AMERICAN EXPRESS PUBLISHING CORPORATION
©1994 American Express Publishing Corporation

Published by American Express Publishing Corporation
1120 Avenue of the Americas, New York, New York 10036

Library of Congress Catalog Card Number: 94-77976

ISBN 0-916103-23-4

Manufactured in the United States of America

CONTENTS

FOREWORD

Pasta is at the top of almost any cook's list of foods that please everyone. I have never met a child who didn't love pasta, especially when it was called macaroni, nor a man who didn't thank me for preparing it even when it *was* macaroni. Hence this book, a collection of pasta recipes gathered from around the world. Each recipe is sure to become an instant favorite.

In addition to Italian classics like Spaghetti Carbonara and Lasagne Bolognese, we have pasta recipes for dishes that meld Italian technique with French ingredients, for noodle dishes from Southeast Asia plus a wonderfully eclectic collection gathered from American chefs. These great cooks have contributed inventive recipes that might shock a traditional Italian cook, but would surely please an innovative one.

We wish you all the pleasure that a plate of pasta brings.

MARY SIMONS
Editor in Chief
Food & Wine Magazine

A WORD ABOUT CHOOSING WINE

The wine suggestions in this book are exactly that: suggestions. None of them is offered as the one and only right choice—if any such thing exists. They are intended to provide you with an idea or two that will narrow the field and give you a place to start.

Choosing a wine to drink with a particular dish should be fun. The key to enjoying food and wine matching is simply an open mind. Don't hesitate to experiment with wines you've never tried before or with combinations that are new to you.

While time-honored matches and principles are reflected in the suggestions here, particularly for the regional Italian recipes, many of the dishes are from areas with no real wine tradition or are a mix of traditional cuisines. These recipes should be among the most exciting to pair with wine, since they often allow for possibilities that are a bit more off the beaten track than those that go well with classic recipes.

Resist the temptation to open that same favorite wine for every dish in this book. Instead, use the suggestions, even if that means buying a bottle you've never tried before. See if you like the way the wine tastes. Think about whether and how the food and wine complement each other, or perhaps how they battle for control of your palate. From the general categories of wine suggested, try different producers, vintages and vineyard areas to see the considerable differences these factors make. Give some thought to whether one or another quality enhances or detracts from a dish.

If you're willing to experiment, rather than just buy a particular vintage from a specific producer because someone told you to do so, you'll learn a lot about wine and about the interplay of food and wine. You'll also enjoy pairing a wine with a recipe as much as you do preparing the dish itself.

RICHARD A. MARMET

MAKING GREAT PASTA AND OTHER BASICS

Buckwheat
Pasta

Whole-
Wheat Pasta

Fresh Pasta

Herb Pasta

Tomato
Pasta

Saffron
Pasta

Spinach
Pasta

Egg Pasta

Cracked-Pepper
Pasta

Egg Pasta Dough

We think this is the easiest possible pasta dough—both to put together and to roll out. It's quite soft, hence the ease in rolling by hand, but is nevertheless authentically chewy when cooked, not at all flabby like so many store-bought fresh pastas. If you use a pasta machine to roll the dough, it should be a little drier so that it moves smoothly through the rollers. An additional two tablespoons of flour should do the trick. Though we give exact quantities in each of our pasta-dough recipes, you may find you need to adjust the amount of flour or egg from one day to the next. Every egg is a little different, and the amount of moisture in your flour can vary depending on the brand you use, where it's stored both in the market and your home, and even on the weather. You'll find suggestions in this recipe to help you get the consistency just right every time. You can make this dough in the food processor in two minutes. Of course, if you don't have a processor, or are simply a purist, the dough can be made by hand. It's equally good either way.

3-EGG QUANTITY
(equivalent to about ¾ pound dry pasta)

1¾ cups plus 2 tablespoons unbleached all-purpose flour
3 extra-large eggs

2-EGG QUANTITY
(equivalent to about ½ pound dry pasta)

1¼ cups unbleached all-purpose flour
2 extra-large eggs

WITH A FOOD PROCESSOR

1. Put the flour and the eggs in the food processor. If you'll be rolling the dough by machine, use 2 cups of flour. Process until the dough forms a ball, about 45 seconds. If the dough comes together in a sticky mass in just a few seconds, it is too moist. Pull the dough into several pieces, sprinkle with about two tablespoons flour and process for another 30 seconds. If the pasta forms large crumbs and does not come together in a mass, press some of the crumbs together. If they stick, then the dough is the right consistency. If the crumbs are small and dry, we like to add a few teaspoons beaten egg, but you can also use water. Process again for about 30 seconds.

2. Transfer the dough to a work surface and knead about 5 seconds. If rolling the dough by hand, dust with flour, wrap in plastic wrap and let it rest at least 30 minutes so that the gluten will relax and the pasta will be easier to roll. If using a pasta machine, you can roll the dough out at once. ➤

11

By Hand

1. Put the flour in a large bowl and make an indentation in the center. Beat the eggs to combine them and pour them into the indentation.

2. With a fork, gradually pull the flour into the egg mixture. You can also use your fingers to do this. When the dough is a rough mass, transfer it to a floured work surface. Knead the dough, sprinkling with more flour if the dough is sticky. Work the dough until it forms a smooth and elastic ball, about 10 minutes. If rolling the dough by hand, dust with flour, wrap in plastic wrap and let it rest about 30 minutes. If using a pasta machine, you can use the dough immediately.

Variations

Though water or another ingredient takes the place of one of the eggs in some of these variations, they are all equivalent to the three-egg and two-egg quantities in the Egg Pasta Dough recipe.

CRACKED-PEPPER PASTA DOUGH

3-EGG QUANTITY
1¾ cups plus 2 tablespoons unbleached all-purpose flour
1½ teaspoons black peppercorns, crushed and added to the flour
3 extra-large eggs

2-EGG QUANTITY
1¼ cups unbleached all-purpose flour
1 teaspoon black peppercorns, crushed and added to the flour
2 extra-large eggs

HERB PASTA DOUGH

3-EGG QUANTITY
1¾ cups plus 2 tablespoons unbleached all-purpose flour
3 tablespoons chopped mixed fresh herbs (such as tarragon, chives, rosemary, thyme, parsley or chervil), added to the flour
3 extra-large eggs

2-EGG QUANTITY
1¼ cups unbleached all-purpose flour
2 tablespoons chopped mixed fresh herbs (such as tarragon, chives, rosemary, thyme, parsley or chervil), added to the flour
2 extra-large eggs

SAFFRON PASTA DOUGH

3-EGG QUANTITY EQUIVALENT

- 1¾ cups plus 2 tablespoons unbleached all-purpose flour
- 2 extra-large eggs
- 3 tablespoons warm water
- ¼ teaspoon saffron threads, crumbled, stirred into the water and added along with the eggs

2-EGG QUANTITY EQUIVALENT

- 1¼ cups unbleached all-purpose flour
- ⅓ cup beaten eggs, about 1¼ extra-large eggs
- 2 tablespoons warm water
- 1 large pinch saffron threads, crumbled, stirred into the water and added along with the eggs

SPINACH PASTA DOUGH

3-EGG QUANTITY EQUIVALENT

- 1¾ cups plus 2 tablespoons unbleached all-purpose flour
- 2 extra-large eggs
- 3 tablespoons chopped frozen spinach, squeezed dry and added along with the eggs

2-EGG QUANTITY EQUIVALENT

- 1¼ cups unbleached all-purpose flour
- ⅓ cup beaten eggs, about 1¼ extra-large eggs
- 2 tablespoons chopped frozen spinach, squeezed dry and added along with the eggs

TOMATO PASTA DOUGH

3-EGG QUANTITY EQUIVALENT

- 1¾ cups plus 2 tablespoons unbleached all-purpose flour
- 2 extra-large eggs
- ¼ cup tomato paste, added along with the eggs

2-EGG QUANTITY EQUIVALENT

- 1¼ cups unbleached all-purpose flour
- ⅓ cup beaten eggs, about 1¼ extra-large eggs
- 2½ tablespoons tomato paste, added along with the eggs

BUCKWHEAT PASTA DOUGH

3-EGG QUANTITY
1½ cups unbleached all-purpose flour
6   tablespoons buckwheat flour, added to the all-purpose flour
3   extra-large eggs

2-EGG QUANTITY
1   cup unbleached all-purpose flour
¼   cup buckwheat flour, added to the all-purpose flour
2   extra-large eggs

WHOLE-WHEAT PASTA DOUGH

3-EGG QUANTITY
1   cup plus 2 tablespoons whole-wheat flour
¾   cup unbleached all-purpose flour, added to the whole-wheat flour
3   extra-large eggs

2-EGG QUANTITY
¾   cup whole-wheat flour
½   cup unbleached all-purpose flour, added to the whole-wheat flour
2   extra-large eggs

DON'T RINSE IT

Contrary to popular belief, you usually should not rinse cooked pasta to prevent it from sticking together. The starch that makes the pasta stick to itself also helps the sauce stick to the pasta. If you're going to toss the pasta with the sauce immediately, sticking shouldn't be a problem. Two exceptions: We do suggest you rinse the wide pasta, such as lasagne noodles, used in many of our baked dishes. Otherwise, you're likely to have a hard time separating the pieces without tearing them. Making pasta salads is another time when rinsing is in order. The thin coating of starch on cooked pasta has an unpleasant, sticky texture when cold.

Rolling, Cutting and Cooking Pasta

ROLLING PASTA DOUGH

ROLLING PASTA BY HAND

A long, relatively narrow rolling pin is the only special equipment required. When you're learning, it's easier to roll a small piece of dough. Cut the dough in half and wrap one piece in plastic. If you're adept at rolling pasta, you may want to try working with the entire piece at once. However, when you're making stuffed pasta, you'll always be better off with a smaller piece of dough so that it remains moist enough to stick together and seal in the filling. The classic Italian method of stretching the dough in addition to rolling gives a better texture than just flattening the dough. Be assured that once you get used to the process it's much faster and easier than reading about it.

1. Lightly dust the work surface with flour. Roll the dough with a back and forth motion, giving it a quarter turn every few rolls. When the dough is a flat disk, about ¼ inch thick, it is ready for its first stretching.

2. Wrap the top quarter of the dough over the rolling pin and hold securely with one hand. With the other hand hold the bottom of the dough in place as you stretch the dough away from you.

Give the dough a quarter turn and repeat this stretching motion 7 more times.

3. Now put the pin in the middle of the round and roll away from you. Repeat several times. Give the dough a quarter turn, roll and continue turning and rolling until the sheet is ⅛ to 1/16 inch thick.

4. For the second stretching, start with the far edge and roll ⅓ of the dough around the rolling pin. Put your

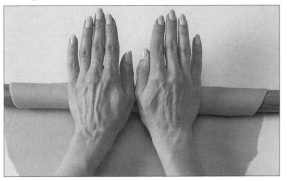

palms on top of the dough so that your thumbs are touching and your fingers are extended and pointing slightly toward the ceiling. With your palms, press down on the dough as you slide your hands apart along the top of the pin so that the dough stretches outward. Then move your hands back to the center. At the same time as you stretch the dough sideways, roll the pin toward you bit by bit. The motion is really more jiggling than rolling. Keep sliding and rolling until the dough is completely rolled around the pin.

5. Now unroll the dough and give it a quarter turn. Wind a third of the dough back onto the pin and repeat the sliding and rolling motion. Continue until the dough is less than $\frac{1}{16}$ inch thick.

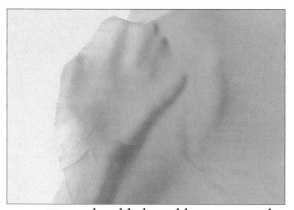

6. You should be able to see the shape of your hand clearly through the dough. Work quickly so that the dough doesn't become too dry. If making filled pasta, use the dough while still moist. If cutting the dough into noodles, let it dry about 10 minutes on one side. Flip the dough and let it dry about 10 minutes longer. When the dough is ready to cut, it should look somewhat leathery but should not be so dry that it cracks.

ROLLING PASTA WITH A MACHINE
The stainless-steel pasta machine—with two rollers, notches that regulate their distance, and a crank—is a convenient alternative to hand rolling.

1. Cut a 3-egg quantity of pasta dough into 3 pieces or a 2-egg quantity into 2 and wrap what you're not working with in plastic. Set the rollers of the pasta machine on the widest notch. Flatten a piece of dough with your hands and pass it through the rollers of the pasta machine. Fold the dough in thirds, press it together and dust lightly with flour. Feed one of the open ends of dough through the machine. Repeat the whole process about 8 times.

2. Move the setting of the pasta machine to the next notch. This time, don't fold the dough. Dust with flour on one side and roll it through. Continue to flatten the pasta, moving the rollers one notch closer each time. When the rollers are on the thinnest setting, dust the dough with flour on both sides and then pass it through the machine.

3. If making filled pasta, use the dough at once while it is still moist. If cutting the dough into noodles, let it dry about 10 minutes on one side. Flip the dough and let it dry about 10 minutes longer. When the dough is ready to cut, it should look somewhat leathery but not be so dry that it cracks.

CUTTING ROLLED PASTA

No matter which way you choose to roll the pasta dough, we suggest cutting the noodles by hand rather than with a pasta machine. Cutting by machine saves very little work and seems to intensify the slickness that makes machine-rolled pasta less desirable than hand-rolled.

FETTUCCINE OR TAGLIATELLE

1. Loosely roll the pasta into a flattened cylinder about 2 inches wide.

2. With a large knife, cut the rolled sheet crosswise into ¼-inch-wide strips. Unravel the strips and put on a baking sheet dusted with flour.

PAPPARDELLE

1. Loosely roll the dough into a flattened cylinder about 2 inches wide.

2. With a large knife, cut the rolled sheet crosswise into ¾-inch-wide strips. Unravel the strips and put on a baking sheet dusted with flour. If you want to use a fluted pastry wheel, cut the sheet flat, not rolled, or it will stick together.

LASAGNE

1. With a chef's knife, cut the pasta into 4-by-8-inch rectangles.

2. Put them on a baking sheet dusted with flour.

COOKING PASTA

A large pot of boiling water and a handful of salt are all you need to cook pasta. For a ¾-pound batch of pasta use about 3 quarts of water and 1½ tablespoons of salt. Though this may seem like a lot of salt, it's just enough to give the water a slightly salty flavor. Taste the water; if it doesn't taste like anything, neither will your cooked pasta.

Virtually every batch of fresh pasta dough and every brand of dry pasta will cook a little differently. We suggest pasta cooking times in all our recipes, but they're just guidelines. It's up to you to determine when the pasta is cooked, and tasting is really the only way to know for sure. When the pasta has boiled almost as long as we suggest, take a piece out of the pot and bite into it. It should be slightly chewy but shouldn't have an opaque, uncooked center.

THE PASTA POSSIBILITIES

◆ HOMEMADE HAND-ROLLED: The texture of hand-rolled pasta is superior to that of pasta rolled in the machine. Hand-rolled is slightly bumpy rather than perfectly smooth, and so sauces cling to it instead of slipping off. The little bit of roughness also feels more pleasant on the tongue than the slickness of machine-rolled.

◆ HOMEMADE MACHINE-ROLLED, HAND-CUT: Hands down, hand-rolled pasta is the best, but machine-rolled, hand-cut is a close second. The surface is not flattened to as slippery a slickness as you'll find in pasta that's not only rolled but also cut with the machine (see next entry).

◆ HOMEMADE MACHINE-ROLLED AND MACHINE-CUT: We prefer a good brand of dry pasta to that rolled and cut by machine. Entirely machine-made noodles lack the tiny bumps and indentations of hand-rolled and therefore have a slippery quality, and the sauce slides right off the pasta onto the plate.

◆ HOMEMADE MACHINE-EXTRUDED: We do not recommend the home extrusion machines. The dough is kneaded neither uniformly nor enough. Thus the texture of the pasta within a single batch is inconsistent and flabby.

◆ STORE-BOUGHT FRESH: Some specialty shops sell their own homemade fresh egg pasta, and it can be excellent. The pasta sold in the refrigerated section of most supermarkets isn't worth the money. The noodles have neither good surface texture nor enough body. Buy a dry pasta instead.

◆ FACTORY-MADE DRY EXTRUDED PASTA: All of the round and shaped pastas, such as spaghetti and macaroni, are best left to factory production. Made without eggs, these extruded pastas are simply semolina flour and water.

◆ FACTORY-MADE DRY EGG PASTA: Flat egg pasta in various widths from angel hair to pappardelle is usually produced with semolina, as is extruded pasta. While not so exceptional as hand-made, dry egg pasta is very good indeed and is what most of us mortals use for everyday meals. Do look for the brands that include egg rather than just flour and water. Believe it or not, some companies make egg pasta without egg.

Crespelle

An oddity among pastas, this batter version made in a frying pan is well worth knowing on several counts. It's quick and easy, and you don't have to roll it out or cut it. Even more important, it's delectably rich, light and tender. Since our recipes call for twelve crespelle, the amount below allows for a couple of mistakes. The crespelle can be cooked in advance and stored in the refrigerator for several days or the freezer for a month. Allow to defrost completely before pulling the crespelle apart.

MAKES ABOUT 14 CRESPELLE

¾ cup unbleached all-purpose flour
½ teaspoon salt
3 eggs
1½ cups milk
3 tablespoons olive oil, plus more for cooking

1. Put the flour, salt, eggs, milk and oil in a blender or food processor and whir until smooth. Pour the batter into a bowl. Cover and let rest 30 minutes.

2. Heat a 6- or 7-inch frying pan over moderately high heat. Brush the pan lightly with oil. Ladle in about 3 ta-

blespoons of the batter. Tilt and swirl to coat the bottom of the pan completely,

working quickly before the batter sets.

3. Cook until the batter stiffens and just begins to brown around the edge, about 30 seconds. Loosen the crespelle from the pan by running a knife or

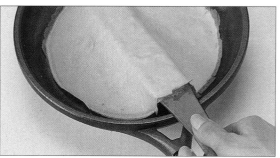

metal spatula around the edge. With a spatula or your fingers, flip the crespelle. Cook about 5 seconds longer.

4. Remove and repeat with the remaining batter, adding more oil only if necessary. Stack the finished crespelle.

Dried Pasta

Large Shells

Cavatappi
(Corkscrews)

Elbow
Macaroni

Penne

Fusilli
(Rotini)

Angel
Hair

Vermicelli

Spaghetti

Spaghettini

Perciatelli
(Bucatini)

Linguine

Orzo

Orecchiette

Ziti

Fettuccine

Fettuccine

Ditali

Wagon Wheels
(Rotelle)

Pappardelle

Penne Rigate

Stelline

Bow Ties

Rigatoni

Pastina
(Acini di Pepe)

Medium
Shells

Egg Noodles

Tomato Sauces

BASIC ITALIAN TOMATO SAUCE

Chunky and flavorful, this is a good all-purpose sauce. For a smoother texture, puree it in a food processor or blender.

MAKES ABOUT 3 CUPS

2	tablespoons olive oil
1	onion, chopped
1	clove garlic, minced
3½	cups canned tomatoes with their juice (28-ounce can), chopped
¾	cup water
2	tablespoons tomato paste
1½	teaspoons salt
⅛	teaspoon fresh-ground black pepper
1	tablespoon chopped fresh basil

1. In a medium saucepan, heat the oil over moderately low heat. Add the onion and garlic and cook, stirring occasionally, until the onion is translucent, about 5 minutes.

2. Add the tomatoes and juice, water, tomato paste and salt and bring to a boil. Reduce the heat to low and simmer, partially covered, for 35 minutes.

3. Uncover, add the pepper and basil and continue simmering until thick, about 10 minutes longer.

VARIATION

Basic Italian Tomato Sauce with Pancetta: Add 2 ounces chopped pancetta to the pan with the onion and garlic.

FRESH VS. CANNED TOMATOES

Plump and sweet, good vine-ripened tomatoes are available in most parts of the country only from June through September. The pale specimens found in supermarkets the remaining eight months of the year bear little resemblance to the delectable summer fruit. Mealy and flavorless, hothouse tomatoes usually turn into mush during cooking. If you can't get good vine-ripened ones use canned tomatoes instead. For two pounds of fresh tomatoes substitute 3½ cups or a 28-ounce can of tomatoes in their juice, or vice versa.

CLASSIC AMERICAN-STYLE TOMATO SAUCE

Thick, robust and fragrant with thyme, oregano and bay, this sauce is de rigueur with spaghetti and meatballs and is also good on its own over spaghetti or in lasagne.

MAKES ABOUT 2½ CUPS

1	tablespoon olive oil
1	onion, chopped
2	cloves garlic, minced
2½	cups canned crushed tomatoes
¾	cup water
1	tablespoon tomato paste
1½	teaspoons sugar
¼	teaspoon dried thyme
½	teaspoon dried oregano
1	bay leaf
1¼	teaspoons salt
⅛	teaspoon fresh-ground black pepper

1. In a medium saucepan, heat the oil over moderately low heat. Add the onion and garlic and cook, stirring occasionally, until the onion is translucent, about 5 minutes.

2. Add the tomatoes, water, tomato paste, sugar, thyme, oregano, bay leaf and salt. Bring to a boil. Reduce the heat and simmer, partially covered, until thickened, for about 1 hour. Add the pepper.

CANNED TOMATOES: OUR FAVORITE BRAND

Imported canned tomatoes cost about twice as much as the average domestic brand. Are they worth it? Sometimes. Many imported brands are excellent. Others are watery and short on flavor. Our favorite brand of all is the domestic Muir Glen Organic Whole Peeled Tomatoes. They're packed in enamel-lined cans, which eliminate the metallic taste that tomatoes pick up so easily. The difference between sauces made with tomatoes from lined and unlined cans is astounding. We think the higher price is worth every penny. If you don't, a couple of good unlined-can brands to try are Progresso Italian-Style Peeled Tomatoes and Redpack Italian-Style Tomatoes. Find your own favorite by testing different possibilities. The better the flavor, the better your sauce will taste.

LIGHT TOMATO SAUCE

Smooth, mild and mellow with butter, this sauce is refined. It's especially appropriate when you want to avoid overpowering a subtly flavored dish.

MAKES ABOUT 2 CUPS

4   tablespoons butter
1   onion, chopped
3½   cups canned tomatoes with their
     juice (28-ounce can), chopped
1   cup water
1   teaspoon salt
¼   teaspoon fresh-ground black pepper

1. In a medium saucepan, melt 2 tablespoons of the butter over moderately low heat. Add the onion and cook, stirring occasionally, until translucent, about 5 minutes. Add the tomatoes with their juice, water and salt. Reduce the heat to low and simmer 1½ hours.

2. Puree the sauce in a food processor or blender. Return it to the pan and stir in the pepper and remaining 2 tablespoons butter.

ZESTY TOMATO SAUCE

Plenty of garlic and a shot of wine give this smooth sauce character. Serve it over plain pasta or in more complex dishes such as The Best Cheese Cannelloni, page 87.

MAKES ABOUT 2 CUPS

2   tablespoons olive oil
1   onion, chopped
2   cloves garlic, minced
½   cup dry white wine
3½   cups canned tomatoes with their
     juice (28-ounce can), chopped
1   teaspoon salt
¼   teaspoon fresh-ground black pepper

1. In a medium saucepan, heat the oil over moderate heat. Add the onion and cook, stirring occasionally, until golden, about 5 minutes. Stir in the garlic and cook 1 minute longer.

2. Add the white wine and simmer until almost evaporated. Add the tomatoes with their juice and the salt. Bring the sauce to a simmer and cook, partially covered, 1½ hours.

3. Add the pepper and puree the sauce in a food processor or blender.

FRESH TOMATO SAUCE

As simple as they come, this sauce is a highlight of the summer months. Toss with spaghettini and a few fresh herbs, sprinkle with Parmesan and you'll have a feast.

MAKES ABOUT 2 CUPS

⅓ cup olive oil
1½ pounds tomatoes, about 3, peeled, seeded and chopped (3 cups)
1 clove garlic, minced
1 teaspoon salt
¼ teaspoon fresh-ground black pepper

1. In a large frying pan, heat the oil over moderately high heat. Add the tomatoes, garlic and salt. Cook, uncovered, stirring occasionally, for 5 minutes. Add the pepper.

PASTA PORTIONS

Most of the pasta quantities in this book serve four as a main course. Figure each recipe will make enough for six if you're serving it as a first course. A few of the dishes are better suited for appetizers than main courses, such as the rich Lobster Semolina Ravioli with Tomato Basil Broth, page 43, and the Salmon and Cabbage Filled Buckwheat Agnolotti, page 68. In such cases we indicate that they're to be served as appetizers, and we have reduced the portion sizes accordingly.

DON'T DROWN YOUR PASTA

Italians complain that Americans serve pasta swimming for its life in sauce. The Italian way is to toss pasta with just enough sauce to coat it without leaving a puddle on the bottom of the plate. The idea is to enjoy the flavor and texture of the pasta as well as of the sauce. If you've taken the time to roll out your own fresh pasta, or if you've spent a little extra money on an imported brand of dry pasta, don't drown it in sauce.

Ragù alla Bolognese

Virtually every Italian who prepares this rich meat sauce boasts a different version. Pork is the meat of choice for many cooks, while others claim that the sauce should be made with beef, veal and even sausage. Everyone seems to agree, however, on the long, slow cooking. In Italy the sauce would be prepared with the Italian version of stock, an all-purpose broth made from meat and chicken. We find that chicken or beef stock works just as well. Use whatever you have on hand. Ragù alla Bolognese is used in lasagne or tossed with filled or plain pasta. This amount is enough for one three-egg quantity of fresh pasta, page 11, or three-quarters pound dry pasta. Be sure to top it with fresh-grated Parmigiano-Reggiano cheese.

MAKES 2½ CUPS

3   ounces pancetta or bacon, chopped
4   tablespoons butter
2   tablespoons olive oil
1   onion, minced
2   cloves garlic, minced
1   carrot, minced
1   rib celery, chopped
½   pound ground beef
½   pound ground pork
1½   cups dry white wine
1½   cups Chicken Stock, page 29, or beef stock or canned low-sodium broth
¾   teaspoon salt
2   tablespoons tomato paste
¼   teaspoon grated nutmeg
¼   teaspoon fresh-ground black pepper
½   cup milk

1. In a large saucepan, cook the pancetta over moderate heat until golden, about 5 minutes. Remove the pancetta and discard the fat.

2. Heat the butter and oil in the same pan over moderately low heat. Add the onion, garlic, carrot and celery to the pan and cook, stirring occasionally, until the vegetables have softened, about 10 minutes.

3. Add the pancetta, ground beef and pork. Cook, breaking up the meat, until browned, about 5 minutes.

4. Add the wine. Increase the heat to high and simmer until almost evaporated. Stir in the stock and salt and cook at a bare simmer, stirring occasionally, until almost all of the liquid has evaporated, about 2¼ hours. Stir the tomato paste, nutmeg, pepper and milk into the ragù and simmer 15 minutes longer.

Pesto alla Genovese

This popular fresh basil sauce comes from the northern Italian region of Liguria where the basil is said to be sweeter than that grown anywhere else. The best pesto in the world can be found in Genoa, the major Ligurian city. Traditionally the sauce is pounded in a mortar with a pestle. Make it by this time-honored method or the easy way—with a food processor. In either case, the ingredients are the same. This recipe makes enough pesto to dress one pound of pasta. If you don't want to use it all at once, you can store it in the refrigerator for about a week, or you can freeze it.

MAKES 1 CUP PESTO

2 cloves garlic, chopped
1½ cups packed fresh basil leaves
¾ teaspoon salt
½ cup olive oil
¼ cup pine nuts
½ cup grated Parmesan cheese
1 tablespoon butter, at room temperature

1. In a food processor, mince the garlic and the basil with the salt.

2. With the machine on, add the oil in a thin stream and continue processing until well blended. Add the pine nuts, Parmesan and butter and process until the nuts are chopped.

GARLIC POINTERS

◆ To peel a garlic clove, use a large knife. Put the flat of the blade over the garlic and smack the blade with the heel of your hand. The clove will crack, and the skin will loosen and come off easily.
◆ You may find that the center of a garlic clove is green. Many chefs take the time to remove this shoot because they feel it imparts a too pungent flavor to food. We think you can leave the cloves intact when cooking garlic. However, if you plan to eat the garlic raw, as in the Pesto alla Genovese on this page, take a minute to remove the little green sprout-to-be.
◆ Once it browns past golden, garlic has an unpleasant, bitter flavor that can ruin a dish. So take care and keep a close eye when cooking.

Thin Fresh
Chinese
Egg
Noodles

Dried Wheat Vermicelli

Medium
Fresh
Chinese Egg
Noodles

Fresh
Udon

Wide
Dried
Udon

Medium
Dried Rice
Noodles

Asian Pasta

Fine Dried
Rice Noodles
(Vermicelli or
Rice Sticks)

Thin
Dried
Udon

Cellophane
Noodles
(Bean
Threads)

Fresh Rice-
Noodle
Sheets
(Vermicelli
Sheets)

Wide Soba
(Japanese
Buckwheat
Noodles)

Thin Soba

Fresh Wheat
Noodles

Chicken Stock

Making chicken stock is a cinch. All you do is dump the ingredients in a pot and cook them for a long time. If you freeze carcasses and stray parts as they come your way until you have enough for a pot of stock, you don't even have to buy the major ingredient. Keep stock frozen in one-cup containers for a convenient supply.

MAKES 1 QUART

4	pounds chicken carcasses, backs, wings and/or necks and gizzards
1	large onion, halved
2	carrots, cut in thirds
2	ribs celery, cut in thirds
4	sprigs fresh parsley
1	bay leaf
½	teaspoon black peppercorns
1½	quarts cold water

1. In a large saucepan, combine all the ingredients. Bring to a boil over high heat. Reduce the heat and skim the foam that rises to the surface. Simmer, partially covered, for 2 hours.

2. Strain the stock, pressing the bones and vegetables with a spoon to extract all the liquid before throwing them away. Refrigerate for up to a week or freeze. Scrape off the fat before using.

VARIATION
Turkey Stock: Substitute 4 pounds turkey carcasses, backs, wings and/or necks and gizzards for the chicken.

CANNED CHICKEN BROTH

Homemade chicken stock is better than anything you can find in a can. If you don't have stock, though, canned broth will certainly do, especially if the quantity is small or the other ingredients are strong. We used unsalted stock to develop and test the recipes in this book, an especially important point when the flavor is concentrated by reducing the stock for a sauce, as in Gratinéed Potato Gnocchi in Sage Cream, page 143. Low-sodium broth is the closest substitute for unsalted stock. If you have only regular canned broth on hand, just use less salt in the recipe than we suggest.

Vegetable Stock

Here's a quick stock you can make with ingredients on hand. More and more chefs are using vegetable stock in place of chicken or fish stock, and it certainly is a convenience.

1½ quarts water
2 whole leeks, cut in half lengthwise, sliced crosswise and washed well
1 onion, chopped
2 carrots, chopped
2 ribs celery, chopped
2 cloves garlic, unpeeled
½ teaspoon black peppercorns
1 teaspoon tomato paste
5 sprigs fresh parsley
2 sprigs fresh thyme, or ½ teaspoon dried
1 bay leaf

1. Combine all the ingredients in a large saucepan and bring to a boil. Lower the heat and simmer, partially covered, until reduced to 1 quart, about 1 hour.

2. Strain the stock, pressing the vegetables with a spoon to extract all the liquid before throwing them away.

FILLED PASTA

Sweet-Potato Ravioli with Brown Butter

Here is our version of the wonderful pumpkin ravioli, called cappellacci, from the Emilia-Romagna and Veneto regions of Italy. Many of the traditional variations use a filling made with Italian pumpkin and amaretti cookies. If the cookies are not added to the filling, they are scattered over the finished ravioli. This unusual combination contrasts pleasantly with the saltiness of the Parmesan and the bite of fresh-ground pepper. Our version calls for sweet potatoes because they're more like Italian pumpkin than American pumpkin is, in both flavor and texture. The ravioli are also delicious without the amaretti.

SERVES 4

1   pound sweet potatoes
3   imported Italian amaretti cookies
½   cup grated Parmesan cheese, plus more for serving
1½   tablespoons chopped fresh flat-leaf parsley
     Pinch grated nutmeg
¾   teaspoon salt
     Fresh-ground black pepper
     Egg Pasta Dough (3-egg quantity), page 11
¼   pound butter

WINE RECOMMENDATION: THIS DISH WILL BENEFIT FROM A FRUITY WHITE WINE WITH NOTICEABLE ACIDITY, TO PLAY AGAINST ITS SWEET FLAVORS. TRY A SAUVIGNON BLANC FROM EITHER THE FRIULI OR EMILIA-ROMAGNA REGION OF ITALY.

1. Heat the oven to 400°. Bake the sweet potatoes until soft, about 1¼ hours. Turn off the oven. Cut the sweet potatoes in half lengthwise and put the halves back in the still warm oven for 10 minutes to dry.

2. In a food processor, pulverize the amaretti. Peel the sweet potatoes and add the flesh to the food processor. Process until the mixture is smooth. Scrape the filling into a bowl and stir in ¼ cup of the Parmesan, the parsley, nutmeg, ¼ teaspoon of the salt and ¼ teaspoon pepper. Cool to room temperature.

3. Roll, fill and cut the ravioli as directed on page 35. They should be 2-

inch squares with about ¾ teaspoon of filling in each one.

4. In a large pot of boiling, salted water, cook the ravioli until just done, about 7 minutes. Drain.

5. In a large frying pan, melt the butter and the remaining ½ teaspoon salt over moderate heat. Cook until the butter turns golden brown, about 2 minutes. Add the ravioli, the remaining ¼ cup Parmesan and a large pinch of pepper. Toss and serve with extra Parmesan.

CHOOSING THE SWEETEST SWEET POTATOES

Look closely at sweet potatoes. You'll sometimes see two or more types sold side by side that look similar from the outside but are quite different inside. These tubers, often mistakenly called yams, are all from the same family. Some have a light-brown skin and yellow to medium-orange flesh that is somewhat dry, even mealy, once cooked. The most common kind has a reddish-brown skin and a deep-orange flesh that is moist and sweet. It's the one that is best for this recipe because it most nearly resembles Italian pumpkin.

MAKING RAVIOLI

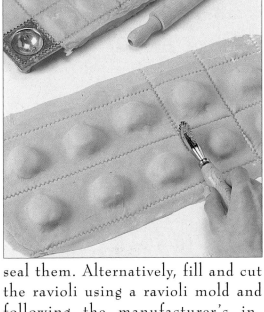

1. Working with a third of the dough at a time, roll it out to less than ¹⁄₁₆ inch thick by hand or with a pasta machine. If rolling the dough by hand, cut it into 5-inch-wide strips. If using a pasta machine cut the length of dough crosswise in half.

2. Arrange one strip of dough on a floured work surface. Drop ¾-teaspoon mounds of filling in two rows, about 2 inches apart, down the length of the dough. Drape the second sheet of dough over the filling. Firmly press around each mound of filling, taking care to press out any air that may be trapped inside.

3. With a fluted pastry cutter, cut the ravioli into 2-inch squares. Firmly press around the edges to seal them. Alternatively, fill and cut the ravioli using a ravioli mold and following the manufacturer's instructions. Put the finished ravioli on a baking sheet dusted with flour. Continue with the remaining dough and filling.

Eggplant and Goat-Cheese Ravioli in a Brown-Butter Walnut Sauce

Eggplant and goat cheese strike a perfect balance in these delectable ravioli. They need no more sauce than some brown butter. The crunch of a scattering of nuts completes the dish.

SERVES 4

⅓   cup olive oil
2   pounds eggplant (about 2 medium), peeled and cut crosswise into ½-inch slices
2   cloves garlic, minced
6   ounces soft goat cheese, such as Montrachet
⅓   cup chopped fresh flat-leaf parsley
1¾   teaspoons salt
     Fresh-ground black pepper
     Egg Pasta Dough (3-egg quantity), page 11
¼   pound butter
½   cup walnuts, chopped fine

1. In a large frying pan, heat 2 tablespoons of the oil over moderate heat. Fry the eggplant in several batches, adding the remaining oil as necessary. Cook each batch until lightly browned, about 4 minutes a side.

2. In a food processor, puree the eggplant, garlic, goat cheese, parsley, 1¼ teaspoons of the salt and ½ teaspoon pepper.

3. Roll, fill and cut the ravioli as directed on page 35. They should be 2-inch squares with ¾ teaspoon filling in each one.

4. In a large pot of boiling, salted water, cook the ravioli until just done, about 7 minutes. Drain.

5. In a large frying pan, melt the butter over moderate heat. Add the walnuts

and the remaining ½ teaspoon salt. Cook until the butter turns golden brown, about 2 minutes. Add the ravioli and a pinch of pepper and toss.

BROWN BUTTER

Butter that is cooked to a golden brown makes a simple and delicious sauce. Italians call this classic from France and Northern Italy *burro nocciola*, which means hazelnut butter, or *burro d'oro*, golden butter. It's traditionally tossed with stuffed pasta, gnocchi and occasionally with fresh fettuccine. To make it, melt butter over moderate heat. Cook just until the butter turns golden brown and gives off a nutty fragrance. Take it off the heat as soon as it gets to this point or you'll risk burning it.

GOAT CHEESE

Goat cheese, or chèvre, comes in myriad forms including cylinders, pyramids, disks and logs; and it ranges from fresh, soft and mild to aged, hard and pungent. Officially chèvre refers to goat cheese produced in France, but it has come to indicate all French-style goat cheeses, including those made domestically. The soft varieties (such as Montrachet from France, the log made by Coach Farms in New York State, or Laura Chenel's chabis or log from California) melt to make a smooth creamy sauce, such as in Bow Ties with Chèvre and Rosemary, page 137. When melting chèvre, avoid prolonged cooking, which can cause the mixture to separate.

Asparagus Ravioli with Hazelnut Sauce

Bursting with flavor, these little pasta pillows are a delightful way to serve spring asparagus. If hazelnuts are hard to find, walnuts will also complement the asparagus and make the recipe quicker as well. You needn't skin them as you do hazelnuts; just roast for about five minutes to bring out the flavor.

SERVES 4

2   pounds asparagus, peeled and cut into 1-inch lengths
11   tablespoons butter
1¼   teaspoons salt
    Fresh-ground black pepper
¾   cup hazelnuts
    Egg Pasta Dough (3-egg quantity), page 11
¼   cup grated Parmesan cheese

WINE RECOMMENDATION:
SAUVIGNON BLANC IS A PERFECT MATCH FOR THIS ASPARAGUS DISH, AND THE MORE AGGRESSIVE THE FLAVORS IN THE WINE THE BETTER. TRY TO FIND A BOTTLE NO MORE THAN TWO OR THREE YEARS OLD FROM NEW ZEALAND OR FROM SANCERRE IN THE LOIRE VALLEY OF FRANCE.

1. In a pan of boiling, salted water, cook the asparagus until just tender, about 4 minutes. Drain. Put back in the pan over moderate heat and cook, stirring, until dry, about 5 minutes. Puree in a food processor or blender until smooth.

2. Melt 3 tablespoons of the butter in the pan over moderate heat. Add the asparagus puree, 1 teaspoon of the salt and ¼ teaspoon pepper. Cook, stirring, until the mixture thickens and begins to stick to the bottom of the pan, about 5 minutes. Transfer the filling to a bowl to cool.

3. Heat the oven to 350°. Put the hazelnuts on a baking sheet and roast in the oven until the skins are cracked and

loose and the nuts are golden brown, about 10 minutes. Wrap the hot hazelnuts in a kitchen towel and firmly rub them together to loosen most of the skins. Discard the skins. Chop the hazelnuts when cool.

4. Roll, fill and cut the ravioli as directed on page 35. They should be 2-inch squares with about ¾ teaspoon filling in each one.

5. In a large pot of boiling, salted water, cook the ravioli until just done, about 7 minutes. Drain.

6. In a large frying pan, melt the remaining 8 tablespoons butter with the remaining ¼ teaspoon salt and a pinch of pepper over moderate heat. Cook until the butter turns golden brown, about 2 minutes. Toss the ravioli and hazelnuts in the butter. Sprinkle with the Parmesan.

—Joan Husman and Catherine Whims
Genoa

Morel-Mushroom Ravioli in Wild-Mushroom Broth

Many chefs are experimenting with wonton wrappers in place of egg pasta for ravioli. The wrappers are lighter and certainly easier. You could use either here. Dried mushrooms add their intense, nutty flavor to the chicken and cream in this excellent filling. The fresh mushrooms in the broth can be whatever type is in season, but for a real treat choose morels when they're available in spring and early summer.

SERVES 8 AS A FIRST COURSE

1½ tablespoons cooking oil
3   tablespoons minced shallot
5   ounces dried morels, rinsed
2   cups heavy cream
½   pound boneless, skinless chicken breast, cut into 1-inch pieces
2   teaspoons salt
    Fresh-ground black pepper
80 wonton wrappers
4   tablespoons butter
⅔   pound fresh wild mushrooms, stems reserved, caps sliced
1   large clove garlic, minced
1   quart Vegetable or Chicken Stock, pages 29 and 30, or canned low-sodium chicken broth
3   tablespoons chopped fresh chives, or scallion tops

WINE RECOMMENDATION: LOOK FOR A SERIOUS, EARTHY RED WINE TO COMPLEMENT THE MUSHROOM FLAVORS HERE. FROM ITALY'S PIEDMONT REGION, TRY A BARBARESCO OR BAROLO THAT'S AT LEAST FIVE YEARS OLD.

1. In a medium saucepan, heat the oil over moderately low heat. Add 2 tablespoons of the shallot and cook until translucent, about 5 minutes. Add 4 ounces of the dried morels and the heavy cream and bring to a boil. Lower the heat and simmer until the mixture is reduced to 1 cup, about 8 minutes. Remove from the heat and let stand 15 minutes. Strain the cream and reserve the mushrooms. Let the cream cool completely and chop the morels fine.

2. Put the chicken in a food processor and pulse 2 or 3 times. With machine running, add the cooled cream in a steady stream, scraping the bowl as needed. Transfer the mixture to a bowl and add the chopped morels, 1 teaspoon of the salt and ¼ teaspoon pepper.

3. On a clean work surface, lay out a few of the wonton wrappers and brush lightly with water. Put 2 teaspoons of the chicken mixture in the center of each wrapper. Top with a second wonton wrapper and press around the filling to seal and to remove any air that may be trapped inside. With a 2½-inch cutter, stamp out a round. Put on a baking sheet dusted with flour and continue making the ravioli.

4. Heat 2 tablespoons of the butter in a large frying pan over moderately high heat. Add the sliced wild mushrooms, ½ teaspoon of the salt and ⅛ teaspoon pepper and sauté, stirring occasionally, until golden, about 8 minutes. Cover and keep warm.

5. In a large saucepan, heat the remaining 2 tablespoons butter over moderately low heat. Add the remaining tablespoon shallot, the 1 ounce dried morels, the reserved mushroom stems and the garlic. Cook, stirring occasionally, until the shallot is translucent, about 5 minutes. Add the stock and simmer until reduced to 2 cups, about 15 minutes. Season with the remaining ½ teaspoon salt. Strain the stock and keep warm until ready to use.

6. In a large pot of boiling, salted water, cook the ravioli until just done, about 3 minutes.

7. To serve, arrange the ravioli in shallow bowls and cover with broth. Top with the mushrooms and chives.

—Alfred Portale
Gotham Bar and Grill

Lobster Semolina Ravioli with Tomato Basil Broth

Everything about these ravioli is luxurious. The creamy filling with bits of lobster meat and the basil-infused broth are well worth the effort. Try to buy a female lobster (see page 45) so that you can use the roe for decoration.

SERVES 6 AS A FIRST COURSE

1	leek, white and light green parts only, cut in half lengthwise and washed well
3	carrots
2	onions
4	shallots
12	cloves garlic
4	ribs celery
1	teaspoon salt
1	teaspoon black peppercorns
1½	cups dry white wine
1½	cups canned crushed tomatoes
1½	quarts plus ⅔ cup water
2	cups lightly packed chopped fresh basil leaves and stems
1⅓	cups Chicken Stock, page 29, or canned low-sodium chicken broth
⅛	teaspoon fresh-ground black pepper
1	live lobster (1 pound)
⅔	cup heavy cream
⅓	cup semolina flour*
72	wonton wrappers
2	tablespoons chopped fresh chives, or scallion tops

* Available at specialty food stores and Italian markets

WINE RECOMMENDATION: THIS RICH DISH SHOULD BE PAIRED WITH AN EXPANSIVE, YOUNG WHITE WINE, SUCH AS A GOOD-QUALITY CHARDONNAY FROM EITHER CALIFORNIA OR AUSTRALIA.

1. In a food processor, in several batches, chop the leek, 2 of the carrots, 1 of the onions, 2 of the shallots, 6 cloves garlic and the celery. Put the chopped vegetables in a large saucepan. Add ½ teaspoon of the salt, the peppercorns, wine, tomatoes and 1½ quarts of the water. Bring to a boil. Reduce the heat and simmer until the mixture is reduced by half, about 2 hours.

2. Add the basil and let steep 30 minutes. Strain the broth, pressing the vegetables with a spoon to extract the juices.

3. Chop the remaining carrot, onion, 2 shallots and 6 garlic cloves. Put the vegetables in a medium saucepan with ¼ teaspoon of the salt, the remaining ⅔ cup water and the chicken stock. Simmer until the vegetables are very soft and almost all the liquid is evaporated, about 1 hour. Add the ground pep-

per. In a food processor or blender, puree the vegetables until smooth.

4. In a large pot of boiling, salted water, cook the lobster until almost done, about 9 minutes. When cool enough to handle, twist the lobster to separate the tail section and the large legs with the claws from the body. Turn the tail upside down. Use a large, sharp knife to cut the tail in half lengthwise. Remove the tail meat from the shell. Crack the knuckles and claws and remove the meat from the shells. Chop all the lobster meat.

5. In a small saucepan, combine the cream, semolina and the remaining ¼ teaspoon salt. Boil, stirring, until very thick, 3 to 5 minutes. Remove the pan from the heat, add ⅔ cup of the vegetable puree and let cool. Fold the chopped lobster into the cooled semolina mixture.

6. On a clean work surface, lay out a few of the wonton wrappers and brush lightly with water. Put about 1 tablespoon filling in the center of each. Top with a second wonton wrapper and press around the edges to seal, taking care to press out any air that may be trapped inside. With a 2½-inch fluted or plain round cutter, stamp out the ravioli. Press firmly around the edges to make sure they're sealed. Put the finished ravioli on a baking sheet dusted with flour. Continue until you have made 36 ravioli.

7. Bring the tomato basil broth to a simmer. In a large pot of boiling, salted water, cook the ravioli 1 minute. With a slotted spoon, transfer them to the broth and simmer 2 minutes longer. Serve topped with lobster roe if available and chopped chives.

—Jim Galileo
Oceana

LOBSTER CORAL

Female lobsters contain the delicious and decorative roe, also descriptively called coral. It can be served in situ with a whole or split lobster, removed and added to sauces, or used as a garnish. Unlike caviar, coral is eaten cooked. Cut a lobster in half lengthwise, and you'll see the roe in the body cavity and the upper portion of the tail. A soft, greenish-black, congealed mass when raw, it becomes firm and red when cooked. The coral won't usually be done if the lobster is undercooked, which it should be if you plan to heat the meat again as in the ravioli here. If the roe is still dark and you want to use it as a garnish, remove it carefully and simmer it in an inch of water until it's a beautiful coral color, about three minutes. Remove and rub it between your fingers or mash it with a fork to separate the eggs.

BUYING AND KEEPING WONTON WRAPPERS

Wonton wrappers are available in most supermarkets, either fresh or frozen. They usually come in twelve-ounce packages with fifty or more wrappers. You can't always count on there being that many, though, and so it's a good idea to buy extra. Look for wrappers that are white or off-white. A darker color indicates coloring has been added. You can keep them in the refrigerator for a couple of days; beyond that, store them in the freezer.

Potato and Chive Ravioli with Mascarpone Sauce

Presented this way, with chives and rich mascarpone cheese, the humble potato reaches new heights. If you want to go all the way, shave some fresh truffle over the top.

SERVES 4

1	pound baking potatoes, peeled and cut in half
1¼	cups mascarpone cheese
2	tablespoons butter
¼	cup grated Parmesan cheese
2	tablespoons chopped fresh chives, or scallion tops, plus more for garnish
1¼	teaspoons salt
	Fresh-ground black pepper
1	egg
	Herb Pasta Dough (3-egg quantity), page 12
1	cup heavy cream

WINE RECOMMENDATION: THE RICHNESS OF THIS MASCARPONE-DOMINATED DISH CALLS FOR A SIMPLE, LIVELY RED WINE MEANT TO BE DRUNK YOUNG, SUCH AS A BARDOLINO FROM ITALY. A BOURGUEIL FROM FRANCE'S LOIRE VALLEY WILL ALSO PAIR NICELY WITH THIS DISH.

1. Put the potatoes in a saucepan of salted water. Bring to a boil and simmer until the potatoes can be pierced easily with a fork, about 20 minutes. Drain. Push them through a sieve or ricer. Put the potato puree in a pot over moderate heat and cook, stirring, until dry, about 3 minutes.

2. Transfer the potatoes to a bowl and add ¼ cup of the mascarpone, the butter, Parmesan, chives, ½ teaspoon of the salt and ⅛ teaspoon pepper. Let cool, then add the egg.

3. Roll, fill and cut the ravioli as directed on page 35. They should be 2-inch squares with about ¾ teaspoon filling in each one.

4. In a large pot of boiling, salted water, cook the ravioli until just done, about 7 minutes. Drain.

5. Meanwhile, in a large frying pan, melt the remaining 1 cup mascarpone. Add the cream, the remaining ¾ teaspoon salt and ¼ teaspoon pepper and bring to a boil. Toss the ravioli with the sauce and serve sprinkled with chives.

MASCARPONE

Mascarpone is soft, falling between cream cheese and sour cream in texture. With its sixty percent butterfat, mascarpone has a nutty, buttery flavor and behaves more like thickened cream than cheese. It melts into a most delicious sauce that needs nothing more than salt and also combines well with other cheeses. Originally from the Lombardy and Tuscany regions of Italy, mascarpone is now produced all over Italy and is made domestically as well. While the domestic varieties are good and are slightly cheaper than the imported, those from Italy have a fuller flavor. Look for a pale cream color and sweet, buttery taste. If the mascarpone is yellowed and sour tasting, return it.

Cheese-Stuffed Raviolacci in Sage Cream

Four Italian cheeses are combined with scallions and Swiss chard in a creamy filling for these large ravioli. If you can't find Swiss chard, spinach is a fine alternative; you'll need about one-half pound. Cook it just until the leaves wilt, about one minute.

SERVES 4

¼ pound Swiss chard, cut into 2-inch pieces
1½ teaspoons olive oil
3 scallions including green tops, minced
1 cup (about ½ pound) ricotta cheese
¼ cup mascarpone cheese
2 ounces ricotta salata cheese, grated
½ cup grated Parmesan cheese
2 tablespoons chopped fresh flat-leaf parsley
¼ teaspoon salt
  Fresh-ground black pepper
1 egg
  Egg Pasta Dough (3-egg quantity), page 11
¼ pound butter
¼ cup milk
¼ cup heavy cream
8 fresh sage leaves, or ½ teaspoon dried

WINE RECOMMENDATION: A WHITE WINE WITH PLENTY OF ACIDITY AND LOTS OF PERSONALITY WILL PAIR WELL WITH THE LEAFY VEGETABLES AND THE MILD CHEESES AND CREAM. TRY A RIESLING FROM EITHER THE ALTO ADIGE REGION OF ITALY OR ALSACE IN FRANCE.

1. In a large pot of boiling, salted water, cook the Swiss chard until the stems are tender, about 4 minutes. Drain and rinse with cold water. Drain again and squeeze a handful at a time to remove as much water as possible. Chop the Swiss chard fine. You should have about ¼ cup.

2. In a small frying pan, heat the oil over moderately low heat. Add the scallions and cook until soft, about 3 minutes. Remove from the heat, add the Swiss chard and let cool.

3. In a bowl, combine the ricotta, mascarpone, ricotta salata, ¼ cup of the Parmesan, the parsley, salt and ¼ teaspoon pepper. Stir in the reserved vegetables and the egg.

4. Roll, fill and cut the pasta as

directed for ravioli on page 35. The raviolacci should be approximately 2½-by-3-inch rectangles with about 2 teaspoons filling in each one.

5. In a large pot of boiling, salted water, cook the raviolacci until just done, about 7 minutes. Reserve ¼ cup of the pasta water. Drain the pasta.

6. Meanwhile, in a deep frying pan, melt the butter over moderately high heat. Add the milk, cream, sage leaves, the reserved pasta water and a pinch of pepper and bring to a simmer. Add the cooked raviolacci and stir gently with a wooden spoon. Shake the pan until the sauce thickens slightly and coats the raviolacci, about 2 minutes. Add the remaining ¼ cup Parmesan.

—Lidia Bastianich
Felidia

Spinach and Ricotta Ravioli

The mild flavors of fresh spinach and ricotta cheese are the base for this creamy filling. A light tomato sauce complements the classic pair perfectly.

SERVES 4

1	pound spinach, stems removed, leaves washed
2	cups (about 1 pound) ricotta cheese
¼	cup grated Parmesan cheese
2	egg yolks
	Pinch grated nutmeg
¾	teaspoon salt
¼	teaspoon fresh-ground black pepper
	Egg Pasta Dough (3-egg quantity), page 11
2	cups Light Tomato Sauce, page 24

WINE RECOMMENDATION: THE STRAIGHTFORWARD FLAVORS OF THIS DISH WILL PAIR WELL WITH A SIMPLE, MEDIUM-BODIED WHITE WINE. TRY IT WITH A YOUNG BOTTLE OF EITHER PINOT GRIGIO FROM FRIULI IN ITALY OR CÔTES DU RHÔNE FROM FRANCE.

1. In a large pot of boiling, salted water, cook the spinach just until the leaves wilt, about 1 minute. Drain and rinse with cold water. Drain again and squeeze a handful at a time to remove as much water as possible.

2. Put the spinach in a food processor with the ricotta, Parmesan, egg yolks, nutmeg, salt and pepper. Puree until smooth.

3. Roll, fill and cut the ravioli as directed on page 35. They should be 2-inch squares with about ¾ teaspoon filling in each one.

4. In a large pot of boiling, salted water, cook the ravioli until just done, about 7 minutes. Meanwhile, reheat the tomato sauce if necessary. Drain the ravioli. Toss with the sauce.

Cheese, Spinach and Egg Raviolo with Brown Butter

Dramatically large, a raviolo is served on its own, just one per person. This version is even more special than most because it has a surprise soft egg yolk in the center. When you cut into your raviolo, the yolk runs out, mixing with the brown butter to form a delicious sauce. Don't separate the eggs until you're ready to use the yolks; it's important that each yolk remains intact until the raviolo is cooked. Impressive though a raviolo is, it's actually easy, especially since you make only one per person.

SERVES 4 AS A FIRST COURSE

½   pound spinach, stems removed, leaves washed
½   cup ricotta cheese
5   egg yolks
5   tablespoons grated Parmesan cheese
¼   teaspoon salt
¼   teaspoon fresh-ground black pepper
⅛   teaspoon grated nutmeg
     Egg Pasta Dough (2-egg quantity), page 11
6   tablespoons butter
1   small white truffle, optional

WINE RECOMMENDATION:
A LUSH WHITE WINE WILL WORK WELL WITH THIS VERY RICH DISH. TRY A PINOT GRIS FROM ALSACE IN FRANCE OR A SPÄTLESE RIESLING FROM THE MOSEL-SAAR-RUWER REGION OF GERMANY.

1. In a large pot of boiling, salted water, cook the spinach just until the leaves wilt, about 1 minute. Drain and rinse under cold water. Drain again and squeeze a handful of the spinach at a time to remove as much water as possible. Chop the spinach fine. You should have about ¼ cup.

2. In a medium bowl, combine the spinach, ricotta, 1 of the egg yolks, 3 tablespoons of the Parmesan, the salt, pepper and nutmeg.

3. Roll the pasta dough out to less than 1⁄16 inch thick by hand or with a pasta machine. Cut the dough into eight

6-inch squares. Loosely cover 6 of the squares with plastic wrap while filling the first raviolo as shown on page 53. Put the finished raviolo on a baking sheet dusted with flour and continue making the rest.

4. In a small pot, melt the butter over moderate heat until golden brown, about 2 minutes.

5. Put the stuffed pasta in a large pot of boiling, salted water. Bring the water back to a boil and then cook the pasta exactly 4 minutes. With a slotted spoon, transfer to individual plates.

6. If necessary, reheat the butter. Pour some over each raviolo. Sprinkle with the remaining 2 tablespoons Parmesan, top with thin shavings of the truffle, if using, and serve immediately.

—Paul Bartolotta
Spiaggia

NOBLE PASTA

Nino Bergese, private chef to Vittorio Emanuele III, the last king of Italy, created this raviolo in the 1930s. It reflects the fashion for rich, French-inspired food among the Italian nobility of that time. With the fall of the monarchy, Chef Bergese opened a restaurant in Genoa, wrote a cookbook and eventually worked as a consultant for Ristorante San Domenico in Imola. There, Bergese taught the dish to Chef Valentino Marcattilii, who in turn taught Paul Bartolotta, the young American chef of SanDomenico NY in New York City, how to make it. The raviolo is still on the menu at SanDomenico NY and is also served at Spiaggia in Chicago, where Bartolotta is now the executive chef.

MAKING A RAVIOLO

1. Spoon one-quarter of the spinach filling in the center of a pasta square. With a teaspoon, make

an indentation in the middle of the filling. The indentation should be just big enough to hold an egg yolk.

2. Carefully drop an egg yolk into the center of the spinach filling. The yolk must remain unbroken.

ken. Sprinkle it with a pinch each of salt and pepper.

3. Brush the edges of the pasta with water. Top with a second pasta square. Carefully seal the edges, tak-

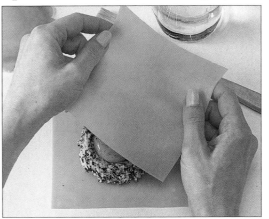

ing care to press out any air that may be trapped inside.

4. With a 4-inch fluted, round pastry cutter or tartlet pan, stamp out a round raviolo. If using a tartlet pan, the sides must be high

enough to cut the pasta without breaking the egg yolk.

Artichoke and Sun-Dried-Tomato Tortellini

Because of the tangy filling spiked with garlic and lemon zest, this filled pasta needs only a simple sauce. You can use the briefly cooked fresh-tomato sauce suggested here or toss the tortellini with cream and grated Parmesan cheese.

SERVES 4

1	9-ounce package frozen artichoke hearts, thawed
½	cup grated Parmesan cheese
⅓	cup sun-dried tomatoes
3	tablespoons olive oil
1	tablespoon chopped fresh parsley
1	clove garlic, minced
½	teaspoon grated lemon zest
½	teaspoon salt
¼	teaspoon fresh-ground black pepper Egg Pasta Dough (3-egg quantity), page 11
2	cups Fresh Tomato Sauce, page 25

WINE RECOMMENDATION:
ARTICHOKES ARE TOUGH TO MATCH WITH WINE, AS ARE SUN-DRIED TOMATOES. TWO ASSERTIVE WHITE WINES FROM THE LOIRE VALLEY IN FRANCE—THE SAUVIGNON BLANC-BASED SANCERRE AND THE MORE ACIDIC CHENIN BLANC-BASED SAVENNIÈRES—HAVE ENOUGH PERSONALITY TO ATTEMPT THE DIFFICULT MATCH. THE SANCERRE SHOULD BE A VERY RECENT VINTAGE, WHILE THE SAVENNIÈRES SHOULD IDEALLY BE AT LEAST FIVE YEARS OLD.

1. Squeeze the artichokes a handful at a time to remove any water. In a food processor, puree the artichokes, Parmesan, sun-dried tomatoes, oil, parsley, garlic, lemon zest, salt and pepper.

2. Roll, cut, fill and shape the tortellini as directed on page 55. Use a 2-inch cutter and about ½ teaspoon filling.

3. In a large pot of boiling, salted water, cook the tortellini until just done, about 7 minutes. Meanwhile, reheat the tomato sauce if necessary. Drain the tortellini and toss with the tomato sauce.

MAKING TORTELLINI

1. Working with a third of the dough at a time, roll to less than $1/16$ inch thick by hand or with a pasta machine. With a 2-inch cutter, stamp out about 6 circles. Loosely cover the uncut portion of dough with plastic wrap.

2. Drop about $1/2$ teaspoon of filling in the center of each round.

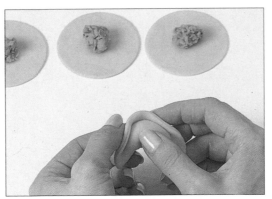

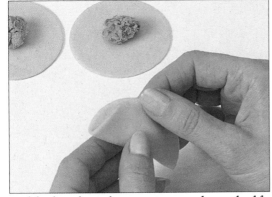

Fold the dough over to make a half-circle. Firmly press the edges to seal them, taking care to press out any air that may be trapped inside.

3. Bring the pointed ends of each half-circle toward you. The cut edge of the half-circle should naturally fold up.

4. Slightly overlap the ends and pinch to seal. Put on a baking sheet

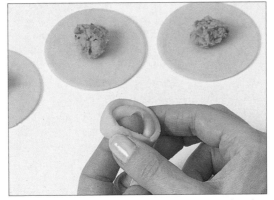

dusted with flour. Continue with the rest of the pasta and filling.

Chicken Tortellini with Asparagus in Lemon Cream Sauce

Usher in spring and the arrival of tender young asparagus with this delicious dish. The lemon juice, lemon zest and cream combine to make a lush sauce that is both satisfying and refreshing.

SERVES 4

14	ounces boneless chicken thighs
2⅓	cups heavy cream
½	cup grated Parmesan cheese
1	shallot, minced
1	egg
2	tablespoons chopped fresh flat-leaf parsley
	Pinch grated nutmeg
1	teaspoon salt
½	teaspoon fresh-ground black pepper
	Egg Pasta Dough (3-egg quantity), page 11
1	pound asparagus, peeled and cut into 1½-inch lengths
6	tablespoons butter
1	tablespoon lemon juice
1	teaspoon grated lemon zest

1. Put the chicken in a food processor and pulse until almost smooth, about 20 times. Add ⅓ cup of the cream, ¼ cup of the Parmesan, the shallot, egg, parsley, nutmeg, ½ teaspoon of the salt and ¼ teaspoon of the pepper. Pulse until thoroughly combined, about 8 times.

2. Roll, cut, fill and shape the tortellini as directed on page 55. Use a 2-inch round cutter and about ½ teaspoon filling.

3. In a large pot of boiling, salted water, cook the asparagus until just tender, about 4 minutes. Drain, rinse with cold water and drain thoroughly.

4. In a large pot of boiling, salted water, cook the tortellini until just done, about 7 minutes. Drain. ➤

5. In a large frying pan over moderate heat, melt the butter with the lemon juice and lemon zest. Add the remaining 2 cups cream and bring the sauce to a boil. Simmer, stirring occasionally, until slightly thickened, about 3 minutes. Do not cook too long after the cream is added or the sauce may curdle. Add the remaining ½ teaspoon salt, ¼ teaspoon pepper, the tortellini and asparagus and toss until hot. Sprinkle with the remaining ¼ cup Parmesan.

Polenta-Filled Tortelloni in Gorgonzola Cream Sauce

Here's a new way to feature polenta—inside tortelloni, a larger version of tortellini. This dish is rich, cheesy and very comforting. You can substitute plain egg pasta for the tomato pasta here.

SERVES 4

3   cups plus 2 tablespoons water
¾   cup coarse or medium cornmeal
½   teaspoon salt
3   tablespoons grated Parmesan cheese
5   ounces Gorgonzola cheese, chopped
1   egg yolk
⅛   teaspoon fresh-ground black pepper
      Tomato Pasta Dough (3-egg equivalent), page 13
1   cup heavy cream

WINE RECOMMENDATION:
CHOOSE A LIGHT-BODIED, FRUITY RED WINE TO CONTRAST WITH AND ENLIVEN THE HEARTY, RICH FLAVORS OF THIS DISH. A YOUNG VALPOLICELLA OR BARDOLINO FROM THE VENETO REGION OF ITALY WOULD BE A GOOD CHOICE.

1. In a heavy, medium saucepan, bring the water to a boil. Add the cornmeal in a slow stream, whisking constantly. Reduce the heat to moderate and add the salt. Simmer, stirring frequently with a wooden spoon, until the polenta is very thick, about 20 minutes. Transfer it to a medium bowl.

2. Stir in the Parmesan and 1 ounce of the Gorgonzola. Cool slightly and then stir in the egg yolk and pepper.

3. Roll, cut, fill and shape the pasta as directed for tortellini on page 55. Use a 3½-inch round cutter and fill each tortelloni with about 1 tablespoon filling.

4. In a large pot of boiling, salted water, cook the tortelloni until just done, about 7 minutes. Drain. ➤

5. In a medium saucepan over moderately high heat, bring the cream and the remaining 4 ounces of Gorgonzola just to a boil, whisking. Toss the tortelloni with the sauce.

CORNMEAL FOR POLENTA

Cornmeal comes in a variety of grinds ranging from coarse to fine, and it may or may not contain the germ. For polenta we recommend coarse or medium cornmeal without the germ. Fine meal is too smooth, and whole-grain cornmeal, which contains the germ, gives polenta a bitter, earthy flavor that is not to everyone's taste. Both imported and domestic cornmeal labeled polenta are available in specialty stores and Italian markets. Instant polenta is a pale substitute. A better alternative is supermarket cornmeal, a blend of medium and fine grind with the germ removed. If you do use whole-grain cornmeal, it's a good idea to store it in the refrigerator or freezer because the oil in the germ turns rancid quickly.

Pork-Filled Cappelletti with Creamy Parmesan Sauce

Chopped mortadella gives this classic filling its distinctive flavor. We like to use spinach pasta because it looks so nice with the cream sauce, but plain egg pasta is fine, too.

SERVES 4

½   pound ground pork

¼   pound mortadella, chopped fine

6   tablespoons grated Parmesan cheese, plus more for serving

     Pinch grated nutmeg

¾   teaspoon salt

½   teaspoon fresh-ground black pepper

     Spinach Pasta Dough (3-egg equivalent), page 13

1   cup heavy cream

4   tablespoons butter

WINE RECOMMENDATION: PAIR THE CREAMINESS AND MEATINESS OF THIS DISH WITH AN EQUALLY FLAVORFUL WHITE WINE, SUCH AS A RICH CHARDONNAY FROM CALIFORNIA OR A PINOT GRIS FROM FRANCE'S ALSACE REGION.

1. In a medium bowl, combine the pork, mortadella, ¼ cup of the Parmesan, the nutmeg, ½ teaspoon of the salt and ¼ teaspoon of the pepper.

2. Roll, cut, fill and shape the cappelletti as directed on page 65. Use a 2½-inch square of pasta and about ½ teaspoon filling.

3. In a small saucepan, simmer the heavy cream and butter until slightly thickened, about 5 minutes. Stir in the remaining 2 tablespoons Parmesan, ¼ teaspoon salt and ¼ teaspoon pepper.

4. In a large pot of boiling, salted water, cook the cappelletti until just done, about 7 minutes. Drain.

5. Reheat the sauce if necessary and toss it with the cappelletti. Serve with additional Parmesan cheese.

Asian-Style Cappelletti in a Tomato Ginger Sauce

East meets West in this delightfully different pasta dish. The Asian flavors of the filling—dried shiitakes, pork, crab, bamboo shoots and soy sauce—are all wrapped up in Italian pasta and tossed with a spicy ginger and cilantro tomato sauce. Altogether a great combination. Since the other ingredients are so full-flavored, good-quality canned crabmeat works as well as fresh here.

SERVES 4

½ ounce dried Chinese black mushrooms or dried shiitake mushrooms (about 6 medium mushrooms)
½ pound ground pork
½ cup minced bamboo shoots
6 ounces fresh or canned crabmeat, picked clean of shells
2 tablespoons dry sherry
2 tablespoons soy sauce
1 teaspoon sugar
¾ teaspoon salt
1 egg
1 teaspoon minced fresh ginger, plus one 6-ounce piece
Egg Pasta Dough (3-egg quantity), page 11
3 cups Basic Italian Tomato Sauce, page 22, basil omitted, pureed and strained through a coarse sieve
3 tablespoons chopped fresh cilantro, plus whole leaves for garnish

WINE RECOMMENDATION: PAIR THE ASIAN FLAVORS IN THIS DISH WITH A GEWÜRZTRAMINER FROM FRANCE'S ALSACE REGION OR A COLD BEER.

1. In a medium bowl, soak the mushrooms in hot water until softened, about 20 minutes. Drain, rinse and squeeze to extract as much water as possible. Remove and discard the stems and mince the caps. Put them in a bowl and stir in the pork, bamboo shoots, crab, sherry, soy sauce, sugar, ½ teaspoon of the salt, the egg and the minced ginger. Chill the filling for at least 15 minutes.

2. Roll, cut, fill and shape the cappelletti as directed on page 65. Use a 2½-inch square of pasta and about ½ teaspoon filling.

3. Peel the piece of ginger. Cut it into 1-inch pieces and puree in a food processor. Squeeze to extract 3 tablespoons ginger juice and discard the pulp. Put juice in a saucepan with the tomato sauce, cilantro and the remaining ¼ teaspoon salt and heat through. ➤

4. In a large pot of boiling, salted water, cook the cappelletti until just done, about 7 minutes. Meanwhile, reheat the sauce if necessary. Drain the cappelletti. Toss with the sauce and garnish with cilantro leaves.

CRAB: FRESH VS. CANNED

There is no question about it: Fresh jumbo-lump crabmeat is the best. It tastes good and has the least amount of shell of any grade. But it's expensive and unnecessary for most dishes, especially in pasta fillings. For cooking, consider the alternatives. The lower grades, ranging from lump down through backfin, special and claw, are excellent choices. Lump crabmeat provides good-size chunks of meat, just not quite so large as jumbo-lump. This grade is perfect for the Shellfish Cannelloni with Tarragon Sauce, page 91. Even claw meat, the lowest grade, is flavorful and works well when combined with other ingredients. We can't be so enthusiastic about canned crab, though it's convenient and considerably cheaper. Some of it is fine for cooking. Quality varies tremendously, however, and many brands taste like salty sawdust. We recommend Seafare brand, sold in different grades, all of which are good. Another possibility you may not be aware of is pasteurized crab, a close second to fresh. In fact it's often the best bet in markets with a low turnover of fresh fish. Pasteurized crab, sold in sealed, refrigerated containers, costs about the same as fresh.

MAKING CAPPELLETTI

1. Working with a third of the dough at a time, roll to less than $\frac{1}{16}$ inch thick by hand or with a pasta machine. Cut the dough into 2½-inch squares. Loosely cover all but 4 squares with plastic wrap.

2. Drop about ½ teaspoon of filling in the center of the 4 squares.

3. Fold each square over so that the opposite corners meet to make a triangle. Firmly press the edges to seal them, taking care to press out any air that may be trapped inside.

4. Bring together the opposite corners of the triangle so that they

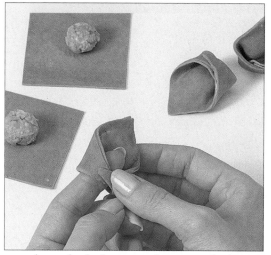

overlap slightly. Pinch to seal them. Put on a baking sheet dusted with flour. Continue with the rest of the pasta and filling.

Kale and Fontina Agnolotti

The traditional union of kale and bacon is joined here by Fontina cheese to make a delicious pasta filling. One caution: Kale often harbors lots of sand; wash it well in several changes of water.

SERVES 4

2   strips bacon, chopped fine
1   small onion, chopped fine
½   pound kale, stems removed, leaves washed well
2   ounces Fontina cheese, grated (about ½ cup)
½   teaspoon salt
¼   teaspoon fresh-ground black pepper
     Egg Pasta Dough (3-egg quantity), page 11
2   cups Light Tomato Sauce, page 24

WINE RECOMMENDATION: THE ASSERTIVE AND DIFFICULT TO MATCH FLAVORS OF KALE AND BACON ARE BEST PAIRED WITH AN EASYGOING, LIGHT AND CRISP WHITE WINE, SUCH AS ORVIETO OR SOAVE, BOTH FROM ITALY.

1. In a medium frying pan, cook the bacon over moderately low heat until the fat is rendered, about 5 minutes. Add the onion and cook until translucent, about 5 minutes longer. Transfer the mixture to a large bowl and let cool.

2. In a large pot of boiling, salted water, cook the kale until tender, about 5 minutes. Drain and rinse with cold water. Drain again and squeeze a handful at a time to remove as much water as possible. Chop the kale fine. Stir into the bacon mixture along with the Fontina, salt and pepper.

3. Roll, fill and cut the agnolotti as directed on page 67. Use a 2½-inch cutter and about 1 tablespoon filling.

4. In a large pot of boiling, salted water, cook the agnolotti until just done, about 7 minutes. Meanwhile, reheat the sauce if necessary. Drain the agnolotti and toss with the tomato sauce.

MAKING AGNOLOTTI

1. Working with a third of the dough at a time, roll to less than $\frac{1}{16}$ inch thick by hand or with a pasta machine. Cut hand-rolled pasta into strips 4 inches wide. Loosely cover all but one strip of dough with plastic wrap.

2. Drop 1-tablespoon mounds of filling, about $2\frac{1}{2}$ inches apart, down the length of the dough. Fold the dough lengthwise in half and press around the filling to seal the agnolotti and to remove any air that may be trapped inside.

3. With a $2\frac{1}{2}$-inch fluted pastry cutter, stamp out the agnolotti

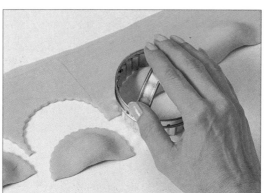

along the folded side of the dough into half-moon shapes.

4. Press firmly all around the edges to make sure they're sealed. Put the agnolotti on a baking sheet dusted with flour. Continue with the rest of the pasta and filling.

Salmon and Cabbage Filled Buckwheat Agnolotti

Cabbage may seem like an unlikely partner for salmon, but when the lowly vegetable is cooked until soft and golden it makes a perfect match for the rich fish, especially when the two are wrapped together in nutty buckwheat pasta.

SERVES 6 AS A FIRST COURSE

1	tablespoon butter
10	ounces green cabbage (about ¼ head), shredded
1	leek, white and light green parts only, cut in half lengthwise, sliced crosswise and washed well
¾	teaspoon salt
	Fresh-ground black pepper
1	cup plus 2 tablespoons crème fraîche
2	tablespoons chopped fresh chives, or scallion tops
½	pound skinless salmon fillet, cut into ¼-inch dice
	Buckwheat Pasta Dough (2-egg quantity), page 14

WINE RECOMMENDATION: THE SALMON TOGETHER WITH THE EARTHY FLAVORS OF THE CABBAGE AND BUCKWHEAT PASTA WILL BE DELIGHTFUL WITH A GLASS OF PINOT GRIS. A YOUNG BOTTLE FROM OREGON OR ALSACE IS IDEAL.

1. In a large frying pan, melt the butter over low heat. Add the cabbage, leek, ½ teaspoon of the salt and ⅛ teaspoon pepper. Cook, covered, stirring occasionally, until the vegetables are very soft and just beginning to brown, about 30 minutes. Transfer to a medium bowl and let cool. Stir in 2 tablespoons of the crème fraîche, 1 tablespoon of the chives and the salmon.

2. Roll, fill and cut the pasta as directed on page 67. Use about 1 tablespoon filling in each agnolotti and a 2½-inch round cutter.

3. In a large pot of boiling, salted water, cook the agnolotti until just done, about 7 minutes. Drain.

4. Return the hot pot to the stove and add the remaining 1 cup crème

fraîche, 1 tablespoon chives, ¼ teaspoon salt and a pinch of pepper. Simmer 2 minutes. Add the agnolotti to the pan and cook another minute.

 CRÈME FRAÎCHE

Thick, tangy, nutty crème fraîche, or *panna doppia* as it's called in Italy, has a fuller, more complex flavor than sour cream. Also, it doesn't curdle when heated as sour cream does. Both imported and domestic varieties are available in specialty shops and many super-markets. You can also make it at home: Heat one cup of heavy cream with a teaspoon of butter-milk until lukewarm. Transfer to a jar or plastic container, cover loosely and let sit at room temper-ature until thick, about 24 hours. Then refrigerate. It will continue to thicken as it chills.

Crab Agnolotti with Braised Fennel and Smoky Tomato Sauce

Chef Scott Cohen uses wonton wrappers to make agnolotti—a great short cut. He serves this for a first course. As a main dish, the quantity would be right for four.

SERVES 8 AS A FIRST COURSE

1	6-ounce baking potato, peeled and cut into chunks
½	cup milk
¼	pound cod fillet
½	teaspoon chopped fresh rosemary, or ¼ teaspoon dried
4	cloves garlic, minced
1¼	teaspoons salt
	Fresh-ground black pepper
¾	pound crabmeat, picked clean of shells
	Pinch grated nutmeg
½	cup plus 2 tablespoons olive oil
48	wonton wrappers
2½	pounds tomatoes, about 5
2	shallots, chopped
¾	cup water
½	teaspoon chopped fresh oregano, or ¼ teaspoon dried
½	teaspoon chopped fresh thyme, or ¼ teaspoon dried
4	tablespoons butter
1	fennel bulb (about 1 pound), sliced, feathery tops reserved

WINE RECOMMENDATION:
A SIMPLE WHITE WINE WILL WORK BEST WITH THE UNUSUAL FLAVORS OF THIS DISH. TRY A WHITE WINE FROM NEAR THE SHORE, SUCH AS VERDICCHIO FROM THE MARCHES REGION OF ITALY.

1. Put the potato in a saucepan of salted water. Bring to a boil and simmer until the potato can be pierced easily with a fork, about 20 minutes. Drain and push through a sieve. You will need ½ cup potato puree.

2. In a small saucepan, heat the milk. Add the cod, rosemary, garlic, ½ teaspoon of the salt and ¼ teaspoon pepper. Bring to a boil and simmer until the fish is done, about 5 minutes. Transfer the mixture to a medium bowl.

3. With an electric mixer, beat the fish mixture at low speed. Add the potato, ½ pound of the crabmeat and the nutmeg. Heat ½ cup of the oil until hot. Beat the oil into the fish mixture, adding it in a slow, steady stream.

4. On a clean work surface, lay out a few of the wonton wrappers and brush

lightly with water. Place about 2 teaspoons filling in the center of each wrapper. Fold over the opposite corners of each to form a triangle. Press around the filling to remove any air that may be trapped inside. With a 2½-inch cutter, cut the triangles into half-circles. Press firmly around the edges to make sure the agnolotti are sealed. Put on a baking sheet dusted with flour. Continue until you have 48 agnolotti.

5. Smoke the tomatoes in a hot smoker for an hour. Alternatively, cook in a covered grill with wood chips for about 25 minutes. Or you can roast the tomatoes in a 400° oven until slightly charred, about 25 minutes. Chop the tomatoes.

6. In a medium saucepan, heat the remaining 2 tablespoons oil over moderately low heat. Add the shallots and cook, stirring occasionally, until translucent, about 5 minutes. Add the toma-

toes with any juice, ½ cup of the water, the oregano, thyme, ½ teaspoon of the salt and ¼ teaspoon pepper. Simmer until the sauce thickens, about 30 minutes. Puree the sauce in a food processor and then strain it.

7. In a medium saucepan, melt the butter over moderately low heat. Add the fennel, remaining ¼ cup water, ¼ teaspoon salt and a pinch of pepper. Cook, stirring occasionally, until the fennel is very soft and the water has evaporated, about 10 minutes.

8. In a large pot of boiling, salted water, cook the agnolotti until just done, about 3 minutes. Drain. To serve, ladle the tomato sauce into shallow bowls and put a scoop of fennel in the center of each. Arrange the agnolotti around the fennel. Top with some of the reserved crabmeat and fennel sprigs.

—Scott Cohen
Tatou

71

Herb Fazzoletti with Fresh Tomatoes and Butter

These elegant pasta squares can be made with any of the soft-leaved herbs, such as chervil, tarragon, chives or basil, but we think that flat-leaf parsley is the prettiest. Sturdier herbs, such as thyme and rosemary, break through the delicate pasta dough. To save time we suggest cutting a portion of the dough into plain fazzoletti. The plain and herb fazzoletti are cooked separately so that the more attractive herb squares can be easily arranged on top. When you've made a sensational pasta like this, a simple presentation is best. Here fazzoletti is served with chopped herbs, butter and raw-tomato dice.

SERVES 6 AS A FIRST COURSE

Egg Pasta Dough (3-egg quantity), page 11

18 whole fresh flat-leaf parsley leaves

1 large tomato, peeled, seeded and diced (1 cup)

¾ teaspoon salt
 Fresh-ground black pepper

¼ pound butter

2 tablespoons chopped mixed fresh herbs, such as flat-leaf parsley, chives and basil

WINE RECOMMENDATION:
A FRESH, YOUNG SAUVIGNON BLANC, WITH ITS GRASSY AROMA AND AGGRESSIVE FLAVOR, IS AN IDEAL CHOICE TO ACCOMPANY THIS DISH. LOOK FOR A BOTTLE FROM CALIFORNIA OR NEW ZEALAND.

1. Divide the pasta dough into thirds. Roll out two pieces of the dough to less than $1/16$ inch thick by hand or with a pasta machine. Cut them into 2½-inch squares. You should have about 36 squares. Put on a baking sheet dusted with flour.

2. Roll and cut the remaining third with the parsley, as directed on page 74.

3. In a small bowl, toss the tomato with ¼ teaspoon of the salt and a pinch of pepper.

4. In a small pan, melt the butter over low heat. Stir in the chopped herbs, the remaining ½ teaspoon salt and ¼

teaspoon pepper. Remove the pan from the heat.

5. In two separate pots of boiling, salted water, cook the plain and herb fazzoletti until just done, about 4 minutes. Drain separately. Toss the plain fazzoletti with about half the butter and toss the herb fazzoletti with about a quarter of it.

6. To serve, put the plain fazzoletti on plates and top with the herb fazzoletti. Scatter the diced tomatoes and drizzle the remaining herb butter over all.

—Judith Sutton

MAKE-AHEAD PASTA

Although the herb fazzoletti on this page should be cooked within two or three hours of rolling, most pasta can be made ahead. If you're going to keep homemade noodles for more than a few hours, it's best to dry them. After you cut the noodles, gather several strands together and curl them loosely to form nest shapes. Let them dry on a baking sheet sprinkled with flour for twenty-four hours and then layer the nests between sheets of paper towels in a large box or tin. They'll keep for about three weeks in a dry spot. Filled pasta, such as ravioli, takes some time to make; so it's a good idea to prepare them several hours in advance of cooking. Once filled, put the pasta shapes in a single layer on a baking sheet sprinkled with flour. Let dry for half an hour, turning occasionally to prevent sticking, and refrigerate them, uncovered, for up to eight hours. For longer storage freeze them. They keep beautifully for about a month before starting to dry out. Freeze in a single layer on a floured baking sheet. Then put them in a plastic bag or container and seal well.

1. Roll one-third of a 3-egg quantity of Egg Pasta Dough to a 10-by-14-inch rectangle by hand. Cut the dough in half lengthwise. Or, using a pasta machine, roll out the dough to the second thinnest setting and cut in half crosswise. Set one piece of dough aside on a floured surface. Sprinkle with flour and cover loosely with plastic wrap.

2. Put the other piece of dough on a floured surface, roll to a 6-by-16-inch rectangle and trim the ends if necessary. Or roll the other half out through the pasta machine to the thinnest setting.

3. Arrange 9 parsley leaves at 1¾-inch intervals about ½ inch up

from the bottom of the pasta strip. Fold the dough over to cover the leaves and press firmly all along the dough with your fingertips to seal it.

With a sharp knife, cut the strip into individual squares. Roll out each square, first in one direction,

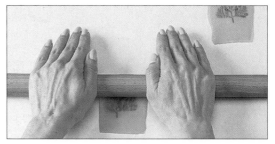

and then in the other direction to less than ¹⁄₁₆ inch thick by hand

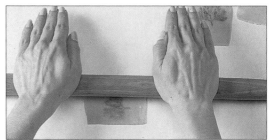

or with the pasta machine, pressing each one firmly before you roll it.

4. Trim the edges if necessary to make 2½-inch squares. Lay the

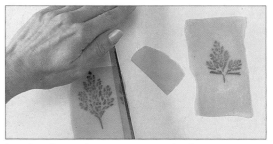

herb fazzoletti on a baking sheet dusted with flour. Repeat with the remaining dough and parsley. You should have 18 herb fazzoletti.

DO-AHEAD BAKED DISHES

Lasagne with Oven-Roasted Vegetables

Roasting gives vegetables so much flavor that no one will miss the meat in this vegetarian version of an old favorite. You can play with the vegetable combination to include those you like best.

SERVES 6

1   red bell pepper, cut into ¾-inch squares

1   yellow bell pepper, cut into ¾-inch squares

1   eggplant (about ¾ pound), cut into ¾-inch dice

2   zucchini (about ½ pound), cut into ¾-inch dice

2   yellow summer squash (about ½ pound), cut into ¾-inch dice

½   pound portobello or other mushrooms, cut into ¾-inch dice

2   shallots, unpeeled, halved lengthwise

1   sprig fresh rosemary or ¼ teaspoon dried

3   tablespoons olive oil

1¾   teaspoons salt
     Fresh-ground black pepper

1   cup (about ½ pound) ricotta cheese

½   pound mozzarella cheese, grated (about 2 cups)

¼   cup grated Parmesan cheese
     Pinch grated nutmeg

1   egg
     Egg Pasta Dough (3-egg quantity), page 11, or ¾ pound dry lasagne noodles (about 15 noodles)

5   cups Classic American-Style Tomato Sauce, page 23 (double recipe)

WINE RECOMMENDATION:
A SIMPLE RED WINE, SUCH AS A SALICE SALENTINO FROM ITALY OR A CÔTES DU RHÔNE FROM FRANCE, WILL WORK WELL WITH THE STRAIGHTFORWARD FLAVORS OF THIS LASAGNE.

1. Heat the oven to 450°. In a large roasting pan, combine the bell peppers, eggplant, zucchini, summer squash, mushrooms, shallots and rosemary. Toss with the oil, 1¼ teaspoons of the salt and ¼ teaspoon pepper. Roast, stirring occasionally, until softened and beginning to brown, about 25 minutes.

2. Discard the rosemary sprig, if using. When the shallots are cool enough to handle, peel and chop them. Combine the chopped shallots, ricotta, 1 cup of the mozzarella, 2 tablespoons of the Parmesan, the nutmeg, egg, the remaining ½ teaspoon salt and ⅛ teaspoon pepper.

3. If using fresh pasta, roll out the dough to less than 1/16 inch thick, by hand or with a pasta machine. Cut into 4-by-8-inch rectangles. ➤

4. In a large pot of boiling, salted water, cook the lasagne until almost tender but still slightly underdone, about 3 minutes for fresh pasta or 10 minutes for dry. Drain. Rinse with cold water and dry on paper towels.

5. Heat the oven to 350°. Oil a 9-by-13-inch baking dish. Spread about ½ cup of the tomato sauce over the bottom of the dish. Lay several sheets of the pasta, slightly overlapping, on the sauce. Dot with half the ricotta mixture. Spread half of the roasted vegetables on top of the cheese. Pour about 1 cup of sauce over the vegetables. Top the sauce with a second layer of pasta. Dot with the remaining ricotta mixture and cover with the remaining vegetables and about 1 cup of sauce. Top the sauce with a final layer of pasta and the remaining sauce. Sprinkle with the remaining 1 cup of mozzarella and 2 tablespoons Parmesan.

6. Bake until golden and bubbling, about 45 minutes. Let rest 15 minutes before cutting into squares.

—Grace Parisi

MOZZARELLA

Try a good fresh, handmade mozzarella once and you'll see what a difference there is between it and the rubbery commercial variety available in supermarkets. The fresh is moist and soft, quick-melting and delicate tasting. Mozzarella was originally made from water-buffalo milk in the Campania region of Italy, and still is today. Prized for its sweet, rich flavor, this pricey mozzarella is rarely used for cooking. Most fresh mozzarella now comes from cow's milk, both in Italy and here. It's delicious tossed into hot pasta, the heat of which is just enough to melt the cheese. It also melts beautifully layered in baked pastas. You'll usually see unsalted mozzarella in a container of water. Refrigerate it in its water and don't expect it to last longer than a few days. The salted version, which is just as good or even better, keeps a bit longer.

Lasagne Bolognese with Meat Sauce and Spinach Pasta

Though the ricotta and tomato-sauce version of lasagne is better known, this luscious classic with creamy Bolognese sauce should not be overlooked. The spinach pasta called for here looks especially nice, but plain can be substituted without harm to the flavor of the dish.

SERVES 6

6	tablespoons butter
6	tablespoons flour
1	quart milk
	Pinch grated nutmeg
1	teaspoon salt
¼	teaspoon fresh-ground black pepper
	Spinach Pasta Dough (3-egg equivalent), page 13
1½	cups Ragù alla Bolognese, page 26
1	cup grated Parmesan cheese

WINE RECOMMENDATION: For this dish, seek a simple, young red wine, such as a Chianti Classico from Italy or an inexpensive cabernet sauvignon from California or Australia.

1. In a large saucepan, melt the butter over moderate heat. Add the flour and cook, whisking, for 1 minute. Whisk in the milk. Still over moderate heat, bring to a boil, whisking. Reduce the heat and simmer the béchamel sauce for about 5 minutes, stirring occasionally. Stir in the nutmeg, salt and pepper.

2. Roll out the pasta dough to less than 1/16 inch thick by hand or with a pasta machine. Cut into 4-by-8-inch rectangles.

3. In a large pot of boiling, salted water, cook the pasta until almost tender but still slightly underdone, about 3 minutes. Drain. Rinse with cold water and dry on paper towels.

4. Heat the oven to 350°. Butter a 9-by-13-inch baking dish. Spread about ½ cup béchamel sauce over the bottom

of the dish. Lay several sheets of pasta, slightly overlapping, on the béchamel. Spread a quarter of the remaining béchamel on the pasta and top with half of the ragù. Sprinkle with ¼ cup Parmesan. Cover with a second layer of pasta. Spread another quarter of the béchamel on the pasta. Sprinkle with ¼ cup Parmesan and top with a third layer of pasta. Spread another quarter of the béchamel on the pasta and top with the remaining ragù. Sprinkle with ¼ cup Parmesan cheese and top with a final layer of pasta. Spread the remaining béchamel on the pasta and top with the remaining ¼ cup Parmesan.

5. Bake the lasagne until golden and bubbling, about 40 minutes. Let rest 15 minutes before cutting into squares.

LASAGNE—
THE FRESH PASTA DIFFERENCE

Lasagne is one dish where the difference between fresh and dry pasta is critical. Lasagne made with thick, store-bought noodles simply cannot compare to the subtle, delicate dish made from paper-thin sheets of handmade pasta. Don't go so far as to avoid lasagne recipes because you don't have time to make fresh noodles. But at least once in a while take the time to make lasagne noodles from scratch, just to experience what this fine dish was truly meant to be.

Lasagne Carnevale

The Italians treat themselves to this lasagne once a year during their pre-Lenten celebration. There are many versions even more rococo than ours, with additions such as chopped vegetables, meat sauce and hard-cooked eggs.

SERVES 6

½   pound ground beef
½   pound ground pork
⅔   cup grated Parmesan cheese
¼   cup fresh bread crumbs
6   tablespoons chopped fresh flat-leaf parsley
1   egg
2   cloves garlic, minced
½   teaspoon grated lemon zest
2   teaspoons salt
½   teaspoon fresh-ground black pepper
¼   cup olive oil
½   pound mild Italian sausage
3   cups (about 1½ pounds) ricotta cheese
¼   teaspoon dried thyme
    Egg Pasta Dough (3-egg quantity), page 11, or ¾ pound dry lasagne noodles (about 15 noodles)
5   cups Basic Italian Tomato Sauce with Pancetta, page 22 (double recipe)
¾   pound mozzarella cheese, grated (about 3 cups)

WINE RECOMMENDATION:
STAY WITH A SIMPLE AND QUAFFABLE WINE TO MATCH THE OPEN, FAMILIAR FLAVORS AND TEXTURES OF THIS DISH. A YOUNG DOLCETTO FROM THE PIEDMONT REGION IN ITALY WILL REFRESH THE PALATE AS WILL A RECENT VINTAGE OF CORBIÈRES FROM SOUTHERN FRANCE.

1. In a medium bowl, combine the ground beef and pork, ⅓ cup of the Parmesan, the bread crumbs, ¼ cup of the parsley, the egg, garlic, lemon zest, 1 teaspoon of the salt and ¼ teaspoon of the pepper.

2. Shape the mixture into about 40 meatballs. In a large frying pan, heat the oil over moderately high heat. Fry the meatballs in batches until brown on all sides, about 3 minutes.

3. Discard all but 1 tablespoon of the oil. Return pan to heat. Add the sausage and cook until browned, about 6 minutes. Let cool. Cut into 1-inch pieces.

4. In a medium bowl, combine the ricotta, the remaining ⅓ cup Parmesan, the remaining 2 tablespoons parsley, the thyme, the remaining 1 teaspoon salt and ¼ teaspoon pepper. ➤

5. If using fresh pasta dough, roll out the dough to less than 1⁄16 inch thick, by hand or with a pasta machine. Cut the dough into 4-by-8-inch rectangles.

6. In a large pot of boiling, salted water, cook the lasagne until almost tender but still slightly underdone, about 3 minutes for fresh or 10 minutes for dry. Drain. Rinse with cold water and dry on paper towels.

7. Heat the oven to 350°. Oil a 9-by-13-inch baking dish. Spread about 1 cup of the tomato sauce over the bottom of the dish. Lay several sheets of the pasta, slightly overlapping, on the sauce. Spread half of the ricotta mixture on the pasta and dot with half the meatballs and sausage. Pour about 1½ cups of the sauce over the meatballs and sausage and sprinkle with about one-third of the mozzarella. Top the cheese with a second layer of pasta. Spread with the remaining ricotta mixture and dot with the remaining meatballs and sausage. Top with 1½ cups of the sauce and half the remaining mozzarella. Top the cheese with a final layer of pasta and the remaining sauce.

8. Cover with aluminum foil and bake 45 minutes. Uncover the lasagne, sprinkle with the remaining mozzarella and bake 15 minutes longer. Let rest 15 minutes before cutting into squares.

Roasted-Asparagus Lasagne

The flavor of fresh asparagus is concentrated in roasting, and its intensity is complemented by the nutty Parmesan and creamy sauce. This dish could be a first course, in which case it would serve six, or take center stage at lunch or supper, accompanied by a simple salad and crusty bread.

SERVES 4

5	tablespoons butter
1½	teaspoons salt
2	tablespoons flour
1½	cups milk
3	tablespoons olive oil
2	onions, cut into thin slices
2	pounds fresh asparagus, peeled
	Egg Pasta Dough (2-egg quantity), page 11
½	cup plus 1 tablespoon heavy cream
¼	pound fresh mozzarella cheese, cut into thin slices
1¼	cups grated Parmesan cheese

WINE RECOMMENDATION:
THE FORCEFUL FLAVOR OF ASPARAGUS MAKES A CLASSIC PAIRING WITH YOUNG, AGGRESSIVE SAUVIGNON BLANC. LUCKILY, THAT WINE WILL ALSO GO NICELY WITH THE PARMESAN. TRY EITHER AN ITALIAN SAUVIGNON BLANC FROM THE FRIULI REGION OR THE SAUVIGNON BLANC-BASED SANCERRE FROM FRANCE'S LOIRE VALLEY.

1. In a medium saucepan, melt 3 tablespoons of the butter with ½ teaspoon of the salt over moderate heat. Add the flour and cook, whisking, for 1 minute. Whisk in the milk. Still over moderate heat, bring to a boil, whisking. Reduce the heat and simmer the béchamel sauce for 5 minutes, stirring occasionally.

2. Heat the oven to 500°. In a large frying pan, melt the remaining 2 tablespoons butter with 1 tablespoon of the oil over moderately low heat. Add the onions and ¾ teaspoon of the salt. Cook, covered, until the onions are very soft, about 15 minutes.

3. On a baking sheet, toss the asparagus with the remaining 2 tablespoons oil and the remaining ¼ teaspoon salt until evenly coated. Spread in a single

layer and roast until tender, about 10 minutes. Remove from the oven and let cool slightly. Cut the asparagus stalks into thin diagonal slices and add them and the tips to the onions.

4. Roll the pasta dough to less than 1/16 inch thick, by hand or with a pasta machine. Cut into approximately 4-by-8-inch rectangles.

5. In a large pot of boiling, salted water, cook the lasagne until almost tender but still slightly underdone, about 3 minutes. Drain. Rinse with cold water and dry on paper towels.

6. Heat the oven to 375°. Oil an 8-inch square baking dish. Spread about a fifth of the béchamel sauce on the bottom of the dish and drizzle 2 table-spoons of heavy cream on top. Cover with 2 pasta rectangles and spread on another fifth of the béchamel. Spread a third of the asparagus and onions on the sauce, cover with a third of the mozzarella and sprinkle ¼ cup of the Parmesan on top. Drizzle with 2 tablespoons of the cream. Top with 2 more pasta rectangles and repeat the layering twice. Cover with 2 final pasta rectangles and top with the remaining béchamel, 1 tablespoon cream and ½ cup Parmesan.

7. Cover the lasagne with aluminum foil and bake for 10 minutes. Uncover and bake until golden and bubbling, about 35 minutes longer. Let rest 5 minutes before cutting.

—Johanne Killeen and
George Germon
Al Forno

Baked Semolina Gnocchi

Baked with a simple topping of Parmesan cheese and butter, these gnocchi make an easy and delicious appetizer or side dish. Semolina is the pale-yellow flour made from durum wheat.

SERVES 4

3   cups milk
¾   cup semolina flour*
3   tablespoons butter
⅔   cup grated Parmesan cheese
2   egg yolks
     Pinch grated nutmeg
½   teaspoon salt
     Pinch fresh-ground pepper

* Available at specialty food stores and Italian markets

WINE RECOMMENDATION:
THE SIMPLE FLAVORS OF THIS DISH ARE BEST SUITED TO A YOUNG, SLIGHTLY RUSTIC RED WINE. TWO IDEAS FROM ITALY ARE A SANGIOVESE DI ROMAGNA OR A MONTE-PULCIANO D'ABRUZZO.

1. In a medium saucepan, bring the milk just to a simmer over moderate heat. Reduce the heat to low and add the semolina in a thin, steady stream, whisking constantly. Simmer for 15 minutes, stirring constantly with a wooden spoon. The mixture will become very thick.

2. Remove from the heat and cool 5 minutes. Stir in 1½ tablespoons of the butter, ⅓ cup of the Parmesan, the egg yolks, nutmeg, salt and pepper.

3. Lightly oil a baking sheet. Spread the gnocchi mixture on the sheet, about ½ inch thick. Refrigerate until cold, about 20 minutes.

4. Heat the oven to 400°. Butter a shallow 1-quart baking dish. With a 1½-inch-round cutter, stamp out 24 gnocchi. Arrange them in the dish slightly overlapping. Sprinkle with the remaining ⅓ cup Parmesan and dot with the remaining 1½ tablespoons butter. Bake until golden brown, about 15 minutes.

The Best Cheese Cannelloni

Using rich and tender crespelle to hold the cheese filling, rather than stodgy, store-bought cylinders, makes all the difference in this recipe. Try them once, and you'll be convinced.

Serves 4

1	tablespoon olive oil
1	onion, chopped
2	cloves garlic, minced
	Pinch dried red-pepper flakes
2	cups (about 1 pound) ricotta cheese
6	tablespoons grated Parmesan cheese
2	eggs
3	tablespoons chopped fresh flat-leaf parsley
½	teaspoon salt
¼	teaspoon fresh-ground black pepper
2	cups Zesty Tomato Sauce, page 24
12	Crespelle, page 19

WINE RECOMMENDATION: The richness of this ricotta-based dish calls for a wine with a lot of exuberance to refresh the palate. Try either a young Beaujolais or a young, inexpensive sauvignon blanc-based wine from the Graves region of France.

1. In a medium frying pan, heat the oil over moderately low heat. Add the onion and cook, stirring occasionally, until golden, about 10 minutes. Add the garlic and red-pepper flakes and cook 2 minutes longer. Let cool.

2. In a medium bowl, combine the onion mixture, ricotta, ¼ cup of the Parmesan, the eggs, parsley, salt and pepper.

3. Heat the oven to 350°. Butter a 9-by-13-inch baking dish. Spread ½ cup of the tomato sauce on the bottom of the baking dish.

4. Put a crespelle, brown-side up, on the work surface. Spoon about 3 tablespoons filling in the center. Fold in 1 inch from opposite sides of the crespelle. Starting from an unfolded side, roll up the crespelle to form a cylinder. Transfer to the prepared baking dish, seam-side down. Continue filling and rolling until

all the cannelloni are completed.

5. Pour the remaining sauce over the filled cannelloni and sprinkle with the remaining 2 tablespoons Parmesan. Bake until hot and bubbling, about 30 minutes.

RICOTTA— GOOD, BETTER, BEST

While commercial brands are good, handmade ricotta, prepared and sold in some cheese shops, specialty stores and Italian markets, has a better flavor— rich and almost sweet tasting rather than bland. Because the handmade variety contains no preservatives, it spoils more quickly than the manufactured type. Some of the best ricotta is not only handmade but from Italy. It is imported to North America, but because of its perishability, few cheese shops stock it. Look for Italian ricotta in early spring, when more is available than usual because it's part of several traditional Italian Easter dishes.

Veal, Sausage and Mushroom Cannelloni

Make these refined cannelloni the classic way with white mushrooms, or add a new flavor dimension by using shiitakes. Either way the dish is perfect for a special first course or an intimate dinner with friends.

SERVES 4

5	tablespoons butter
½	onion, chopped fine
¼	pound white mushrooms, chopped fine
¼	pound mild Italian sausage
¼	pound ground veal
1	egg
½	cup grated Parmesan cheese
1½	tablespoons chopped fresh flat-leaf parsley
1½	teaspoons salt
	Fresh-ground black pepper
	Egg Pasta Dough (2-egg quantity), page 11, or 12 dried pasta tubes
3	tablespoons flour
1	quart milk
	Pinch grated nutmeg

WINE RECOMMENDATION: ANY NUMBER OF MORE SERIOUS, FULL-BODIED RED WINES, SUCH AS A BARBARESCO FROM ITALY OR A CABERNET SAUVIGNON FROM CALIFORNIA, WILL GO WELL WITH THIS DISH.

1. In a medium frying pan, melt 2 tablespoons of the butter over moderately low heat. Add the onion and cook, stirring occasionally, until translucent, about 5 minutes. Raise the heat to moderate. Add the mushrooms and cook, stirring, until brown, about 5 minutes. Remove from the pan.

2. Remove the sausage meat from its casing. Put the sausage meat in a food processor and pulse until chopped fine, about 8 times. Add the sausage and veal to the pan and cook, stirring, until brown, about 5 minutes. Transfer to a medium bowl, cool slightly and add the mushroom mixture, egg, ¼ cup of the Parmesan, the parsley, ¾ teaspoon of the salt and ¼ teaspoon pepper.

3. Roll out the fresh pasta dough, if using, to less than ¹⁄₁₆ inch thick, by hand or with a pasta machine. Cut the dough into twelve 4-inch squares. ➤

4. In a large pot of boiling, salted water, cook the pasta until almost tender but still slightly underdone, about 3 minutes for fresh or 12 minutes for dry. Drain. Rinse with cold water and dry on paper towels.

5. In a medium saucepan, melt the remaining 3 tablespoons butter over moderate heat. Add the flour and cook, whisking, for 1 minute. Whisk in 1½ cups of the milk. Still over moderate heat, bring to a boil, whisking. Reduce the heat and simmer for 5 minutes, stirring occasionally. Stir in the remaining ¾ teaspoon salt, ⅛ teaspoon pepper and the nutmeg. Add ½ cup of this béchamel sauce to the meat filling. Whisk the remaining 2½ cups milk into the

sauce and return to a boil, stirring occasionally. Remove from the heat.

6. Heat the oven to 350°. Oil a 9-by-13-inch baking dish and spread 1 cup of the sauce on the bottom. Put a pasta square on the work surface. Spoon about 2½ tablespoons of the filling along one edge and roll up to form a cylinder. Transfer to the baking dish, seam-side down. Continue until all the cannelloni are filled.

7. Pour the remaining sauce over the filled pasta. Cover the baking dish with aluminum foil and bake for 20 minutes. Remove the foil. Sprinkle with the remaining ¼ cup Parmesan and broil until golden brown, about 2 minutes.

Shellfish Cannelloni with Tarragon Sauce

Delicate crespelle are stuffed full of shrimp, scallops and crab and covered with a creamy tarragon sauce—a luxurious dish indeed.

SERVES 4

¾ cup dry white wine
½ pound medium shrimp
½ pound sea scallops
½ pound lump crabmeat
1 teaspoon salt
  Fresh-ground black pepper
1¾ cups milk, more if needed
6 tablespoons butter
4 tablespoons flour
2 teaspoons chopped fresh tarragon
  or ¾ teaspoon dried
12 Crespelle, page 19

WINE RECOMMENDATION:
THE LUSH TASTES AND TEXTURES OF THIS DISH ARE BEST MIRRORED IN THE WINE TO ACCOMPANY IT. TRY TO FIND A RICH, EXPANSIVE CHARDONNAY FROM CALIFORNIA OR, FROM THE HUNTER VALLEY REGION IN AUSTRALIA, A CHARDONNAY OR CHARDONNAY-SÉMILLON BLEND. IN EITHER CASE, LOOK FOR A VERY RECENT VINTAGE.

1. In a medium saucepan, bring the wine to a simmer. Add the shrimp. Cover and cook until pink, about 2 minutes. Remove with a slotted spoon. Shell the shrimp.

2. Add the scallops to the pan. Cover and cook just until opaque, about 2 minutes. Remove with a slotted spoon. Cut the shellfish into ¼-inch pieces. Reserve the cooking liquid.

3. In a medium bowl, combine the shrimp, scallops, crab, ½ teaspoon of the salt and ¼ teaspoon pepper.

4. Pour the reserved cooking liquid into a measuring cup and add enough milk to measure 2½ cups. In a medium saucepan, melt 4 tablespoons of the butter over moderate heat. Add the flour and cook, whisking, for 1 minute. Whisk in the milk mixture and dried tar-

ragon, if using. Still over moderate heat, bring to a boil, whisking. Reduce the heat and simmer the sauce for 5 minutes, stirring occasionally. Stir in the remaining ½ teaspoon salt and ⅛ teaspoon pepper. Add the fresh tarragon, if using.

5. Heat the oven to 350°. Stir ½ cup of the sauce into the seafood filling. Butter a 9-by-13-inch baking dish. Put one crespelle at a time, brown-side up, on the work surface. Spoon about 3 tablespoons filling in the center. Fold in 1 inch from opposite sides of the crespelle. Starting from an unfolded side, roll up the crespelle to form a cylinder. Transfer to the baking dish, seam-side down.

6. Melt the remaining 2 tablespoons butter. Brush the cannelloni with the butter. Bake until hot, 15 to 20 minutes. Heat the sauce and pour over the cannelloni.

Ricotta Cheese and Chive Stuffed Shells

Pasta shells filled with creamy cheese are perfectly complemented by a zesty tomato sauce. This is the kind of old-fashioned dish beloved by children and adults alike.

SERVES 4

¾   pound jumbo pasta shells
4   cups (about 2 pounds) ricotta cheese
½   cup grated Parmesan cheese
½   pound Fontina cheese, grated (about 2 cups)
2   tablespoons chopped fresh chives, or scallion tops
1   tablespoon chopped fresh flat-leaf parsley
2   eggs
½   teaspoon salt
¼   teaspoon fresh-ground black pepper
     Pinch grated nutmeg
3   cups Basic Italian Tomato Sauce, page 22, pureed

WINE RECOMMENDATION:
THIS SIMPLE CLASSIC IS BEST ACCOMPANIED BY A SIMILARLY UNCOMPLICATED RED WITH PLENTY OF UP-FRONT CHARM, SUCH AS A BEAUJOLAIS NOUVEAU OR AN ITALIAN VINO NOVELLO.

1. In a large pot of boiling, salted water, cook the shells until almost tender but still slightly underdone, about 14 minutes. Drain, rinse with cold water and drain thoroughly.

2. In a medium bowl, combine the ricotta, Parmesan, Fontina, chives, parsley, eggs, salt, pepper and nutmeg.

3. Heat the oven to 350°. Butter a 9-by-13-inch baking dish and cover the bottom with 1 cup of the tomato sauce. Fill the pasta shells with the ricotta filling and put them in the dish. Pour the remaining sauce over the shells. Cover with aluminum foil and bake until the shells are piping hot, about 15 minutes.

Baked Shells with Fresh Spinach and Pancetta

Creamy tomato sauce is caught in the curves of the shell-shaped pasta so that each bite is filled with flavor.

SERVES 4

3	tablespoons butter
1½	cups heavy cream
6	tablespoons tomato puree
6	tablespoons grated Parmesan cheese
1	teaspoon salt
¼	teaspoon fresh-ground black pepper
¼	pound pancetta or prosciutto, cut into small dice
¾	pound fresh spinach, stems removed, leaves washed and torn
¾	pound medium pasta shells

WINE RECOMMENDATION:
CONTRAST THE CREAMY TEXTURE OF THIS DISH WITH A CRISP, WHITE WINE, SUCH AS PINOT BIANCO FROM ITALY'S ALTO ADIGE REGION OR KABINETT (DRY) RIESLING FROM THE MOSEL-SAAR-RUWER REGION OF GERMANY.

1. In a medium saucepan, bring 2 tablespoons of the butter, the heavy cream and tomato puree to a boil. Reduce the heat to moderately low and simmer until reduced to 1¼ cups, about 15 minutes. Remove from the heat and stir in 3 tablespoons of the Parmesan, ½ teaspoon of the salt and ⅛ teaspoon of the pepper.

2. In a large frying pan, melt the remaining 1 tablespoon butter over moderately high heat. Add the pancetta, if using, and cook until slightly crisp, about 3 minutes. Add the spinach in batches and cook, tossing, until wilted. Season with the remaining ½ teaspoon salt and ⅛ teaspoon pepper.

3. Heat the oven to 350°. Butter a 2-quart shallow baking dish. In a large pot of boiling, salted water, cook the shells until almost tender, but slightly underdone, about 8 minutes. Drain.

4. Combine the tomato sauce, spinach, prosciutto, if using, and shells. Transfer to the baking dish and top with the remaining 3 tablespoons Parmesan. Bake until very hot, 15 to 20 minutes.

—Nancy Verde Barr

COOKING PASTA FOR BAKED DISHES

Because it's cooked twice—boiled first and then combined with other ingredients and cooked in the oven—pasta in baked dishes often ends up a characterless mush. To ensure that the finished dish is not overcooked, the pasta should be boiled for less time than normal, until just flexible but still quite firm. To test, cut into a piece. There should be a white uncooked core. Begin testing dried pasta after about 5 minutes of cooking. Fresh pasta, depending on its shape and size, will be ready in even less time.

Baked Rigatoni with Meat Sauce and Mozzarella

This rustic combination of pasta in meat sauce layered with cheese is easy and quick. Ground fennel seed gives the sauce its special flavor.

SERVES 4

2	tablespoons olive oil
2	tablespoons butter
1	onion, chopped
1	carrot, chopped fine
1	rib celery, chopped fine
2	cloves garlic, minced
¼	cup chopped fresh flat-leaf parsley
2	tablespoons chopped fresh basil
1	pound ground beef
1	teaspoon ground fennel seed or 1½ teaspoons whole fennel seed
1½	teaspoons salt
¼	teaspoon fresh-ground black pepper
½	cup dry white wine
4	cups canned tomatoes with their juice (32-ounce can), chopped
6	tablespoons grated Parmesan cheese
¾	pound rigatoni
½	pound mozzarella cheese, grated (about 2 cups)

WINE RECOMMENDATION: THIS RIGATONI WILL PAIR WELL WITH ANY NUMBER OF RUSTIC REDS FROM ITALY OR FRANCE. TWO POSSIBILITIES ARE CHIANTI CLASSICO AND CÔTES DU RHÔNE.

1. Heat the oven to 350°. In a medium frying pan, heat the oil and butter over low heat. Add the onion, carrot, celery, garlic, parsley and basil and cook until very soft, about 20 minutes.

2. Raise the heat to moderate, add the ground beef, fennel seed, salt and pepper and cook, stirring, until the meat is no longer pink, about 5 minutes. Add the wine and cook until almost evaporated, about 5 minutes. Add the tomatoes with their juice and simmer, covered, for 30 minutes. Stir in the Parmesan.

3. In a large pot of boiling, salted water, cook the rigatoni until almost done, about 12 minutes. Drain.

4. Lightly oil a 3-quart oval baking dish. Toss the pasta with the meat sauce and put half of it in the baking dish. Top with half of the mozzarella. Cover with the remaining pasta and top with the remaining mozzarella. Bake until the pasta is piping hot, about 20 minutes.

Baked Penne with Swiss Chard and Ham

A comforting dish on a cold winter night, this simple combination is a great introduction to Swiss chard. The buttered bread crumbs turn crisp in the oven making a delicious topping.

SERVES 4

8   tablespoons butter
1   clove garlic, minced
¾   pound Swiss chard, cut into thin strips
1   teaspoon salt
3   tablespoons flour
3   cups milk
⅛   teaspoon fresh-ground black pepper
¾   pound penne
½   pound Fontina cheese, grated (about 2 cups)
⅓   cup grated Parmesan cheese
½   pound ham, diced
1½   cups fresh bread crumbs

WINE RECOMMENDATION:
LOOK FOR A WHITE WINE WITH DECENT BODY AND GOOD ACIDITY TO PAIR WITH THE HEARTY SWISS CHARD AND HAM FLAVORS. AN INTERESTING PAIRING WOULD BE A YOUNG, DRY, NOT OVERLY AMBITIOUS RIESLING FROM ITALY'S ALTO ADIGE OR FRANCE'S ALSACE.

1. Heat the oven to 350°. Butter a 9-by-13-inch baking dish. In a large frying pan, melt 2 tablespoons of the butter over moderately low heat. Add the garlic and cook 1 minute. Raise the heat to moderate. Stir in the Swiss chard and ¼ teaspoon of the salt and cook until the Swiss chard is tender, 5 to 10 minutes.

2. In a medium saucepan, melt 4 tablespoons of the butter over moderate heat. Add the flour and cook, whisking, for 1 minute. Whisk in the milk. Still over moderate heat, bring to a boil, whisking. Reduce the heat and simmer the béchamel sauce for 5 minutes, stirring occasionally. Stir in the remaining ¾ teaspoon salt and the pepper.

3. In a large pot of boiling, salted water, cook the penne until almost tender but still slightly underdone, about 9 minutes. Drain.

4. Combine the Swiss chard, béchamel, penne, Fontina, Parmesan and ham and transfer to the baking dish. Cover with aluminum foil and bake 45 minutes.

5. Meanwhile, melt the remaining 2 tablespoons butter in a medium frying pan. Add the bread crumbs and stir until coated with butter. Increase the oven temperature to 400°. Uncover the pasta, sprinkle with the bread crumbs and bake until golden brown, about 15 minutes.

—Jan Newberry

MAKING FRESH BREAD CRUMBS

Stale bread makes great crumbs. If you don't have any bread hanging around, leave slices of fresh French, Italian or good-quality commercial bread out for a few hours. Or you can put the bread in a 300° oven to dry it a bit. Bake for about fifteen minutes, turning once. Pulverize the bread in a food processor or blender, or push it through a sieve. There's no need to remove the crusts, unless they're very hard or burned, or you want completely white crumbs. Other types of bread can be used, such as sourdough, whole wheat or rye, or you can make a blend. Store in the refrigerator or freezer. You don't need to thaw the crumbs before using.

Pastitsio

A ground-lamb-and-tomato sauce is gently spiced with cinnamon and baked between layers of macaroni and feathery-light cheese custard. This comforting casserole hails from the Greek islands.

SERVES 6

1	tablespoon olive oil
1	onion, chopped
2	cloves garlic, minced
1	pound ground lamb
3½	cups canned tomatoes with their juice (28-ounce can), chopped
2	teaspoons dried oregano
¼	teaspoon ground cinnamon
1¾	teaspoons salt
½	teaspoon fresh-ground black pepper
6	tablespoons butter
6	tablespoons flour
1	quart milk
½	pound elbow macaroni
2	eggs
1	cup grated kefalotyri or Parmesan cheese

WINE RECOMMENDATION: LOOK FOR A REFRESHING RED WINE WITH PLENTY OF SWEET FRUIT TO PAIR WITH THE SPICED LAMB HERE. A GOOD CHOICE WOULD BE A YOUNG RIOJA FROM SPAIN OR EVEN A FAIRLY STRAIGHTFORWARD CALIFORNIA OR OREGON PINOT NOIR. IN EITHER CASE, THE WINE WILL BE DELIGHTFUL IF SERVED SLIGHTLY CHILLED.

1. In a deep frying pan, heat the oil over moderately low heat. Add the onion and garlic and cook, stirring occasionally, until translucent, about 5 minutes. Raise the heat to moderate. Add the ground lamb and cook, breaking up the meat, until browned, about 5 minutes.

2. Add the tomatoes and juice, oregano, cinnamon, 1 teaspoon of the salt and ¼ teaspoon of the pepper. Simmer the sauce, uncovered, stirring occasionally until thickened, about 40 minutes.

3. In a medium saucepan, melt the butter over moderate heat. Add the flour and cook, whisking, for 1 minute. Whisk in the milk. Still over moderate heat, bring to a boil, whisking. Reduce the heat and simmer the béchamel sauce for 5 minutes, stirring occasionally. Stir in the remaining ¾ teaspoon salt and ¼ teaspoon pepper. Let cool.

4. Heat the oven to 375°. Butter an 8-by-12-inch baking dish. In a large pot of boiling, salted water, cook the macaroni until almost tender but still slightly chewy, about 7 minutes. Drain.

5. Beat the eggs to mix. Whisk the eggs and ¾ cup of the grated cheese into the slightly cooled béchamel sauce.

6. Spread half of the macaroni in the baking dish. Pour 1½ cups cheese sauce over the macaroni and spread it evenly with a rubber spatula. Spread the lamb mixture on top and then the remaining macaroni. Top with the remaining cheese sauce.

7. Rap the baking dish several times on the counter so that the layers settle together. Sprinkle with the remaining ¼ cup grated cheese. Bake until a golden crust forms, about 30 minutes. Let rest 15 minutes before cutting into squares.

Fazzoletti with Lemon Cream, Pistachios and Oven-Dried Cherry Tomatoes

Highly original and attractive, this dish uses homemade pasta to make the folded sheets called *fazzoletti* (literally handkerchiefs). The shaping of the pasta is simple, though, since there's no stuffing or crimping. The combination would still taste great and be even easier made with a good-quality fettuccine rather than fazzoletti and just tossed together.

SERVES 4

10	cherry tomatoes
3	tablespoons butter
2	shallots, minced
1½	cups heavy cream
1	teaspoon grated lemon zest
½	teaspoon salt
¼	teaspoon fresh-ground black pepper
	Egg Pasta Dough (2-egg quantity), page 11
½	pound spinach, stems removed
¼	cup grated Parmesan cheese
3	tablespoons shelled pistachio nuts, chopped

WINE RECOMMENDATION:
THE VARIOUS RICH FLAVORS OF THIS QUIRKY DISH WILL WORK WELL WITH AN EXPANSIVE WHITE WINE. TRY A CHARDONNAY EITHER FROM THE TRENTINO REGION OF ITALY OR FROM CALIFORNIA.

1. Heat a gas oven to 300°, or an electric to 175°. Cut the tomatoes in half through the stem end and put them on a cake rack, cut-side up. If using a gas oven, put the tomatoes in the oven, turn off the heat and leave overnight. If using an electric oven, dry the tomatoes at 175° for 6 to 8 hours. The finished tomatoes should be shriveled and dry on the outside and soft inside. Cut each tomato half in two.

2. Butter a shallow, 9-inch baking or gratin dish. In a medium saucepan, melt 1½ tablespoons of the butter over moderate heat. Add the shallots and cook, stirring, for 2 minutes. Add the cream, lemon zest, ¼ teaspoon of the salt and ⅛ teaspoon of the pepper and bring to a

boil. Reduce the heat and simmer, stirring, until thickened, about 5 minutes.

3. Roll out the pasta dough to less than 1/16 inch thick by hand or with a pasta machine. Cut into twelve 3-inch squares.

4. In a large pot of boiling, salted water, cook the pasta squares until almost done, about 3 minutes. Reserve ½ cup of the pasta water. Drain the pasta. Rinse with cold water and dry on paper towels.

5. Heat the oven to 350°. In a medium frying pan, melt the remaining 1½ tablespoons butter over moderately high heat. Add the spinach, the remaining ¼ teaspoon salt and ⅛ teaspoon pepper and cook, stirring, until just wilted, about 2 minutes.

6. Dip each pasta square in the lemon cream sauce, coating both sides, and fold diagonally into quarters forming triangles. Arrange the triangles in the baking dish in overlapping rows with spinach between each row. Sprinkle with the Parmesan cheese and bake until the fazzoletti are golden brown, about 10 minutes.

7. Heat the remaining lemon cream sauce over low heat. Thin with some of the reserved pasta water if the sauce seems too thick. Stir in the tomatoes and the pistachios and serve over the fazzoletti.

—Jody Adams
Michela's

OVEN-DRIED CHERRY TOMATOES

Simple to make and bursting with flavor, the oven-dried cherry tomatoes in this recipe are a great way to liven up any number of dishes. Use them in salads, tossed with pasta and pesto or cream sauce, or on pizza or crostini. Best of all, this technique makes even out-of-season cherry tomatoes taste great because it concentrates the tomato flavor. They can be packed in olive oil and stored in the refrigerator for weeks.

Macaroni and Cheese

With plenty of sharp cheddar and a crunchy bread-crumb topping, good old macaroni and cheese just doesn't get any better than this.

SERVES 4

5	tablespoons butter
3	tablespoons flour
2	cups milk
¾	pound sharp cheddar cheese, grated (about 3½ cups)
1½	teaspoons Dijon mustard
	Pinch cayenne
1	teaspoon salt
¼	teaspoon fresh-ground black pepper
¾	pound elbow macaroni
1	cup fresh bread crumbs
2	tablespoons chopped fresh parsley

WINE RECOMMENDATION: It's difficult to make a bad wine choice with a dish like this, except by selecting a complex wine. Choose a rough-hewn red wine with plenty of alcohol to play against the sharp creaminess of the cheddar cheese sauce, such as a California zinfandel or a young, lush shiraz from Australia.

1. In a medium saucepan, melt 3 tablespoons of the butter over moderate heat. Add the flour and cook, whisking for 1 minute. Whisk in the milk. Still over moderate heat, bring to a boil, whisking. Reduce the heat and simmer for 5 minutes, stirring occasionally. Remove from the heat. Add the cheese, mustard, cayenne, ¾ teaspoon of the salt and the pepper and whisk until the cheese melts.

2. In a large pot of boiling, salted water, cook the macaroni until almost tender but still slightly underdone, about 7 minutes. Drain.

3. Heat the oven to 350°. Butter a 1½-quart baking dish. Combine the macaroni and cheese sauce. Transfer to the baking dish.

4. Melt the remaining 2 tablespoons butter and combine with the bread

crumbs, chopped fresh parsley and the remaining ¼ teaspoon salt. Sprinkle the bread crumbs over the macaroni. Bake until the top is beginning to brown and the sauce is bubbling, approximately 30 minutes.

PREPARING BAKED PASTA AHEAD

All the pasta dishes in this chapter can be prepared a day ahead. Follow the cooking procedure up to the point where the pasta is put in the oven. Refrigerate the dish, covered tightly with plastic wrap. When ready to bake, simply continue with the recipe, adding 5 to 10 minutes to the baking time if you haven't had time to let the pasta come to room temperature. For cannelloni made with crespelle, such as The Best Cheese Cannelloni, page 87, we recommend refrigerating the filled cannelloni and the sauce separately. This will prevent the delicate crespelle from getting soggy.

Sweet Noodle Kugel

There are many variations on this traditional Jewish pudding. In this one, our favorite sweet version, wide egg noodles are combined with creamy cheeses flavored with lemon and orange zest. The cheesecake-like mixture is studded with raisins and baked until crisp and golden—comfort food par excellence.

SERVES 8

½	pound wide egg noodles
5	tablespoons butter
½	pound farmer, pot or small-curd cottage cheese
½	pound cream cheese
1	cup sour cream
½	cup plus 2 tablespoons sugar
3	eggs
1	teaspoon grated lemon zest
1	teaspoon grated orange zest
1	teaspoon vanilla
½	teaspoon salt
½	cup raisins
1	cup fresh bread crumbs

WINE RECOMMENDATION:
WHEN SERVING KUGEL FOR DESSERT, A LIGHT, FLOWER-SCENTED WINE WILL BE A DELIGHT. IT WOULD BE A MISTAKE, HOWEVER, TO LOOK FOR ANYTHING TOO SWEET OR TOO COMPLEX. ASTI SPUMANTE, THE SWEET, LOW-ALCOHOL SPARKLER FROM ITALY'S PIEDMONT REGION, WOULD BE A GREAT FIRST CHOICE. ALTERNATIVELY, MUSCAT DE BEAUMES-DE-VENISE, A FRENCH STILL WINE FROM THE RHÔNE VALLEY AREA, WOULD ALSO BE EXTREMELY PLEASANT. LOOK FOR THE MOST RECENT VINTAGE OF EACH.

1. Heat the oven to 375°. Butter a 9-inch square baking dish. In a large pot of boiling, salted water, cook the noodles until tender but still slightly underdone, about 7 minutes. Drain. Transfer the noodles to a bowl and stir in 3 tablespoons of the butter.

2. Using an electric mixer set at medium speed, beat the farmer cheese, cream cheese, sour cream and ½ cup of the sugar until smooth. Beat in the eggs, lemon and orange zest, vanilla, salt and raisins. Stir the cheese mixture into the noodles and transfer to the baking dish.

3. Melt the remaining 2 tablespoons butter. In a small bowl, combine the but-

ter, the remaining 2 tablespoons sugar and the bread crumbs. Sprinkle the mixture over the noodles. Bake until the top is golden and the center has set, 35 to 40 minutes. Serve cut into squares, either warm or cooled.

—Ida Bobrow

CITRUS ZEST

The thin, colorful outer layer of a citrus rind is called the zest. A terrific flavor enhancer, zest has a high concentration of aromatic oils and a more intense flavor than citrus juice. When grating zest, be careful not to remove any of the bitter-tasting white pith that lies just beneath it.

PASTA AND VEGETABLES

Spaghetti with Eggplant, Tomatoes and Mozzarella

Cubes of roasted eggplant and fresh mozzarella are tossed with a quick tomato sauce and hot pasta. The mozzarella is added last so it just softens slightly without getting stringy.

SERVES 4

1   large eggplant (about 1¾ pounds), cut into ½-inch cubes
¼   cup olive oil
¾   teaspoon salt
    Fresh-ground black pepper
1   medium onion, chopped
2   garlic cloves, minced
2   pounds tomatoes, about 4, peeled, seeded and chopped (4 cups)
¾   pound spaghetti
3   tablespoons chopped fresh basil
½   pound fresh mozzarella, cut into ½-inch cubes

WINE RECOMMENDATION:
THE PREDOMINANCE OF THE TOMATOES AND EGGPLANT MAKE THIS A TRICKY DISH TO MATCH WITH WINE. STICK WITH A CRISP PINOT GRIGIO FROM ITALY OR THE LIGHTER ORVIETO.

1. Heat the oven to 425°. Toss the eggplant with 2 tablespoons of the oil, ¼ teaspoon of the salt and a pinch of pepper. Spread the eggplant out on a baking sheet. Roast, stirring occasionally, until tender and brown, about 20 minutes.

2. Meanwhile, heat the remaining 2 tablespoons oil in a large frying pan over moderate heat. Add the onion and cook, stirring occasionally, until golden brown, about 8 minutes. Stir in the garlic and cook 1 minute more.

3. Add the tomatoes, the remaining ½ teaspoon salt and ¼ teaspoon pepper. Increase the heat to high and cook, stirring occasionally, until the sauce is thickened, about 10 minutes.

4. In a large pot of boiling, salted water, cook the spaghetti until just done, about 12 minutes. Drain. Toss the pasta with the eggplant, tomato sauce, basil and mozzarella and serve at once.

Rigatoni in Woodsman's Sauce

Presumably, woodsmen found wild mushrooms in the forest, and a mixture of them is a delicious addition to this creamy tomato sauce. If they're in season, choose a few of your favorite varieties. Of course, regular white mushrooms are good, too.

SERVES 4

¼   pound mild Italian sausage

1   tablespoon olive oil

1   small onion, chopped

¼   pound wild or white mushrooms, sliced

2   tablespoons butter

¾   cup canned tomatoes with their juice, chopped

6   tablespoons ricotta cheese

¾   cup cooked fresh or thawed frozen peas

¾   cup half-and-half

1   teaspoon salt

¼   teaspoon fresh-ground black pepper

¾   pound rigatoni

¾   cup grated Parmesan cheese

WINE RECOMMENDATION: A SIMPLE RED WINE WITH PLENTY OF BODY WILL GO NICELY WITH THIS RICH AND HEARTY RIGATONI. LOOK FOR A BARBERA D'ASTI FROM ITALY'S PIEDMONT REGION OR EXPERIMENT WITH AN ALTERNATIVE FROM THE EMERGING WINE REGIONS IN THE SOUTH OF FRANCE, SUCH AS COTEAUX DU LANGUEDOC.

1. Remove the sausage from its casing. In a large saucepan, heat the oil over moderately low heat. Add the onion and cook, stirring occasionally, until translucent, about 5 minutes.

2. Increase the heat to moderate, add the sausage and cook, breaking up the meat, until brown. Drain the fat from the pan.

3. Add the mushrooms and butter and cook 3 minutes. Add the tomatoes and simmer until the sauce has thickened, about 10 minutes. Add 3 tablespoons of the ricotta and mix well. Stir in the peas and the half-and-half, salt and pepper and simmer 5 minutes longer.

4. In a large pot of boiling, salted

water, cook the rigatoni until just done, about 14 minutes. Drain. Return the pasta to the hot pot. Add the sauce to the pasta and mix well over low heat. Stir in the remaining 3 tablespoons ricotta and the Parmesan.

—Lidia Bastianich
Felidia

CLEANING WILD MUSHROOMS

Wild mushrooms often arrive in stores with bits of the forest still clinging to them and almost always require careful cleaning. Discard any stems that are tough and fibrous. Just slice off the earthy base of tender stems. Cut out any damaged parts of the caps. Despite what you may have heard, fresh mushrooms can be washed without damaging their flavor or texture. Simply rinse mushrooms in a colander under cold running water, tossing gently to dislodge dirt. If you soak mushrooms, they will indeed absorb water and get mushy. Any stubborn bits of dirt can be brushed away with a damp cloth or your fingers (most "mushroom brushes" are too abrasive). Take extra care when cleaning mushrooms with pitted surfaces, such as morels, or with deep gills, both of which tend to hoard dirt.

Fusilli with Mushrooms and Sage

Twisted fusilli hold plenty of this delicious, creamy mushroom sauce made from a blend of dried and fresh mushrooms.

SERVES 4

1	ounce dried porcini or other dried mushrooms
2	cups hot water
4	tablespoons butter
3	cloves garlic, minced
2	pounds white mushrooms, cut into ¼-inch slices
1¼	teaspoons salt
¼	teaspoon fresh-ground black pepper
½	teaspoon dried sage
1	cup heavy cream
3	tablespoons grated Parmesan cheese, plus more for serving
¾	pound fusilli

WINE RECOMMENDATION:
THE EARTHY FLAVORS OF THE MUSHROOMS AND SAGE WILL PARTNER NICELY WITH A YOUNG, RICH WHITE WINE, SUCH AS CHARDONNAY EITHER FROM ITALY'S TRENTINO REGION OR FROM CALIFORNIA.

1. In a small bowl, soak the porcini in the water until softened, about 20 minutes. Reserve 1 cup of the soaking liquid and drain the mushrooms. Rinse them under running water to remove any grit. Chop the mushrooms. Strain the soaking liquid through a sieve lined with a paper towel.

2. In a large saucepan, melt the butter over moderately low heat. Add the garlic and cook, stirring, for 1 minute. Increase the heat to moderately high, add the porcini and cook, stirring, for 1 minute. Add the white mushrooms, salt and pepper and cook, stirring frequently, until the mushrooms turn golden brown, about 10 minutes.

3. Add the reserved mushroom soaking liquid, sage and cream and bring to a boil. Reduce the heat to moderate and cook until slightly thickened, about 5 minutes. Stir in the Parmesan.

4. In a large pot of boiling, salted water, cook the fusilli until just done, about 13 minutes. Drain. Toss with the mushroom sauce and serve with Parmesan.

—Judith Sutton

SOAKING OUT THE SAND IN DRIED MUSHROOMS

Dried mushrooms, such as porcini and morels, need to be soaked in hot water to soften them and to remove sand. Begin by rinsing the mushrooms with water to remove surface sand. Then put them in a bowl and cover with about four times the volume of hot water. Let soak until soft, for twenty to thirty minutes, depending on the type of mushroom. Rinse again, squeeze out excess water and the mushrooms are ready to be used. The soaking water is full of flavor and can be added to soups or sauces. Before using, remove any sand by straining the liquid through a sieve lined with a paper towel or coffee filter.

Rigatoni with Provençale Tomato Sauce

Full of vegetables and enlivened with flavors from Provence—fennel, capers, herbs and orange—this rustic pasta is a vegetarian's delight.

SERVES 4

1	large red bell pepper
2	tablespoons olive oil
2	tablespoons butter
1	large fennel bulb, cut into thin slices
2	teaspoons sugar
2	medium leeks, white and light-green parts only, cut in half lengthwise, sliced crosswise and washed well
3	shallots, minced
¼	cup red wine
2½	pounds plum tomatoes, about 12, peeled, seeded and chopped (5 cups), or 3½ cups canned tomatoes with their juice (28-ounce can), chopped
2	tablespoons capers, rinsed
1½	teaspoons herbes de Provence, or a mixture of dried herbs, such as thyme, rosemary, marjoram, oregano and savory
1	tablespoon grated orange zest
2	teaspoons salt
¼	teaspoon fresh-ground black pepper
¾	pound rigatoni
20	fresh basil leaves, cut into fine strips, optional

WINE RECOMMENDATION: PROVENÇALE DISHES ARE MOST ALWAYS ENHANCED BY PROVENÇAL WINES. LOOK FOR A BOTTLE OF A YOUNG RED CÔTES DE PROVENCE OR COTEAUX D'AIX-EN-PROVENCE.

1. Roast the pepper over an open flame or broil 4 inches from the heat, turning with tongs as each side blisters and blackens, about 10 minutes in all. When cool enough to handle, pull off the charred skin. Remove stem, seeds and ribs. Cut the pepper into ¼-inch strips.

2. In a large saucepan, heat the oil and butter over moderately high heat. Add the fennel and sugar and cook, stirring occasionally, until softened and golden brown, about 10 minutes. Add the leeks and shallots and cook until translucent, about 3 minutes. Add the red wine and scrape the pan to dislodge any brown bits. Add the roasted pepper, tomatoes, capers, herbs, orange zest, salt and pepper. Reduce heat and simmer, partially covered, for 20 minutes.

3. In a large pot of boiling, salted water, cook the rigatoni until just done, about 14 minutes. Drain. Toss with the sauce and sprinkle with the basil.

—Grace Parisi

Spaghettini with Caramelized Onions, Olives and Anchovies

Even if you usually turn up your nose at anchovies, you will probably like this dish. Because of the sweet caramelized onions and balsamic vinegar, there's no fishy taste.

SERVES 4

¼ cup olive oil
1 pound onions, cut into thin slices
3 cloves garlic, chopped
1½ teaspoons herbes de Provence, or a mixture of dried thyme, rosemary, marjoram, oregano and savory
1 1¾-ounce can anchovy fillets in oil, drained and chopped
½ cup black olives, pitted and chopped
¼ teaspoon fresh-ground black pepper
¾ pound spaghettini
¼ cup chopped fresh flat-leaf parsley
2 tablespoons balsamic vinegar, or more to taste

WINE RECOMMENDATION:
TRY TO FIND A CRISP WHITE WINE FROM NEAR THE SEASHORE TO ENLIVEN THE CARAMELIZED ONIONS AND ANCHOVIES. AN INTERESTING SELECTION IS VERDICCHIO, FROM ITALY'S MARCHES REGION, ALONG THE ADRIATIC COAST. A WINE FROM THE FRENCH RIVIERA, SUCH AS CASSIS, IS AN ALTERNATIVE. IN EITHER CASE, STAY WITH VERY RECENT VINTAGES, AS FRESHNESS IS THE KEY TO THIS MATCH.

1. In a large frying pan, heat 2 tablespoons of the oil over low heat. Add the onions, garlic, herbes de Provence and anchovies and stir until coated with the oil. Cook, covered, stirring occasionally, until the onions are very soft and just beginning to brown, about 20 minutes.

2. Uncover and cook over moderately high heat, stirring often, until golden brown, about 15 minutes. Add the olives and pepper and cook, stirring occasionally, about 5 minutes longer.

3. In a large pot of boiling, salted water, cook the spaghettini until just done, about 9 minutes. Just before draining, remove about ¾ cup of the

pasta water and add it to the onion mixture. Stir the mixture over high heat, scraping up any brown bits.

4. Drain the spaghettini and return to the hot pot. Add the onion mixture to the pasta with the remaining 2 tablespoons oil, the parsley and vinegar and toss. Add more vinegar if you like.

—Jane Sigal

ABOUT BALSAMIC VINEGAR

Truly great balsamic vinegars, aged for twenty years or more, are dark and sour-sweet, and their flavor is ambrosial. Unfortunately, the years that go into producing such vinegar translate into a high selling price, equal to that of some cognacs. Inexpensive, commercial varieties available in most supermarkets are a different matter. Sometimes aged for less than five years, they are sweet and sour, but have none of the character of the older vinegars. Though we are great admirers of the good stuff, the recipes in this book have been developed and tested with the more mundane variety. If you don't have any, use regular wine vinegar and add a pinch of sugar.

Summer Pasta with Grilled Plum Tomatoes

Make this delicious, quick and easy pasta as an appetizer or side dish when you're grilling steaks or chicken—or any meat, poultry or fish.

SERVES 4

¼ cup chopped fresh basil, plus whole leaves for garnish

¼ cup olive oil

1¾ pounds plum tomatoes, about 8, cored

1½ teaspoons salt

½ teaspoon fresh-ground black pepper

¾ pound bow ties
   Grated Parmesan cheese, for serving

WINE RECOMMENDATION: Serve a chilled rosé wine with this summertime dish, either A Bardolino Chiaretto from Italy or a rosé from Provence.

1. Light the grill. In a large bowl, mix the basil and 3 tablespoons of the oil.

2. Rub the tomatoes with the remaining 1 tablespoon oil to prevent sticking. Grill over a hot fire, turning occasionally, until the tomatoes are very soft and the skins are slightly charred, 20 to 25 minutes. Or roast the tomatoes in the oven: Heat the oven to 400°. Oil a baking sheet. Cut the tomatoes in half lengthwise and put them, cut-side down, on the baking sheet. Roast until the tomatoes are very soft and the skin just starts to char, 20 to 25 minutes.

3. Add the grilled tomatoes with any liquid, the salt and pepper to the basil and oil. Mash the tomatoes with a fork.

4. In a large pot of boiling, salted water, cook the bow ties until just done, about 15 minutes. Drain. Add the pasta to the tomato mixture and toss. Serve with Parmesan.

—Judith Sutton

Bow Ties with Chickpeas and Tomatoes

Cumin, chickpeas, garlic and tomatoes give this easy vegetarian pasta its Middle Eastern flavor.

SERVES 4

3½	cups canned tomatoes with their juice (28-ounce can)
¼	cup olive oil
1	onion, chopped
3	cloves garlic, minced
1	teaspoon ground cumin
⅛	teaspoon cayenne
2	teaspoons salt
1	cup canned chickpeas, rinsed
¾	pound bow ties
¼	cup chopped fresh flat-leaf parsley

WINE RECOMMENDATION:
LOOK FOR A LIGHT, ACIDIC WHITE WINE WITHOUT TOO MUCH PERSONALITY OR AGE TO PAIR WITH THIS DISH. SOME SUGGESTIONS: AN ORVIETO FROM ITALY OR ONE OF THE NEW STYLE OF WINES MADE FROM THE UGNI BLANC GRAPE IN THE GASCOGNE REGION OF FRANCE.

1. Drain the tomatoes, reserving ¾ cup of their juice. Chop the tomatoes.

2. In a large frying pan, heat the oil over moderately low heat. Add the onion, garlic, cumin, cayenne and salt and cook, stirring occasionally, until the onions are translucent, about 5 minutes.

3. Raise the heat to moderate. Add the tomatoes and reserved juice and cook until the sauce thickens, about 20 minutes. Add the chickpeas and cook another 5 minutes.

4. In a large pot of boiling, salted water, cook the bow ties until just done, about 15 minutes. Drain. Toss with the sauce and top with the parsley.

—Jan Newberry

Spicy Penne Charmaine

Mike Fennelly of Mike's on the Avenue in New Orleans brings us this outrageous fusion of flavors from the Orient, Italy and the American Southwest. We think you'll agree, the combination is not at all strange tasting. In fact it's superb. Mike created this pasta for his number-one assistant, Charmaine Morel, using all of her favorite flavors.

SERVES 4

3	tablespoons chopped spinach leaves
1	tablespoon chopped fresh basil
3	tablespoons chopped fresh tomato
2	tablespoons minced sun-dried tomatoes
3	tablespoons heavy cream
3	tablespoons grated Parmesan cheese, plus more for serving
1	scallion including green top, minced
1	tablespoon olive oil
1	tablespoon tomato paste
2	teaspoons Asian fish sauce (nam pla or nuoc mam)*
1	teaspoon minced fresh jalapeño pepper
1	teaspoon lime juice
1	clove garlic, minced
½	teaspoon sugar
½	teaspoon Chimayo or ancho chile powder, or any other medium-hot chile powder, or ¼ teaspoon cayenne and ¼ teaspoon paprika
¼	teaspoon salt
⅛	teaspoon fresh-ground black pepper
¾	pound penne

* Available in Asian markets

WINE RECOMMENDATION:
TRY TO FIND AN EASYGOING, UNDEMANDING WHITE WINE TO DRINK ALONGSIDE THIS DISH. A RELIABLE CHOICE WOULD BE A PINOT GRIGIO FROM JUST ABOUT ANYWHERE IN ITALY OR AN ORVIETO.

1. In a large bowl, combine the spinach, basil, fresh and sun-dried tomatoes, cream, Parmesan, scallion, oil, tomato paste, fish sauce, jalapeño, lime juice, garlic, sugar, chile powder, salt and pepper.

2. In a large pot of boiling, salted water, cook the penne until just done, about 13 minutes. Drain.

3. Add the pasta to the sauce and toss. Serve immediately with extra Parmesan.

—Mike Fennelly
Mike's on the Avenue

Fettuccine with Endive, Mushrooms and Bacon

When cooked quickly as in this recipe, Belgian endive does not become overly bitter. The smoky, salty bacon and rich cream balance the pleasant hint of bitterness.

SERVES 4

Egg Pasta Dough (3-egg quantity), page 11, or ¾ pound dry fettuccine
½ pound bacon, cut crosswise into ½-inch pieces
1 pound mushrooms, sliced thin
2 heads Belgian endive (about ¾ pound), cut crosswise into ½-inch pieces
½ teaspoon dried thyme
1 teaspoon salt
1 cup Chicken Stock, page 29, or canned low-sodium chicken broth
2 cups heavy cream
2 tablespoons chopped fresh flat-leaf parsley

WINE RECOMMENDATION: Look for a young sauvignon blanc to cut through the cream and stand up to the slight bitterness of the endive. A good region for sauvignon blanc in Italy is Alto Adige. Californian or inexpensive French (look for white Graves) versions of this varietal are equally good alternatives.

1. Roll out the pasta dough, if using, to less than ¹⁄₁₆ inch thick by hand or with a pasta machine. Cut into ¼-inch-wide strips and put on a baking sheet dusted with flour.

2. In a large frying pan, cook the bacon over moderate heat until crisp. Drain on paper towels. Discard all but 2 tablespoons of the bacon fat.

3. Put the pan over high heat. Add the mushrooms and sauté, stirring occasionally, until golden and tender, about 8 minutes.

4. Stir in the endive, thyme and salt. Add the chicken stock, reduce the heat to moderate and simmer until the endive softens, about 5 minutes.

5. Add the cream and simmer until the sauce has thickened and reduced by almost half.

6. In a large pot of boiling, salted water, cook the fettuccine until just done, about 4 minutes for fresh pasta or 12 minutes for dry. Reserve ¼ cup of the pasta water. Drain the fettuccine. Add the pasta to the frying pan and toss with the sauce, adding the reserved water if the pasta seems dry. Top with the bacon and parsley and serve at once.

—Jan Newberry

A BETTER WAY TO THIN A SAUCE

Before draining pasta, ladle out a bit of the water in case your sauce is too thick. Because pasta cooking water contains starch, it thins a sauce and adds a bit of body at the same time. Just stir in as much as needed.

Garden-Style
Whole-Wheat Pappardelle

Whole-wheat flour gives a rustic quality to fresh pasta. Here wide noodles are tossed with eight different vegetables for a satisfying main dish or a pleasing first course, in which case it will serve six.

SERVES 4

Whole-Wheat Pasta Dough (3-egg quantity), page 14, or ¾ pound dry whole-wheat pasta

2   small zucchini, cut into ¼-by-2-inch sticks

4   asparagus spears, peeled and cut into 1-inch pieces

¼   pound green beans, cut into 1-inch pieces (about ¾ cup)

¼   pound broccoli, cut into small florets (about 1 cup)

¾   cup shelled fresh or frozen peas

3   tablespoons olive oil

1   small onion, cut into thin slices

3   cloves garlic, minced

2   ounces shiitake mushrooms, stems removed, caps sliced (about ¾ cup)

¾   pound plum tomatoes, about 4, peeled and chopped (1½ cups)

¼   teaspoon dried red-pepper flakes

1   teaspoon salt

¼   teaspoon fresh-ground black pepper

6   tablespoons Chicken Stock, page 29, or canned low-sodium chicken broth

3   tablespoons chopped fresh basil

¾   cup grated Parmesan cheese

WINE RECOMMENDATION:
THIS DISH, WITH ITS MEDLEY OF VEGETABLE FLAVORS AND TOUCH OF HOT PEPPER, WILL BE ENHANCED BY A RICH WHITE WINE, SUCH AS VOUVRAY DEMI-SEC FROM THE LOIRE VALLEY OR PINOT BLANC FROM ALSACE, BOTH IN FRANCE.

1. Roll out the pasta dough, if using, to less than ¹⁄₁₆ inch thick by hand or with a pasta machine. Cut into ¾-inch-wide strips and put on a baking sheet dusted with flour.

2. Bring a large saucepan of salted water to a boil. One vegetable at a time, cook the zucchini, asparagus, green beans, broccoli and fresh peas, if using, in the water just until done. Remove with a slotted spoon. Rinse with cold water. Drain thoroughly.

3. In a large frying pan, heat the oil over moderate heat. Add the onion and garlic and cook, stirring occasionally, until golden, about 3 minutes. Add the mushrooms and sauté 3 minutes. Add the tomatoes, red-pepper flakes, salt and pepper. Reduce the heat to low and cook for 10 minutes, stirring frequently. Add the green vegetables, stock and frozen

peas, if using, and cook for 5 minutes, stirring. Stir in the basil.

4. In a large pot of boiling, salted water, cook the pappardelle until just done, about 4 minutes for fresh pasta or 12 minutes for dry. Drain. Return the pasta to the hot pot. Add half the liquid portion of the sauce, leaving most of the vegetables behind, and toss. Add ½ cup of the Parmesan and toss again. Spoon the remaining sauce and vegetables on top. Sprinkle with the remaining ¼ cup Parmesan and serve.

—Lidia Bastianich
Felidia

Fusilli with Roasted Vegetables, Herbs and Parmesan

The hearty flavor of oven-roasted vegetables set off by piquant red-wine vinegar makes this vegetarian dish particularly satisfying. Vary the recipe with broccoli, cabbage, zucchini, Swiss chard stems or any other vegetable that inspires you at the market.

SERVES 4

1	red bell pepper, cut into 1-inch dice
¼	pound green beans, cut into 1-inch pieces
2	carrots, cut into ¼-inch diagonal slices
10	Brussels sprouts, quartered
1	onion, cut into ¼-inch slices
½	cup olive oil
¾	teaspoon salt
¼	teaspoon fresh-ground black pepper
1	clove garlic, minced
3	tablespoons red-wine vinegar
¾	pound fusilli
¼	cup chopped, mixed fresh herbs, such as basil, tarragon, parsley and chives
½	cup grated Parmesan cheese

WINE RECOMMENDATION: THE VARIOUS VEGETABLE FLAVORS HERE (IN PARTICULAR THE TASTE OF BRUSSELS SPROUTS) GO WELL WITH A WHITE WINE, SUCH AS AN ITALIAN RIESLING FROM FRIULI OR A DRY GERMAN KABINETT RIESLING FROM THE MOSEL-SAAR-RUWER.

1. Heat the oven to 450°. In a large bowl, toss the red pepper, green beans, carrots, Brussels sprouts and onion with 2 tablespoons of the oil, the salt and pepper. Spread the vegetables in one layer on a baking sheet and roast until browned and tender, 15 to 20 minutes. Stir the vegetables 2 or 3 times during cooking.

2. Return the vegetables to the bowl and toss with the garlic and vinegar.

3. In a large pot of boiling, salted water, cook the fusilli until just done, about 13 minutes. Drain. Toss with the remaining 6 tablespoons oil, the herbs and cheese. Top with the roasted vegetables and toss before serving.

—Jane Sigal

Pasta Pomodoro with Capers

Here's a quick tomato sauce made especially flavorful by capers and hot red pepper. If you don't have any fresh basil, substitute half a teaspoon of an herb that dries well, such as marjoram or thyme.

SERVES 4

3½ cups canned tomatoes with their juice (28-ounce can)
3   tablespoons olive oil
1   onion, chopped
3   cloves garlic, minced
¾   teaspoon salt
¼   teaspoon fresh-ground black pepper
¼   teaspoon dried red-pepper flakes
2   tablespoons drained capers
10 fresh basil leaves, cut into fine strips
¾   pound spaghetti
¼   cup grated Parmesan cheese
3   tablespoons chopped fresh flat-leaf parsley

WINE RECOMMENDATION:
THE TOMATO SAUCE, HOT PEPPER AND CAPERS MAKE PAIRING THIS DISH WITH WINE DIFFICULT. TRY A VERY LIGHT-BODIED BEAUJOLAIS FROM FRANCE OR A GRENACHE FROM CALIFORNIA. LOOK FOR A YOUNG VINTAGE AND CHILL WELL.

1. Drain the tomatoes, reserving ½ cup of their juice. Chop the tomatoes.

2. In a medium saucepan, heat the oil over moderately low heat. Add the onion and garlic and cook, stirring occasionally, until the onion is translucent, about 5 minutes.

3. Add the tomatoes and juice, salt and black pepper. Bring to a boil, reduce heat to low and simmer for 15 minutes.

4. Add the red-pepper flakes and capers and simmer about 5 minutes. Stir in the basil.

5. In a large pot of boiling, salted water, cook the spaghetti until just done, about 12 minutes. Drain. Toss the pasta with the sauce. Top with the Parmesan and parsley.

—Jim Flint

Bow Ties with White Beans, Arugula and Sun-Dried Tomatoes

Intensely flavored sun-dried tomatoes and fresh arugula are perfect additions to mellow white beans and bow-tie pasta.

SERVES 4

¼   pound dried cannellini or Great Northern beans (about ½ cup)

3   cloves garlic, 1 left whole, 2 minced

1   teaspoon dried thyme

2   bay leaves

1½   teaspoons salt

3   tablespoons olive oil

1   onion, chopped

2   sun-dried tomato halves, chopped

¼   teaspoon dried red-pepper flakes

¾   pound bow ties

¾   pound arugula, stems removed, chopped

¼   cup grated Parmesan cheese

1   tablespoon red-wine vinegar

WINE RECOMMENDATION:
A CRISP, LIGHT WHITE WINE WILL PAIR WELL WITH THE FLAVORS OF THE BEANS, ARUGULA, GARLIC AND RED-PEPPER FLAKES. GOOD CHOICES WOULD BE A YOUNG ORVIETO OR FRASCATI FROM ITALY.

1. In a medium saucepan, soak the beans overnight in plenty of water. Or cover the beans with water. Bring to a boil. Remove the pan from the heat and let the beans soak for 1 hour.

2. Drain the beans. Return them to the saucepan and add cold water to cover by 2 inches. Add the whole garlic clove, the thyme and bay leaves. Simmer the beans, partially covered, until almost tender, about 1 hour. Add ½ teaspoon of the salt and cook the beans until tender, about 15 minutes longer. Drain. Discard the garlic clove and bay leaves.

3. In a large frying pan, heat the oil over moderately low heat. Add the minced garlic and the onion and cook, stirring occasionally, until the onion is translucent, about 5 minutes. Add the beans, sun-dried tomatoes, red-pepper flakes and the remaining 1 teaspoon

salt. Cook until the beans and tomatoes are heated through, about 2 minutes.

4. In a large pot of boiling, salted water, cook the bow ties until just done, about 15 minutes. Reserve about 2 tablespoons of the pasta water. Drain the bow ties and return them to the hot pot. Add the bean mixture, pasta water, arugula, Parmesan and vinegar and toss.
—Susan Shapiro Jaslove

 BEANS AND SALT

Salt and acidic ingredients, such as tomatoes and vinegar, make it difficult for dried beans to absorb liquid. This means that dried beans must always be cooked until soft in unseasoned water. Otherwise they remain tough. But don't forget the salt completely. When the beans are almost done, season them for optimum flavor.

RECONSTITUTING SUN-DRIED TOMATOES

Imported sun-dried tomatoes marinated in oil and packed in jars are delicious, ready to use—and often quite expensive. The dry tomatoes take a little time to prepare but cost considerably less. To reconstitute them, cover with boiling water, let stand fifteen minutes and drain. If you have extra reconstituted tomatoes, either freeze them or pack in jars, cover with olive oil and store in the refrigerator.

Kasha Varnishkes

Kasha and bow-tie egg noodles are a classic Jewish side dish. The recipe can be made several hours ahead and kept at room temperature. Reheat, in a covered ovenproof dish, at 300° for 15 to 20 minutes before serving.

SERVES 4

2	cups Chicken Stock, page 29, or canned low-sodium chicken broth
1	cup kasha
1	egg, lightly beaten
¼	cup rendered chicken fat (schmaltz) or butter
1	teaspoon salt
¼	teaspoon fresh-ground black pepper
1	onion, chopped
6	ounces bow ties

WINE RECOMMENDATION:
THE RICH EARTHINESS OF THIS DISH DEMANDS AN EQUALLY RICH, UNCOMPLICAT-ED, YOUNG WHITE WINE. TRY A PINOT BLANC FROM ALSACE IN FRANCE OR A REASONABLY PRICED, NON-OAKY CHARDONNAY FROM CALIFORNIA.

1. In a medium saucepan, bring the chicken stock to a boil over high heat. Reduce the heat to moderate and cover to keep at a boil.

2. In a medium bowl, combine the kasha and the egg, stirring until the grains are coated. Heat a heavy frying pan over moderately high heat. Add the kasha and cook, stirring constantly, until the grains have separated and have a nutty aroma, about 2 minutes. Add to the boiling chicken stock, stirring. Add 2 tablespoons of the chicken fat, the salt and pepper. Reduce the heat to low, cover and cook until the kasha is tender and the liquid is absorbed, about 20 minutes. Set aside.

3. In a small frying pan, heat the remaining 2 tablespoons chicken fat over moderately low heat. Add the onion and cook, stirring occasionally, until softened and very lightly browned, about

15 minutes. Set aside.

4. In a large pot of boiling, salted water, cook the bow ties until just done, about 15 minutes. Drain. Return the bow ties to the hot pot. Add the kasha and onions and toss.

—Susan R. Friedland

THE SEED THAT ACTS LIKE A GRAIN

Buckwheat is not wheat. In fact, it's not even a grain. It's the seed of a plant in the rhubarb family. Popular in both China and Eastern Europe, buckwheat groats (the hulled seeds) are often called by their Russian name, *kasha*. Usually roasted and used whole, the groats can also be found both raw (albeit with some effort) and crushed to various degrees of fineness. Pancakes made from buckwheat flour have made the earthy, roasted taste familiar to us. If you like the flavor, you're sure to enjoy slightly crunchy kasha.

Pasta and Cheese

Bow Ties with Chèvre and Rosemary

Goat cheese makes a delightfully tangy and creamy sauce for colorful pasta bow ties. Of course, you can use plain bow ties just as well, or, for that matter, another shape of egg pasta, such as fettuccine, either colored or not.

SERVES 6 AS A FIRST COURSE

¾ pound bow ties
4 tablespoons butter
⅓ cup olive oil
¾ pound soft goat cheese, such as Montrachet
4 scallions including green tops, minced
6 tablespoons chopped fresh flat-leaf parsley
2 teaspoons minced fresh rosemary, or 1 teaspoon dried rosemary, crushed
¼ teaspoon salt
¼ teaspoon fresh-ground black pepper
3 tablespoons grated Parmesan cheese, plus more for serving

WINE RECOMMENDATION:
Goat cheese and sauvignon blanc are a classic combination. For this dish, look for a recent vintage of Sancerre or another sauvignon blanc from the Loire Valley in France or try one of the more aggressive sauvignon blancs from New Zealand.

1. In a large pot of boiling, salted water, cook the pasta until just done, about 15 minutes. Reserve 1½ cups of the pasta water. Drain the pasta.

2. In the same pot, melt the butter over moderate heat. Add the oil, goat cheese, scallions, 4 tablespoons of the parsley, the rosemary, salt, pepper and 1¼ cups of the reserved pasta water. Bring to a boil, whisking, until smooth and thickened. If the sauce is too thick, add the remaining pasta water.

3. Add the pasta and Parmesan to the sauce and toss. Sprinkle with the remaining 2 tablespoons parsley and serve with extra Parmesan.

Penne with Goat Cheese and Spicy Tomato Sauce

Aged goat cheese is crumbly rather than creamy like the fresh. If aged cheese is hard to find, try substituting another fairly dry cheese, such as feta or ricotta salata.

SERVES 4

¼   cup olive oil
1   red bell pepper, chopped
1   onion, chopped
2   cloves garlic, minced
2   anchovies, chopped
⅛   teaspoon dried red-pepper flakes
1   teaspoon salt
¼   teaspoon fresh-ground black pepper
2   cups canned tomatoes with their juice
¼   cup red-wine vinegar
¾   pound penne
½   pound aged goat cheese, such as Boucheron, crumbled (about 1½ cups)
2   tablespoons chopped fresh parsley

WINE RECOMMENDATION: SAUVIGNON BLANC IS THE PERFECT MATCH FOR GOAT CHEESE, AND IT WILL HOLD ITS OWN WITH THE OTHER CHALLENGING INGREDIENTS IN THIS DISH. LOOK FOR A YOUNG SAUVIGNON BLANC FROM CALIFORNIA OR WASHINGTON STATE.

1. In a large frying pan, heat the oil over moderate heat. Add the bell pepper, onion, garlic, anchovies, red-pepper flakes, salt and black pepper. Cook, stirring occasionally, until the vegetables are soft, about 8 minutes.

2. Drain the tomatoes, reserving ½ cup of their juice. Chop the tomatoes. Add the tomatoes with the reserved tomato juice to the pan with the vinegar and cook over low heat until the sauce thickens, 20 to 25 minutes.

3. In a large pot of boiling, salted water, cook the penne until just done, about 13 minutes. Drain and toss with the sauce. Sprinkle with the goat cheese and parsley.

—Jan Newberry

Bow Ties with Ricotta and Asparagus

Celebrate the advent of spring asparagus with this couldn't-be-simpler pasta. To make it really special, use handmade ricotta cheese from a specialty shop.

SERVES 4

¾	pound bow ties
1	pound asparagus, peeled and cut into 1-inch lengths
1	cup (about ½ pound) ricotta cheese
2	tablespoons butter
½	cup grated Parmesan cheese
½	teaspoon salt
¼	teaspoon fresh-ground black pepper

 WINE RECOMMENDATION: LOOK FOR AN ACIDIC, ASSERTIVE WHITE WINE, SUCH AS A RIESLING FROM ALSACE OR A VOUVRAY FROM THE LOIRE VALLEY, TO PAIR WITH THE ASPARAGUS HERE.

1. In a large pot of boiling, salted water, cook the pasta for 12 minutes. Add the asparagus and cook until the pasta and asparagus are just done, about 3 minutes longer.

2. Drain. Toss with the ricotta, butter, Parmesan, salt and pepper. Serve immediately.

—Jan Newberry

PEELING ASPARAGUS

Even the earliest plump, green asparagus that appears in late February and early March may have a somewhat tough outer skin. The same goes for the more unusual purple variety. While they're generally not unpleasant to eat with the skin left on, they're all the better if you peel the stalks with a knife or vegetable peeler. Thin green asparagus, that with a diameter of about a quarter inch, need not be peeled, because it's tender through and through. While it has the advantage of not requiring peeling, we prefer the wider green variety for its more juicy interior. White asparagus, which can be found in specialty markets, has an inedible, woody skin that must be peeled.

Ricotta Pinwheels with Sage Cream

When the combination is perfectly harmonious, a few simple ingredients can add up to a dish that is much more than the sum of its parts. Here spinach pasta holds ricotta and Parmesan and is sauced with sage-infused cream. Perfection. You can make these rolls with plain pasta too. They're just not quite so pretty.

SERVES 4

Spinach Pasta Dough (2-egg equivalent), page 13
2 cups (about 1 pound) ricotta cheese
¼ cup grated Parmesan cheese
1½ teaspoons salt
Fresh-ground black pepper
2 cups heavy cream
2 tablespoons butter
1 tablespoon chopped fresh sage or 1 teaspoon dried

WINE RECOMMENDATION:
A BRACINGLY ACIDIC WHITE WINE WILL CONTRAST NICELY WITH THE RICH FLAVORS AND CREAMY TEXTURE OF THIS DISH. LOOK FOR A CHENIN BLANC FROM VOUVRAY IN THE LOIRE VALLEY, EITHER SEC (DRY) OR SPARKLING.

1. Roll the pasta dough out to less than 1/16 inch thick by hand or with a pasta machine. Cut the dough into twelve 4-inch squares.

2. In a large pot of boiling, salted water, cook the pasta until just done, about 4 minutes. Drain. Rinse with cold water and dry on paper towels.

3. Butter a shallow baking dish. In a medium bowl, stir together the ricotta, 2 tablespoons of the Parmesan, ¾ teaspoon of the salt and ¼ teaspoon pepper.

4. Heat the oven to 375°. Lay several pasta squares on a work surface. Spread about 1 tablespoon of the ricotta mixture on each one. Roll into thin cylinders and arrange them, seam-side down, in the baking dish. Continue until

all the pasta and filling has been used.

5. In a medium saucepan, boil the cream, butter and sage until reduced to about 1½ cups. Stir in the remaining 2 tablespoons Parmesan, ¾ teaspoon salt and ⅛ teaspoon pepper. Pour the sauce over the pasta. Bake until bubbling and golden around the edges, 10 to 15 minutes. Serve immediately.

BUYING PARMESAN CHEESE

While ready-grated Parmesan cheese is convenient, we recommend grating it yourself. The cheese will have more flavor. Even further, if you have the choice, buy it not only by the piece instead of grated but in a wedge just cut from the wheel rather than in a pre-cut chunk. Once cut away from the rest of the wheel, the cheese dries and loses flavor faster. Look for Parmesan that has a uniform pale, creamy color and no dry white patches. The texture should be crumbly, not rock-hard, and the taste should be mellow, neither harsh nor extremely salty.

Gratinéed Potato Gnocchi in Sage Cream

Classic, light gnocchi in a smooth sage-infused sauce make a memorable appetizer that is both comforting and elegant. It's especially nice when baked and served in individual gratin dishes so that each person is sure to get some of the golden cheese topping.

SERVES 6 AS A FIRST COURSE

2	large baking potatoes (about 1 pound)
1	egg
½	cup flour
½	cup grated Parmesan cheese
¾	teaspoon salt
¼	teaspoon fresh-ground black pepper
	Pinch grated nutmeg
1½	cups Chicken Stock, page 29, or canned low-sodium chicken broth
20	leaves fresh sage, or ½ teaspoon dried
1	cup heavy cream
2	tablespoons butter

WINE RECOMMENDATION: A FULL-BODIED WHITE WINE, SUCH AS A CHARDONNAY FROM CALIFORNIA OR A SÉMILLON FROM AUSTRALIA, WILL COMPLEMENT THE RICH, CREAMY TASTE AND TEXTURE OF THIS DISH.

1. Put the potatoes in a large saucepan of salted water. Bring to a boil and simmer until the potatoes can be pierced easily with a fork, about 40 minutes. Drain and let cool.

2. Peel the potatoes and work them through a ricer or a coarse sieve. Let them cool completely.

3. Beat the egg and add to the potatoes. Mix in the flour, ¼ cup of the Parmesan, the salt, ⅛ teaspoon of the pepper and the nutmeg.

4. Dust your hands and the work surface with flour and divide the dough into 4 parts. Using both hands, roll each piece of dough into a ½-inch-thick rope and then cut the rope at ½-inch intervals. Shape as directed on page 144.

5. In a large, wide pot of boiling, salt-

ed water, cook half of the gnocchi until they rise to the surface, about 40 seconds. Remove with a slotted spoon and repeat with the remaining gnocchi.

6. In a medium saucepan over moderately high heat, reduce the stock with half of the sage to ½ cup. Strain into a large frying pan and discard the sage. Add the cream, butter, the remaining ⅛ teaspoon pepper and remaining sage. Bring to a boil and cook over moderately high heat until thickened, about 6 minutes. Add the gnocchi, gently toss and simmer 1 minute longer.

7. Spoon the gnocchi into a large shallow gratin dish or divide among individual dishes. Sprinkle with the remaining ¼ cup Parmesan and broil until golden brown.

SHAPING GNOCCHI

For traditional gnocchi, roll one side of each piece of dough along the inside curve of a fork, pressing the opposite side gently with your thumb. The dough will flatten out slightly and then, as it falls off the fork into your hand, will curl in on itself. The finished gnocchi should be oval with ridges on one side and an indentation on the other. It takes a bit of practice to get this right. Don't worry about it. The ridges and indentation are nice to collect the sauce, but even if you just roll the gnocchi into ovals or flatten them by pressing lightly with a fork, they'll taste just as good.

Ricotta Gnocchi with Light Tomato Sauce

Delicate cheese-based gnocchi are an Italian classic. Here they're topped with tomato sauce and glazed with Parmesan.

SERVES 4

2   cups (about 1 pound) ricotta cheese
1¼ cups grated Parmesan cheese
4   egg yolks
¾   cup flour
½   teaspoon salt
¼   teaspoon fresh-ground black pepper
⅛   teaspoon grated nutmeg
2   cups Light Tomato Sauce, page 24

WINE RECOMMENDATION:
A CHIANTI CLASSICO FROM ITALY WOULD BE AN IDEAL ACCOMPANIMENT TO THE CHEESE AND TOMATO SAUCE IN THIS HEARTY DISH.

1. Heat the oven to 400°. Put the ricotta in a medium bowl. Add 1 cup of the Parmesan, the egg yolks, flour, salt, pepper and nutmeg and mix well.

2. With floured hands, taking about 2 teaspoons at a time, shape the mixture into small ovals and drop them onto a plate that has been sprinkled with flour.

3. Carefully drop the gnocchi one by one into a large, wide pot of gently boiling, salted water and cook for 1½ minutes after you add the last one. Remove them with a slotted spoon and drain on paper towels.

4. Butter a shallow 2-quart baking dish. Put in the gnocchi and pour the tomato sauce over them. Sprinkle with the remaining ¼ cup Parmesan and bake until hot, about 10 minutes.

Spinach and Ricotta Gnocchi

That favorite combination of spinach and ricotta cheese comes together again here in a dish that's both delicate and satisfying. These almost fluffy gnocchi are also among the easiest we know since they're shaped by simply rolling ovals of the soft dough in your hands and, once cooked, are just tossed with flavored butter and a bit of grated Parmesan.

SERVES 4

1   pound spinach, stems removed, leaves washed
8   tablespoons butter
1   tablespoon minced onion
¾   cup ricotta cheese
¾   cup flour
2   eggs
1   cup plus 2 tablespoons grated Parmesan cheese
¾   teaspoon salt
¼   teaspoon fresh-ground black pepper
    Pinch grated nutmeg
1   clove garlic, crushed

WINE RECOMMENDATION: THE MILD FLAVORS OF THIS HOMESPUN DISH WILL WORK WELL WITH AN ASSERTIVE SAUVIGNON BLANC FROM NEW ZEALAND OR THE LOIRE VALLEY IN FRANCE.

1. Put the spinach, with just the water that clings to the leaves after washing, in a medium pot. Cover and cook over moderate heat until the leaves wilt, about 5 minutes. Drain and cool. Squeeze out as much water as possible and mince the spinach.

2. In a medium frying pan, melt 2 tablespoons of the butter over moderately low heat. Add the onion and cook, stirring, until translucent, about 5 minutes. Add the spinach and cook, stirring, until the spinach is dry, about 3 minutes. Transfer to a medium bowl and let cool. Stir in the ricotta, flour, eggs, 1 cup of the Parmesan, salt, ⅛ teaspoon of the pepper and the nutmeg.

3. With floured hands, taking about 2 teaspoons at a time, shape the mixture into small ovals and drop them onto a

plate that has been sprinkled with flour.

4. Carefully drop the gnocchi one by one into a large, wide pot of gently boiling, salted water and cook for 2 minutes after you add the last one. Remove them with a slotted spoon.

5. In a large frying pan, melt the remaining 6 tablespoons butter over moderate heat. Add the garlic and cook for 1 minute to flavor the oil. Discard the garlic. Add the gnocchi, the remaining 2 tablespoons Parmesan and ⅛ teaspoon pepper and toss gently.

GNOCCHI VARIETIES

A specialty of Italy, gnocchi are difficult to categorize because there are so many regional and individual variations. Most do, however, fall into one of three categories—potato, cheese or semolina.

◆ By far the most common gnocchi are made from pureed-potato dough, which includes a bit of flour and usually eggs. Cheese or chopped vegetables, such as spinach or mushrooms, can be added to the mix, but potato is the predominant ingredient. The dough is rolled into little curved ovals, poached in salted water and served in any number of sauces (such as Gratinéed Potato Gnocchi in Sage Cream, page 143).

◆ Another major type is based on ricotta cheese, which is bound with flour and eggs to form a soft dough. Vegetables are often included in cheese gnocchi, as in the potato type. The dough is shaped into ovals or balls. These gnocchi are usually poached in salted water and tossed with, or baked in, a sauce (such as Spinach and Ricotta Gnocchi, page 146).

◆ A third variety of gnocchi, hailing from Rome, is made with semolina (flour made from hard durum wheat). The semolina is cooked into a paste with milk, Parmesan and eggs, chilled, cut out in small discs or crescents and baked with butter or a tomato sauce (such as Baked Semolina Gnocchi, page 85).

Fettuccine with Mascarpone, Ricotta and Fresh Herbs

It's hard to believe this delicious dish is so easy to make. The mascarpone and ricotta mixture can be prepared ahead. It becomes a creamy sauce as soon as it's tossed with the hot pasta.

SERVES 4

Egg Pasta Dough (3-egg quantity), page 11, or ¾ pound dry fettuccine
½ cup mascarpone cheese
½ cup ricotta cheese
1 scallion including green top, chopped
1 tablespoon chopped fresh parsley
½ teaspoon chopped fresh thyme, or 1 large pinch dried thyme
1¼ teaspoons salt
½ teaspoon fresh-ground black pepper

WINE RECOMMENDATION: FIND A YOUNG, LIGHT RED THAT WILL REFRESH THE PALATE AND CUT THE RICHNESS OF THE CREAM SAUCE. A GOOD BET WOULD BE AN ITALIAN CHIANTI OR A SIMPLE RED CABERNET FRANC FROM THE LOIRE VALLEY IN FRANCE.

1. Roll out the pasta dough, if using, to less than 1/16 inch thick by hand or with a pasta machine. Cut the dough into ¼-inch-wide strips and put on a baking sheet dusted with flour.

2. In a small bowl, combine the mascarpone, ricotta, scallion, parsley, thyme, salt and pepper.

3. In a large pot of boiling, salted water, cook the fettuccine until just done, about 4 minutes for fresh or 12 minutes for dry. Drain.

4. Return the fettuccine to the hot pot. Add the cheese mixture and stir until melted and smooth. Serve immediately.

Cavatappi with Creamy Tomato and Fontina Sauce

Plenty of cheese melted into basic tomato sauce creates a delicious new creamy-smooth sauce with a distinct flavor of Fontina.

SERVES 4

2 tablespoons olive oil
1 onion, chopped
1 clove garlic, minced
1½ cups Basic Italian Tomato Sauce, page 22 (half recipe)
½ teaspoon salt
⅛ teaspoon fresh-ground black pepper
¾ pound cavatappi
½ pound Fontina cheese, grated (about 2 cups)

WINE RECOMMENDATION:
THE STRONG CHEESE PRESENCE IN THIS DISH DEMANDS A RED WINE, BUT IT SHOULD BE ONE WITH PLENTY OF ACIDITY TO STAND UP TO THE TOMATO SAUCE. A GOOD CHOICE WOULD BE A YOUNG CHIANTI CLASSICO FROM ITALY'S TUSCANY OR A NEBBIOLO D'ALBA FROM ITALY'S PIEDMONT.

1. In a medium frying pan, heat the oil over moderately low heat. Add the onion and cook, stirring occasionally, until translucent, about 5 minutes. Stir in the garlic and cook for 1 minute longer. Add the tomato sauce, salt and pepper and bring to a boil, stirring occasionally. Remove the pan from the heat.

2. In a large pot of boiling, salted water, cook the pasta until just done, about 13 minutes. Drain.

3. Return the pasta to the hot pot. Add the tomato sauce and Fontina and toss over moderate heat just until the cheese melts.

Pasta and Four Cheeses

Spiral pasta in a flavorful sauce featuring four different cheeses—this is the luscious Italian version of macaroni and cheese. The small quantity of Gorgonzola adds just the right amount of sharpness without overpowering the other cheeses.

SERVES 4

¾ pound fusilli
4 tablespoons butter
¼ cup flour
2 cups milk
1 teaspoon salt
¼ teaspoon fresh-ground black pepper
¼ pound mozzarella cheese, grated (about 1 cup)
¼ pound Fontina cheese, grated (about 1 cup)
2 ounces Gorgonzola cheese, chopped
½ cup grated Parmesan cheese

WINE RECOMMENDATION:
PASTA WITH FOUR ITALIAN CHEESES DEMANDS A MEDIUM-BODIED ITALIAN RED WINE (EVEN IF ONE OF THE CHEESES IS GORGONZOLA). TRY A CABERNET SAUVIGNON FROM THE FRIULI REGION OR A BARBERA D'ALBA FROM PIEDMONT.

1. Butter a 7-by-12-inch baking dish or 4 individual baking dishes.

2. In a large pot of boiling, salted water, cook the fusilli until just done, about 13 minutes. Drain.

3. In a medium saucepan, melt the butter over moderate heat. Add the flour and cook, whisking, for 1 minute. Whisk in the milk, salt and pepper. Still over moderate heat, bring to a boil, whisking. Reduce the heat and simmer, stirring occasionally, about 5 minutes. Remove from the heat, add the pasta and cheeses and toss.

4. Put the pasta in the baking dish. Broil until the top turns golden brown, about 3 minutes.

Pasta Fonduta

The combination here of Gruyère cheese, garlic and white wine tastes like Swiss fondue. Pour this creamy sauce over linguine, top with crisp, buttery bread crumbs and you have a delicious dish.

SERVES 4

5	tablespoons butter
½	cup fresh bread crumbs
	Salt
1	clove garlic, minced
¼	cup flour
1	cup milk
½	pound Gruyère cheese, grated (about 2 cups)
½	cup dry white wine
¼	teaspoon fresh-ground black pepper
¾	pound linguine

WINE RECOMMENDATION:
IF PRICE IS NO OBJECT, A RED, GAMAY-BASED DÔLE FROM THE VALAIS REGION OF SWITZERLAND WOULD BE A CLASSIC PAIRING WITH THIS DISH. AS AN ALTERNATIVE, TRY A MORE REASONABLY PRICED GAMAY FROM THE TOURAINE REGION IN THE LOIRE VALLEY OF FRANCE.

1. In a small frying pan, melt 1 tablespoon of the butter over moderate heat. Add the bread crumbs and ⅛ teaspoon salt and cook, stirring occasionally, until golden, about 3 minutes. Set aside.

2. In a medium saucepan, melt the remaining 4 tablespoons butter over moderate heat. Add the garlic and sauté until softened, about 1 minute. Add the flour and cook, whisking, for 1 to 2 minutes. Whisk in the milk, bring to a boil and continue cooking 1 or 2 more minutes. At this point the sauce will be quite thick.

3. Remove the pan from the heat and whisk in the cheese until melted. Stir in the wine, ¾ teaspoon salt and the pepper.

4. In a large pot of boiling, salted water, cook the linguine until just done, about 12 minutes. Drain.

5. Gently reheat the sauce. Divide the pasta among individual plates. Pour the sauce over the pasta and top each serving with toasted bread crumbs.

A WORD ABOUT BUTTER

Salt, originally added to butter as a preservative, is now added for flavor, though many cooks prefer unsalted butter for its clean, unadulterated taste. We've used unsalted butter in developing the recipes for this book, but salted and unsalted can be used pretty much interchangeably, except in sweet recipes.

SEASON TO TASTE

In developing the recipes for this book, we have taken great care to season each one with just the right amount of salt and pepper for maximum flavor. But no amount of testing and tasting in our kitchen can exactly duplicate what will happen in yours. Every time you start a recipe, no matter how many times you've made it before, you are in a sense making a new dish. Each tomato is different— one is sweeter, another has more bite. One slice of ham is saltier than another. The only way to present a perfectly seasoned dish is to taste it as you go along and especially just before serving, adding more salt and pepper if needed. Don't wait until the dish gets to the table. Sprinkling salt (pepper is okay) on top of cooling food can never have the positive effect of adding it during cooking.

Capellini Cake with Caramelized Onions and Cheese

When fried in butter and olive oil, cooked pasta becomes crisp and delicious. This golden cake, flavored with Parmesan and parsley, is a great side-dish alternative to potatoes or rice.

SERVES 4

2	tablespoons butter
2	tablespoons olive oil
3	onions, sliced
1½	teaspoons salt
½	pound capellini or angel hair
2	eggs
¾	cup grated Parmesan cheese
¼	cup chopped fresh parsley
¼	teaspoon fresh-ground black pepper

WINE RECOMMENDATION:
THE SWEET CARAMELIZED ONION FLAVOR OF THIS DISH WILL BE INTERESTINGLY COMPLEMENTED BY A YOUNG, FRUITY WINE, EITHER RED OR WHITE. TRY A GEWÜRZTRAMINER, A WHITE FROM ALSACE IN FRANCE, OR A RED BEAUJOLAIS, ALSO FROM FRANCE.

1. In a large frying pan, melt 1 tablespoon of the butter with 1 tablespoon of the oil over low heat. Add the onions and ½ teaspoon of the salt. Cover and cook the onions until very soft, about 20 minutes. Uncover the onions, increase the heat to moderately high and cook, stirring frequently, until the onions are golden brown, about 10 minutes.

2. In a large pot of boiling, salted water, cook the pasta until just done, about 3 minutes. Drain. Transfer the pasta to a large bowl and let cool slightly.

3. Beat the eggs. Add them to the pasta with the onions, cheese, parsley, the remaining 1 teaspoon salt and the pepper and toss.

4. In a 12-inch nonstick frying pan, melt ½ tablespoon of the butter with ½

tablespoon of the oil over moderately low heat. Add the capellini mixture and press it down to form a flat cake. Cook until a crisp golden crust forms on the bottom, about 15 minutes.

5. Place a large platter or baking sheet over the pan. Invert the pan so the cake drops out. Melt the remaining ½ tablespoon butter with the remaining ½ tablespoon oil in the pan over moderate heat. Slide the cake back into the pan and cook until a golden crust forms on the other side, about 5 minutes. Cut the cake into wedges and serve at once.

—Susan Shapiro Jaslove

CARAMELIZING VEGETABLES

We usually associate caramel with dessert, but in fact the same cooking method used to make caramel sauce can be employed with vegetables. This process, known as caramelization, simply means the browning of sugar by heat. Since all vegetables contain some amount of sugar, you are actually caramelizing the sugar whenever you brown vegetables. Not only does the color change, but so does the flavor as the vegetables develop a fuller, more complex taste. Vegetables high in sugar such as onions and carrots are delicious when caramelized. Sometimes, as in the Fazzoletti with Three Cheeses and Fennel Leek Confit, page 159, a little sugar is added when caramelizing vegetables to supplement the natural sweetness and accentuate the caramel flavor.

Fusilli with Tomatoes, Feta Cheese and Olives

In this easy-to-make summer dish, the hot pasta softens the bits of feta cheese to a creamy consistency, making the combination especially appealing when served warm. But it's good at room temperature too. If you like, substitute another olive, such as Niçoise, for the Greek.

SERVES 4

¾   pound fusilli
¼   cup olive oil
1   clove garlic, minced
1½   pounds tomatoes, about 3, peeled, seeded and chopped (3 cups)
½   pound feta cheese, crumbled (about 1½ cups)
2   dozen Greek olives, pitted and chopped
¼   cup chopped fresh parsley
1   teaspoon salt
¼   teaspoon fresh-ground black pepper

WINE RECOMMENDATION: TRY TO FIND A LIGHT AND CRISP BUT NOT VERY ASSERTIVE WHITE WINE TO COMPLEMENT THE EASTERN MEDITERRANEAN FLAVORS OF THIS DISH. A SOAVE FROM ITALY SHOULD DO NICELY.

1. In a large pot of boiling, salted water, cook the fusilli until just done, about 13 minutes. Drain. Return the pasta to the hot pot.

2. In a small frying pan, heat the oil over moderate heat. Add the garlic and cook until fragrant, about 30 seconds.

3. Add the oil and garlic to the pasta. Toss with the tomatoes, feta cheese, olives, parsley, salt and pepper.

—Jan Newberry

Penne with Gorgonzola Sauce

The pronounced flavor of Gorgonzola cheese is softened with cream to make an irresistible sauce. Penne works well for this dish because the hollow centers trap the sauce.

SERVES 4

6	ounces Gorgonzola cheese
1½	cups heavy cream
½	cup Chicken Stock, page 29, or canned low-sodium chicken broth
⅓	cup dry white wine
2	tablespoons butter
1	teaspoon salt
¼	teaspoon fresh-ground black pepper
¾	pound penne
¼	cup grated Parmesan cheese, plus more for serving
2	tablespoons chopped fresh flat-leaf parsley

WINE RECOMMENDATION:
GORGONZOLA IS A TOUGH CHEESE TO MATCH WITH WINE. TRY AN ACIDIC WHITE, SUCH AS A CHENIN BLANC FROM THE LOIRE VALLEY IN FRANCE, OR AN ACIDIC RED WINE, SUCH AS A YOUNG DOLCETTO FROM THE PIEDMONT REGION IN ITALY.

1. In a medium bowl, mash the Gorgonzola with a fork. Add the cream a little at a time, whisking, until the mixture is fairly smooth. Some lumps of cheese will remain.

2. In a medium frying pan, combine the chicken stock and wine and bring to a boil over moderate heat. Reduce the mixture to about ½ cup. Add the butter.

3. Reduce the heat to moderately low and add the Gorgonzola mixture. Cook, stirring, until the sauce thickens slightly, about 3 minutes. Add the salt and pepper.

4. In a large pot of boiling, salted water, cook the penne until just done, about 13 minutes. Drain.

5. Toss with the Gorgonzola sauce, Parmesan cheese and parsley. Serve immediately with extra Parmesan.

Fazzoletti with Three Cheeses and Fennel Leek Confit

Inventive and delicious, these fazzoletti make a dramatic first course. A cooked square of pasta is topped with a sharp cheese mixture, caramelized fennel and leeks and then another pasta square to make a sort of free-form ravioli. Plain or cracked-pepper pasta can replace the saffron pasta here.

SERVES 6 AS A FIRST COURSE

Saffron Pasta Dough (2-egg equivalent), page 13
¼ pound Gorgonzola cheese, at room temperature
3 tablespoons mascarpone cheese
2 tablespoons grated Parmesan cheese
1 tablespoon butter
1 fennel bulb, cut into thin slices, feathery tops reserved for garnish
2 small leeks, white and light green parts only, cut in half lengthwise, sliced crosswise and washed well
2 cloves garlic, minced
1½ teaspoons sugar
½ teaspoon salt
⅛ teaspoon fresh-ground black pepper
1 tablespoon white-wine vinegar
2 tablespoons Pernod or other anise-flavored liqueur
⅓ cup water
3 cups Vegetable Stock, page 30

WINE RECOMMENDATION: THE COMPLEX MIXTURE OF FLAVORS IN THIS DISH GO WELL WITH A STEELY-DRY ALSATIAN RIESLING OR A TART, YOUNG CHABLIS, BOTH FROM FRANCE.

1. Roll out the pasta dough to less than 1/16 inch thick by hand or with a pasta machine. Cut the dough into twelve 4-inch squares. Put on a baking sheet dusted with flour.

2. In a small bowl, combine the Gorgonzola, mascarpone and Parmesan.

3. In a medium frying pan, melt the butter over moderate heat. Add the fennel, leeks, garlic, sugar, salt and pepper and cook, stirring occasionally, until caramelized, about 15 minutes. Add the vinegar and Pernod and mix well. Add the water, scraping the bottom of the pan to dislodge any brown bits. Cover, reduce the heat and keep warm.

4. In a saucepan, heat the stock over low heat, cover and keep warm. ➤

5. In a large pot of boiling, salted water, cook the pasta until just done, about 4 minutes. Drain thoroughly.

6. Place one square of pasta in each of 6 shallow soup bowls. Scoop ⅙ of the cheese mixture onto the center of each square. Spoon the fennel-leek confit over the cheese and cover with the remaining sheets of pasta. Ladle about ½ cup of the hot vegetable stock over each serving and garnish with the reserved fennel sprigs.

—Grace Parisi

GORGONZOLA

Produced in the Lombardy region of Italy and named after a town near Milan, Gorgonzola is considered one of the top blue cheeses of the world, along with English Stilton and French Roquefort. Actually the veins of this cheese are more green than blue. Young Gorgonzola, labeled *dolce*, is soft, creamy and strong-flavored and is the one we use in all of our recipes. The aged version is firmer and more pungent. When buying young Gorgonzola, look for a warm white color and soft creaminess. Avoid any dry yellow specimens.

PASTA WITH SEAFOOD

Creamy Shrimp and Red Pepper with Ginger

Luscious fare, this rich recipe makes use of stelline, the tiny star-shaped pasta usually reserved for soup. Don't worry about the large quantity of ginger. It's mellowed by the cream and does not overwhelm the other flavors in the dish.

SERVES 4

4	tablespoons butter
2	shallots, chopped
¼	cup chopped fresh ginger
1	cup dry white wine
1½	cups heavy cream
1	teaspoon paprika
1	teaspoon salt
¼	teaspoon fresh-ground black pepper
½	pound stelline, or other small pasta such as orzo
1	pound rock or small shrimp, shelled (if using small shrimp cut them in half)
½	cup red bell pepper, chopped fine
½	cup chopped scallions including green tops
¼	cup grated Parmesan cheese
8	spears fresh chives, optional

WINE RECOMMENDATION:
THE GINGER AND CREAM IN THIS DISH PAIR NICELY WITH A FRUITY BUT ACIDIC WHITE WINE, SUCH AS A GERMAN KABINETT RIESLING FROM THE MOSEL-SAAR-RUWER OR A YOUNG PINOT GRIS FROM OREGON.

1. In a medium saucepan, melt 2 tablespoons of the butter over moderately low heat. Add the shallots and ginger and cook, stirring occasionally, until soft, about 5 minutes. Increase the heat to moderately high. Add the wine and simmer until reduced to about ½ cup. Add the heavy cream and simmer until the mixture is thick enough to coat a spoon, about 10 minutes. Stir in the paprika, salt and pepper. Strain the sauce.

2. In a large pot of boiling, salted water, cook the stelline until just done, about 6 minutes. Drain.

3. In a large frying pan, melt the remaining 2 tablespoons butter over high heat. Add the shrimp, bell pepper and scallions. Cook just until the shrimp turn pink, about 2 minutes. Add the sauce and simmer until slightly thick-

ened, about 3 minutes longer. Stir in the stelline and Parmesan. Serve at once topped with the chives.

—Jimmy Schmidt
The Rattlesnake Club

WHAT ARE ROCK SHRIMP?

Rock shrimp, caught off the coast of mid-Atlantic and southern states and in the Gulf of Mexico, are relatively new to the American cooking scene. Because of their extremely hard shells (hence their name), they were not in much demand until the recent invention of a shelling machine. Now restaurants buy most of them, making them hard to find in fish shops. Rock shrimp have firm meat, much like that of lobster, and are usually sold peeled and often cooked. If you can't find them in your local fish shop, use small shrimp, which work just as well.

Capellini and Shrimp alla Rosa

Slender capellini soak up sauce like a blotter. So toss the pasta first with butter and then ladle the basil-infused sauce over each portion.

SERVES 4

4	tablespoons butter
1	onion, chopped
2	cloves garlic, minced
¼	teaspoon dried red-pepper flakes
1	teaspoon salt
3½	cups canned tomatoes with their juice (28-ounce can), chopped
2	tablespoons heavy cream
¾	pound medium shrimp, shelled
2	tablespoons chopped fresh basil
¾	pound capellini or angel hair

WINE RECOMMENDATION:
Look for a light, crisp white wine to play against the tomato sauce and shrimp, such as a Muscadet from the Loire Valley in France or a vinho verde from Portugal.

1. In a large saucepan, melt 3 tablespoons of the butter over moderately low heat. Add the onion, garlic, red-pepper flakes and salt and cook, stirring occasionally, until the onion is translucent, about 5 minutes. Add the tomatoes and bring to a boil. Reduce the heat and simmer, partially covered, until thick, about 45 minutes. Stir occasionally during cooking.

2. Work the sauce through a food mill or strainer into another saucepan to remove any skin and seeds. Add the heavy cream and bring the sauce to a boil over moderate heat. Add the shrimp and basil and cook just until the shrimp are pink, about 4 minutes.

3. In a large pot of boiling, salted water, cook the pasta until just done, about 3 minutes. Drain. Toss with the remaining 1 tablespoon butter. Serve topped with the sauce.

—Jane Sigal

165

Penne with Garlicky Shrimp and Chorizo

The sweetness of the shrimp and the spiciness of the chorizo combine well in this quick and easy pasta dish.

SERVES 4

1	tablespoon butter
1	carrot, chopped fine
1	rib celery, chopped fine
1	shallot, chopped
1	pound small shrimp, shelled, shells reserved
¼	cup dry white wine
1	tablespoon tomato paste
2	cups water
½	teaspoon black peppercorns
1	slice lemon, about ½-inch thick
2	tablespoons olive oil
½	pound dried chorizo or other dried hot sausage, cut into ½-inch slices
1	clove garlic, minced
1	teaspoon salt
¼	teaspoon fresh-ground black pepper
¾	pound penne
¼	cup chopped fresh parsley

1. In a small saucepan, melt the butter over moderately high heat. Add the carrot, celery and shallot and cook until the vegetables begin to brown, about 3 minutes. Add the reserved shrimp shells. Cook, stirring, until the shells are pink. Add the wine and cook until reduced to about 2 tablespoons. Add the tomato paste, water, peppercorns and lemon slice. Simmer until the liquid is reduced to 1 cup, about 10 minutes. Strain the shrimp stock into a small bowl. Press on the vegetables and shells to get all the liquid.

2. In a large frying pan, heat the olive oil over moderately high heat until very hot. Add the chorizo and cook until well browned, about 3 minutes. Stir in the garlic and cook until fragrant, about 30 seconds. Add the shrimp and sauté until they just begin to turn pink. Pour in the shrimp stock, salt and pepper and scrape the bottom of the pan to dislodge any

brown bits. Simmer 2 minutes.

3. In a large pot of boiling, salted water, cook the penne until just done, about 13 minutes. Drain. Return the pasta to the hot pot and toss with the shrimp mixture and the parsley. Serve in shallow bowls.

—Grace Parisi

DO YOU REALLY NEED TO DEVEIN SHRIMP?

Despite all the gadgets designed to make peeling shrimp easy, the job remains a nuisance. However, you can skip the worst part, removing the so-called vein. It barely affects the flavor, though it does have an impact on appearance.

Noodle Cakes with Shrimp and Roasted-Chile Sauce

For a crisp crust and tender, delicate interior, use fresh Chinese egg or wheat noodles available in Asian stores or large supermarkets. They are sold packed in plastic bags and can be found in the refrigerated produce section near the mung-bean sprouts and tofu. You can also use fresh Italian-style pasta.

SERVES 4

1   pound fresh Chinese egg or wheat noodles, medium or thin width

1   pound medium shrimp, shelled, shells reserved

1   cup water

2   tablespoons soy sauce

1   tablespoon oyster sauce

2   teaspoons cornstarch

1   teaspoon Asian sesame oil

1   teaspoon sake or dry white wine

1   teaspoon sugar

1   large green chile, such as poblano or New Mexico, or 2 fresh jalapeño peppers

6   tablespoons cooking oil

1   onion, sliced

2   cloves garlic, minced

1   tablespoon minced fresh ginger

1   red bell pepper, cut into thin strips

4   canned water chestnuts, cut into thick slices

1   tablespoon lemon juice

1   scallion including green top, cut into thin slices

WINE RECOMMENDATION:
THE WINE ACCOMPANYING THIS DISH SHOULD OFFER QUAFFABLE REFRESHMENT AND LITTLE ELSE. ANYTHING MORE WOULD ONLY GET LOST. LOOK FOR A SIMPLE, FRESH ITALIAN WHITE SUCH AS FRASCATI FROM THE LATIUM REGION OR VERDICCHIO FROM THE MARCHES REGION. BEER IS ALSO AN ALTERNATIVE.

1. In a large pot of boiling, salted water, cook the noodles until tender but still slightly underdone, 30 seconds to 2 minutes, depending on the type of noodle. Drain and allow to cool slightly.

2. Oil a large baking sheet. When the noodles are cool enough to handle, divide them into 4 portions and shape them on the baking sheet into discs about 8 inches in diameter, pressing so that the noodles stick together. Chill for at least an hour or overnight.

3. In a small saucepan combine the shrimp shells and water. Bring to a boil. Reduce the heat and simmer the shrimp stock for 10 minutes. Strain into a measuring cup. Press on the shells to get all the liquid. You should have about ¾ cup

of stock. When the stock has cooled to room temperature, stir in the soy sauce, oyster sauce, cornstarch, sesame oil, sake and sugar.

4. Roast the chile over an open flame or broil 4 inches from the heat, turning with tongs as each side blisters and blackens, about 10 minutes in all. When cool enough to handle, pull off the charred skin; pat dry. Remove the stem and most of the seeds. Cut the chile into medium dice and set aside.

5. In a wok or deep frying pan, heat 2 tablespoons of the cooking oil over moderately high heat until very hot. Add the onion, garlic and ginger and stir-fry until fragrant, about 30 seconds. Add the bell pepper and stir-fry 2 minutes. Add the roasted chile, the water chestnuts and shrimp and stir-fry until the shrimp is almost cooked, 1 to 2 minutes.

6. Stir the shrimp-stock mixture and pour it into the wok. Simmer the sauce, stirring, until thickened, about 1 min-

ute. Remove the wok from the heat.

7. Heat the oven to 300°. In a large frying pan, heat 1½ teaspoons of the cooking oil over moderate heat. When the oil is very hot, slip in one of the noodle cakes and press lightly to keep its shape. Allow the cake to cook undisturbed until golden brown on the bottom, about 5 minutes. Place a large plate over the pan. Invert the pan so the cake drops out. Add another 1½ teaspoons cooking oil, wait a few seconds for it to heat and then slide the cake back into the pan and cook until the second side is brown, about 5 minutes longer. You can use two pans here to save time. Repeat with the remaining noodle cakes using 1 tablespoon oil for each one. Keep the cooked cakes warm in the oven until all four are cooked.

8. Gently reheat the shrimp mixture and add the lemon juice. Serve the noodle cakes topped with the shrimp mixture and sprinkled with the scallion.

—Marcia Kiesel

Angel Hair with Clams

Linguine is the traditional pasta served with clam sauce, but delicate capellini or angel-hair pasta works even better because it melds more thoroughly with the bits of clam and the luscious broth spiked with garlic and hot pepper.

SERVES 4

3   dozen littleneck or cherrystone clams, scrubbed
⅓   cup olive oil
2   cloves garlic, minced
¾   cup dry white wine
¼   cup chopped fresh flat-leaf parsley
    Pinch dried red-pepper flakes
½   teaspoon salt, or to taste
¾   pound angel hair
3   tablespoons butter

WINE RECOMMENDATION: CHOOSE A LIGHT, CRISP AND REFRESHING WHITE WINE FROM A COASTAL AREA IN ITALY, SUCH AS VERDICCHIO FROM THE MARCHES REGION OR PINOT BIANCO FROM THE VENETO REGION. LOOK FOR A YOUNG VERSION OF EITHER OF THESE WINES.

1. Discard any clams that are broken or do not clamp shut when tapped.

2. In a large saucepan, heat the oil and garlic over moderate heat. Cook just until the garlic begins to sizzle. Stir in the clams, white wine, parsley, red-pepper flakes and the salt. Cover and bring to a boil over high heat. Cook, shaking the pan occasionally, just until the clams begin to open, about 3 minutes. Remove the open clams and continue to cook, uncovering the pot as necessary to remove the clams as soon as their shells open. Discard any clams that do not open.

3. Reserve 4 clams for garnish. When cool enough to handle, remove the remaining clams from their shells, holding them over the pan to catch all the juices. Cut the shelled clams in half. Pour the broth through a sieve lined with a paper towel into a large pot. ➤

4. In a large pot of boiling, salted water, cook the angel-hair pasta until just done, about 3 minutes. Drain.

5. Add the butter to the reserved clam-cooking liquid. Bring to a boil over moderate heat. Add the angel-hair pasta and simmer, stirring, for two minutes. Taste and add salt if needed. Remove the pot from the heat, add the clams and toss. Serve, garnished with the 4 reserved clams.

CLEANING FRESH CLAMS

Clam shells harbor lots of sand and should always be scrubbed. First discard any that are broken or that don't close when tapped. Clams can also have some sand inside the shell. If they're to be cooked in liquid that can be strained, as in this recipe, preliminary soaking to purge them of sand is not necessary. If, however, the clams are to be cooked directly in the sauce, they should be soaked first in salted water (one handful salt per each quart of water). Add the clams and let soak for one to two hours. They'll open slightly and release their sand.

Linguine with Tomato Clam Sauce

Pasta and tomato sauce with clams is a classic. For extra body, use canned tomatoes that are packed in puree. The amount of salt you need to add to the sauce will vary depending on your clams, so taste the sauce and add salt if necessary.

SERVES 4

3   dozen littleneck or cherrystone clams, scrubbed
¾   cup dry white wine
¼   cup olive oil
6   cloves garlic, cut into thin slices
3½   cups canned tomatoes in puree (28-ounce can), chopped
1   teaspoon dried oregano
½   teaspoon salt, or to taste
¼   teaspoon fresh-ground black pepper
6   tablespoons chopped fresh flat-leaf parsley
¾   pound linguine

WINE RECOMMENDATION:
PAIR THIS FAVORITE WITH ANY LIGHT, REFRESHING AND NOT OVERLY SERIOUS ITALIAN WHITE WINE, SUCH AS ORVIETO OR FRASCATI.

1. Discard any clams that are broken or do not clamp shut when tapped. In a large saucepan, combine the clams and white wine. Cover and bring to a boil over high heat. Cook, shaking the pan occasionally, just until the clams begin to open, about 3 minutes. Remove the open clams and continue to cook, uncovering the pot as necessary to remove the clams as soon as their shells open. Discard any clams that do not open.

2. When cool enough to handle, remove 2 dozen of the clams from their shells, holding them over the pan to catch all the juices. Set the unshelled clams aside separately. Pour the broth through a sieve lined with a paper towel.

3. In a deep frying pan, heat the oil over moderate heat. Add the garlic and cook until softened, about 1 minute. Add the strained liquid, the tomatoes and puree, oregano, salt and pepper. Boil

the sauce over moderately high heat, stirring occasionally, about 10 minutes. Stir in 4 tablespoons of the parsley.

4. In a large pot of boiling, salted water, cook the linguine until just done, about 12 minutes. Drain. Return the pasta to the hot pot. Add the sauce and shelled clams and toss. Taste and add more salt if needed. Top with the un-shelled clams and remaining parsley.

—Diana Sturgis

STORING DRIED HERBS

Keep dried herbs in the dark. Light, air and moisture are their enemies. Use airtight pottery or dark glass containers; if clear glass containers are your preference, keep them in a dark cabinet. Even under perfect conditions, herbs deteriorate after a year or so. Test by sniffing. If they don't have a pungent aroma, they don't have much flavor either.

Linguine with Clams and Chorizo

A variant of linguine with clam sauce, this recipe adds the Spanish touch of hot chorizo sausage. Use either readily available littleneck or cherrystone clams or, if you can find them, quahogs, or "chowder clams." Quahogs are a great choice—large, flavorful and inexpensive.

SERVES 4

½   pound dried chorizo or other dried hot sausage, cut into ¼-inch pieces

2   tablespoons olive oil

3   cloves garlic, minced

1¾   cups canned tomatoes (14½-ounce can), drained, seeded and chopped

¼   cup dry white wine

3½   dozen littleneck or cherrystone clams, shucked, minced, liquid reserved, or 1 pint minced quahogs with their liquid

½   teaspoon salt, or to taste

⅛   teaspoon fresh-ground black pepper

¾   pound linguine

¼   cup chopped fresh flat-leaf parsley

WINE RECOMMENDATION:
LOOK FOR A WHITE WINE WITH PLENTY OF CHARACTER TO MATCH THE ASSERTIVE FLAVORS OF THIS DISH. AN INTERESTING RANGE OF CHOICES CAN BE FOUND IN SOME OF THE BETTER WINES FROM THE PENEDÈS REGION OF SPAIN. THE TORRES GRAN VIÑA SOL WILL BE AMONG THE EASIEST TO FIND AND A VERY GOOD SELECTION.

1. In a medium frying pan, cook the chorizo over moderate heat until well browned, about 8 minutes. Remove from the pan with a slotted spoon.

2. Add the oil to the pan. When hot, add the garlic and cook 1 minute. Add the tomatoes, wine, ½ cup of the reserved clam liquid, salt and pepper. Simmer until sauce begins to thicken, about 15 minutes. Add the drained clams and increase the heat to high. As soon as the sauce begins to boil, remove the pan from the heat and stir in the chorizo.

3. In a large pot of boiling, salted water, cook the linguine until just done, about 12 minutes. Drain. Toss with the sauce. Taste and add salt if needed. Sprinkle with parsley and serve.

—Jan Newberry

Japanese Noodles with Clams, Ginger and Tomatoes

Udon, the thick Japanese noodles called for in this recipe, are made of wheat flour, salt and water. When cooked, the noodles become soft but retain a pleasant chewiness.

SERVES 4

¾ pound dried Japanese udon noodles or fresh Chinese wheat noodles*

2 dozen littleneck or cherrystone clams, scrubbed

½ cup sake or dry white wine

¼ cup water

2 tablespoons oyster sauce

2 teaspoons soy sauce

1 teaspoon sugar

1 teaspoon Asian sesame oil

2 teaspoons cornstarch

2 teaspoons cooking oil

1 onion, chopped fine

2 tablespoons minced fresh ginger

1 large tomato, chopped (about 1 cup)

¼ teaspoon dried red-pepper flakes, or more to taste

1 scallion, including green top, cut in thin slices

* Available in Asian markets

WINE RECOMMENDATION:
THE BRINE AND SPICINESS HERE MAKE MATCHING A WINE WITH THIS DISH A CHALLENGE. LOOK FOR A VERY YOUNG, FULL-BODIED AND ASSERTIVE WHITE WINE, SUCH AS GEWÜRZTRAMINER, EITHER FROM FRANCE'S ALSACE REGION OR FROM ITALY'S ALTO ADIGE, WHICH MAKES A LIGHTER VERSION THAN THE FRENCH.

1. In a large pot of boiling water, cook the udon, stirring often, until tender but still slightly chewy, about 15 minutes. If using Chinese wheat noodles, cook them in salted water until just done, 1 to 2 minutes. Drain, rinse with cold water and drain thoroughly.

2. Discard any clams that are broken or do not clamp shut when tapped. In a large saucepan, combine the clams, sake and water. Cover and bring to a boil over high heat. Cook, shaking the pan occasionally, just until the clams begin to open, about 3 minutes. Remove the open clams and continue to cook, uncovering the pan as necessary to remove the clams as soon as their shells open. Discard any clams that do not open.

3. When cool enough to handle, remove the clams from their shells, holding them over the pan to catch all the juices. Strain the broth through a sieve lined with a paper towel into a small bowl. Add the oyster sauce, soy sauce, sugar, sesame oil and cornstarch.

4. In a wok or deep frying pan, heat the cooking oil over moderately high heat until very hot. Add the onion and ginger and cook, stirring, until fragrant, about 1 minute. Add the tomato and red-pepper flakes and cook until slightly softened, about 3 minutes. Stir the broth mixture and then pour it into the wok. Simmer until thickened, about 2 minutes. Add the noodles and clams and cook just until heated through, another minute or two. Top with the scallion and serve.

—Marcia Kiesel

Angel Hair with Lobster and Cracked-Pepper Beurre Blanc

A piquant butter sauce is the perfect foil to morsels of sweet lobster meat. We have chosen green and black peppercorns, but you can include red—any combination will do. Be sure to make the beurre blanc just before boiling the pasta. It's a delicate sauce that doesn't hold for long and can't be reheated.

SERVES 4

2	live lobsters (1½ pounds each)
1	teaspoon dried green peppercorns
½	teaspoon black peppercorns
8	tablespoons butter
2	shallots, minced
½	cup dry white wine
¾	teaspoon salt
¾	pound angel hair

WINE RECOMMENDATION:
A CLASSIC PAIRING WITH RICH-TASTING LOBSTER IN A RICH BUTTER SAUCE IS AN EQUALLY RICH WHITE WINE, SPECIFICALLY A WHITE BURGUNDY. THE PEPPERCORNS CHALLENGE BUT DO NOT REFUTE THE LOGIC BEHIND THIS MATCH. THE BEST CHOICE (AND A RELATIVELY AFFORDABLE ONE) WOULD BE A MEURSAULT. A VERY GOOD CALIFORNIA CHARDONNAY (ONE WITH POWER, NOT FINESSE) IS A FINE ALTERNATIVE. LOOK FOR A WINE FROM THREE TO FIVE YEARS OLD.

1. In a large pot of boiling, salted water, cook the lobsters until just done, about 10 minutes after the water returns to a boil.

2. When cool enough to handle, twist to separate the tail sections and the large legs with the claws from the bodies. With the tails upside down, use a large, sharp knife to cut them in half lengthwise. Remove the tail meat from the shells and cut into approximately ¾-inch pieces. Transfer the lobster to a bowl. Crack the knuckles and claws over the bowl to catch any juices. Remove the knuckle

meat, cut into ¾-inch pieces and add it to the bowl. Remove the claw meat, keeping it whole if possible. Set the claw meat aside.

3. Crush the peppercorns. In a small saucepan, melt 1 tablespoon of the butter over moderately low heat. Add the shallots and cook, stirring occasionally, until translucent, about 5 minutes. Add the white wine and cook until the liquid is reduced to about 2 tablespoons. Cut the remaining 7 tablespoons butter into pieces. Over the lowest possible heat, whisk in the butter in 3 batches, adding each batch when the previous one is incorporated. The butter should soften to form a creamy sauce but should not melt completely. Add the green and black pepper and salt.

4. In a large pot of boiling, salted water, cook the angel-hair pasta until just done, about 3 minutes. Drain.

5. Return the angel-hair pasta to the hot pot and toss with the lobster meat (and any liquid it's given off) and the butter sauce. Serve at once, garnished with the claws.

SELECTING LOBSTERS

Choose lively lobsters. While listless lobsters are perfectly all right to eat, they may have been held in the tank for some weeks. Because they're not fed during this time, their meat gradually shrinks, and you wind up with a smaller ratio of meat to shell. To tell how lively a lobster is, pick it up. If it doesn't flip its tail, pick another. If you want lobster roe, choose a female. You can tell the sex of a lobster by looking at the first pair of feelers on the underside of the lobster tail, at the point where the tail meets the body. In males, these two feelers are hard; whereas in females they are soft and feathery. People disagree about size and tenderness, but we find large lobsters to be every bit as tender as small and to be a better buy because there's more meat to shell. Lobsters shed their shells the way blue crabs do, usually during the summer months. While some people prefer the soft-shell lobsters for what they believe to be sweeter-tasting meat, these lobsters have a smaller meat-to-shell ratio, and the shells fill with water during cooking.

Rice Noodles with Lobster, Lemongrass and Tomato

In this delectable Southeast Asian dish, boiled lobster is cracked and then marinated in ginger, garlic and curry powder. A brief stir-frying with tomatoes and lemongrass completes the cooking.

SERVES 4

¾ pound dried rice noodles, medium-width or fine*

2 shallots, minced

2 tablespoons Asian fish sauce (nam pla or nuoc mam)*

6 cloves garlic, minced

3 tablespoons minced fresh ginger

3 tablespoons cooking oil

½ teaspoon fresh-ground black pepper

⅛ teaspoon curry powder

4 live lobsters (1½ pounds each)

2 small red chile peppers, minced, or ½ teaspoon dried red-pepper flakes

1 onion, sliced

6 stalks fresh lemongrass, bottom ⅓ only, smashed and cut into 2-inch lengths*, or six 3-inch strips lemon zest

¼ cup sake or dry white wine

2 pounds tomatoes, about 4, chopped (4 cups)

2 teaspoons lime juice

2 tablespoons chopped fresh basil

2 tablespoons chopped fresh mint

2 tablespoons chopped fresh cilantro

* Available in Asian markets

WINE RECOMMENDATION:
THIS AROMATIC PREPARATION WILL PAIR NICELY WITH A WHITE WINE WITH LOTS OF BODY BUT NOT TOO MUCH FLAVOR. TWO VERY DIFFERENT ITALIAN WINES WILL WORK NICELY WITH THE DISH: A VERNACCIA DI SAN GIMIGNANO FROM TUSCANY OR A GAVI DEI GAVI FROM PIEDMONT. IN EITHER CASE, LOOK FOR A VINTAGE FROM THE PAST THREE YEARS.

1. In a large bowl, cover the rice noodles with cold water and leave to soften, 20 to 30 minutes. Drain and set aside.

2. In a large bowl, combine the shallots, fish sauce, a third of the garlic, 1 tablespoon of the ginger, 1 tablespoon of the oil, the pepper and curry powder.

3. In a large pot of boiling, salted water, cook the lobsters, in 2 batches if necessary, until just done, about 10 minutes after the water returns to a boil.

4. When the lobsters are cool enough to handle, twist to separate the tail sections and the large legs with the claws from the bodies. With the tails upside down, use a large, sharp knife or a pair of kitchen scissors to split the shell on the underside. Cover the claws and

knuckles with a towel, and then whack them in several places with the back of a knife so that the meat will be easy to extract. Put the lobster claws and tails in the bowl and toss until well coated. Marinate 5 to 10 minutes.

5. In a wok or large frying pan, heat the remaining 2 tablespoons oil over moderately high heat until very hot. Add the remaining garlic, 2 tablespoons ginger, the chiles and onion. Cook, stirring, about 1 minute. Add the lemongrass and sake and cook 1 minute. Add half the lobster pieces with half the marinade and stir-fry about 2 minutes. Remove the lobster and add the remaining lobster pieces and marinade. Stir-fry about 2 minutes. Return all the lobster to the wok with any liquid. Add the tomatoes and simmer until the sauce has thickened, about 4 minutes. Turn off the heat. Add the lime juice.

6. In a large pot of boiling, salted water, cook half of the rice noodles, stirring, until translucent but still slightly chewy, 1 to 2 minutes. Lift the noodles from the water with tongs and drain. Cook the remaining noodles in the same way. Top with the lobster pieces. Spoon the sauce over the noodles. Top with the chopped herbs and serve.

—Marcia Kiesel

LEMONGRASS

Woody lemongrass looks something like a stiff scallion but surprises with a delightful lemon scent and flavor. It is sold fresh and dried. When cooking with fresh, strip away the tough outer layers. Cut off the top part of the stalk, using only the lower four to six inches. While the lower part is more tender than the top, it's still quite fibrous. Lemongrass is often cut in large pieces and used as a flavoring, rather like cinnamon sticks. You don't eat it. Either fish it out before serving or just push it to the side of the plate. When minced or ground, it's good to eat, just like powdered cinnamon. If you can't find fresh lemongrass, you can substitute lemon zest. For one stalk of fresh, use a three-inch strip of lemon zest or one-fourth to one-half teaspoon grated. Another alternative is powdered lemongrass. But because the store-bought variety lacks flavor, we recommend that you make your own by pulverizing dried lemongrass chips in a spice grinder, blender or coffee grinder. Sift out any large bits. One teaspoon of the powder is equivalent to one stalk of fresh.

Fettuccine with Squid in Red-Wine Tomato Sauce

Here's a change from the ubiquitous deep-fried squid. The mild-flavored meat benefits from long cooking in a heady red-wine tomato sauce.

SERVES 4

Egg Pasta Dough (3-egg quantity), page 11, or ¾ pound dry fettuccine

2 pounds cleaned squid

¼ cup olive oil

3 cloves garlic, minced

2 cups canned tomatoes, drained and chopped

1 cup red wine

2 teaspoons chopped fresh rosemary, or ½ teaspoon dried rosemary, crushed

⅛ teaspoon dried red-pepper flakes, or more to taste

¾ teaspoon salt

¼ cup chopped fresh parsley

WINE RECOMMENDATION: A REFRESHINGLY LIGHT YOUNG WINE WILL WORK NICELY WITH THIS DISH. TRY A CHILLED ROSÉ FROM PROVENCE IN FRANCE OR A RED CORBIÈRES FROM THE SOUTHERN PART OF FRANCE.

1. Roll out the pasta dough, if using, to less than ¹⁄₁₆ inch thick by hand or with a pasta machine. Cut into ¼-inch-wide strips and put on a baking sheet dusted with flour.

2. Cut the bodies of the squid into ¼-inch rings. Cut the tentacles into halves or quarters, depending on their size. In a deep frying pan, heat the oil over low heat. Add the garlic and cook 1 minute. Raise the heat to moderately high, add the squid and sauté until opaque, about 3 minutes.

3. Add the tomatoes, wine, rosemary, red-pepper flakes and salt. Simmer over moderately low heat, covered, until the squid is tender, about 40 minutes.

4. In a pot of boiling, salted water, cook the pasta until just done, about 4 minutes for fresh or 12 minutes for dry. Drain. Toss with the sauce and parsley.

—Jan Newberry

Spaghettini with Mussels and Pesto

Vibrant basil-and-garlic sauce perks up the subtle blend of spaghettini and mussels steamed in wine. Delectable as this dish is steaming hot, it's also excellent eaten as a salad at room temperature.

SERVES 4

2	pounds small mussels, scrubbed and debearded
½	cup dry white wine
4	tablespoons butter, cut into pieces
1	shallot, chopped
1	tablespoon wine vinegar
¾	pound spaghettini
¾	cup Pesto alla Genovese, page 27

WINE RECOMMENDATION:
THE SUBTLE INTERPLAY OF THE MUSSELS AND PESTO WORK NICELY WITH YOUNG CRISP WHITE WINES, SUCH AS PINOT GRIGIO FROM NORTHERN ITALY OR CÔTES DE PROVENCE FROM FRANCE (IN PARTICULAR, A WHITE WINE FROM CASSIS).

1. Discard any mussels that are broken or do not clamp shut when tapped. In a large pot, combine the mussels, wine, butter, shallot and vinegar. Cover and bring to a boil over high heat. Cook, shaking the pan occasionally, just until the mussels open, about 3 minutes. Remove the open mussels and continue to cook, uncovering the pot as necessary to remove the mussels as soon as their shells open. Discard any mussels that do not open.

2. Reserve about 8 mussels for garnish. When cool enough to handle, remove the remaining mussels from their shells, holding them over the pot to catch all the juice.

3. Pour the cooking liquid through a sieve lined with a paper towel into a measuring cup. Add ½ cup of the strained liquid to the mussels. Discard the re-

maining cooking liquid or save it for another recipe.

4. In a large pot of boiling, salted water, cook the spaghettini until just done, about 9 minutes. Drain. Toss together the spaghettini, mussels and pesto. Top with the reserved mussels and serve hot or at room temperature.

—Jane Sigal

CLEANING MUSSELS

Mussels are often sandy and should be cleaned before cooking. Wash them under cold running water, scraping off barnacles and scrubbing off sand. Pull off and discard the weed-like "beard." Discard any mussels that are broken or that gape open. If a mussel is still alive, it will snap shut when handled. To purge the mussels of sand, soak them according to the method for cleaning fresh clams, page 172.

Tagliatelle with Seafood

The cook at a trattoria in southern Liguria gave this recipe to culinary writer Carol Field, who in turn passed it on to us. Use the freshest possible shellfish, mince the shrimp and squid very fine and use a free hand with the garlic and parsley.

SERVES 4

Egg Pasta Dough (3-egg quantity), page 11, or ¾ pound dry tagliatelle or fettuccine

½	pound cleaned squid, bodies quartered
16	mussels, scrubbed and debearded
16	small clams, scrubbed
½	cup olive oil
4	large cloves garlic, minced
½	cup chopped fresh parsley
⅓	cup dry white wine
¾	pound medium shrimp, shelled and minced
¾	pound tomatoes, peeled, seeded and chopped (about 1½ cups)
½	teaspoon salt
¼	teaspoon fresh-ground black pepper

WINE RECOMMENDATION:
THIS FRESH, LIGHT DISH IS BEST PAIRED WITH A SIMILAR WHITE WINE, PREFERABLY SOMETHING FROM ALONG THE FRENCH OR ITALIAN MEDITERRANEAN COAST. A GOOD CHOICE WOULD BE A BOTTLE OF WHITE WINE FROM THE CÔTES DE PROVENCE IN FRANCE OR A VERDICCHIO FROM THE ITALIAN MARCHES REGION.

1. Roll out the pasta dough, if using, to less than 1/16 inch thick by hand or with a pasta machine. Cut the dough into ¼-inch-wide strips and put on a baking sheet dusted with flour.

2. In a food processor, pulse the squid until minced, or mince it with a knife.

3. Discard any mussels or clams that are broken or do not clamp shut when tapped. In a deep frying pan, combine ¼ cup of the oil, half the garlic and 3 tablespoons of the parsley. Cook over moderate heat until the garlic softens, about 1 minute. Add the mussels, clams and wine. Cover and bring to a boil over high heat. Cook, shaking the pan occasionally, just until the shellfish begin to open, about 3 minutes. Remove the open mussels and clams and continue to cook, uncovering the pan as necessary to

remove the shellfish as soon as they open. Discard any that do not open.

4. When cool enough to handle, remove the mussels and clams from their shells, holding them over the pan to catch all the juice. Strain the broth through a sieve lined with a paper towel and reserve.

5. Pour the remaining ¼ cup olive oil into the pan. Add the remaining garlic and 3 tablespoons of the parsley. Cook over moderate heat until the garlic softens, about 1 minute. Stir in the squid, shrimp, strained liquid, tomatoes and salt. Cook over moderately high heat, stirring, for 5 minutes.

6. In a large pot of boiling, salted water, cook the tagliatelle until just done, about 4 minutes for fresh and 12 minutes for dry. Reserve ½ cup of the pasta cooking water. Drain. Combine the tagliatelle and sauce. Stir in the mussels, clams and the remaining 2 tablespoons parsley and cook over moderate heat, stirring, just 2 minutes longer. If the pasta seems dry, add as much of the reserved pasta liquid as needed. Add the pepper and serve at once.

—Carol Field

Salmon and Asparagus Fettuccine with Orange

For tasty, moist fish in this easy springtime dish, avoid overcooking. The time will depend on how thick the fillet is. Try to take it out of the pan when there's still a thin line of rare salmon in the middle. The fish will keep cooking and be just done when you serve it.

SERVES 4

Egg Pasta Dough (3-egg quantity), page 11, or ¾ pound dry fettuccine

2 tablespoons olive oil

2 tablespoons butter

1½ pounds skinless salmon fillet, cut into 2 pieces

1¼ teaspoons salt

Fresh-ground black pepper

6 scallions including green tops, chopped

3 tablespoons lemon juice

1 teaspoon grated orange zest

¾ pound asparagus, peeled and cut into 1-inch pieces

WINE RECOMMENDATION:
Pair the diverse flavors here with a full-bodied wine, such as a Pinot Blanc from France's Alsace.

1. Roll the pasta dough, if using, to less than ¹⁄₁₆ inch thick by hand or with a pasta machine. Cut into ¼-inch-wide strips and put on a baking sheet dusted with flour.

2. In a large frying pan, heat the oil and butter over moderate heat. Season the fish with ¼ teaspoon of the salt and a pinch of pepper. Cook 3 minutes per side. Remove the salmon and take the pan off the heat. Add the scallions and stir, scraping the pan to dislodge any brown bits, until the scallions wilt. Stir in the juice, zest, the remaining 1 teaspoon salt and ¼ teaspoon pepper. Break the fish into chunks and add to the pan.

3. In a large pot of boiling, salted water, cook the fresh fettuccine 1 minute, add the asparagus and cook until just done, about 3 minutes longer. If using dry fettuccine cook about 9 minutes before adding the asparagus. Drain. Toss gently with the salmon mixture.

Linguine with Fresh Tuna and Sweet-and-Sour Tomato Sauce

Tangy olives and sweet raisins enliven this chunky tomato and tuna sauce. During the warm weather, try grilling the tuna rather than sautéing it. You can substitute strips of sautéed or grilled chicken breasts for an equally delicious dish, or omit the tuna and serve the pasta as a first course or as a side dish with almost any simply prepared fish, poultry or meat.

SERVES 4

1½	pounds fresh tuna steaks, ¾-inch thick
1¼	teaspoon salt
½	teaspoon fresh-ground black pepper
3	tablespoons olive oil
3	tablespoons pine nuts
1	onion, chopped
1	rib celery, chopped
1	fennel bulb (about ¾ pound), sliced
2	tablespoons red-wine vinegar
3½	cups canned tomatoes with their juice (28-ounce can), chopped
2	teaspoons sugar
½	cup green olives, pitted and chopped
¼	cup golden raisins
¾	pound linguine

WINE RECOMMENDATION:
THE GUTSY FLAVORS OF THIS DISH WILL OVERWHELM MANY WINES, SO IT'S BEST TO PAIR IT WITH A LIGHT, EASYGOING WHITE WINE THAT DOESN'T HAVE A LOT OF PERSONALITY, WHICH WOULD BE RUINED BY THE FLAVORS OF THE DISH. TRY A PINOT GRIGIO FROM THE ALTO ADIGE REGION OF ITALY OR AN ALIGOTÉ FROM BURGUNDY IN FRANCE.

1. Season the tuna steaks with ½ teaspoon of the salt and ¼ teaspoon of the pepper. In a frying pan, heat 1 tablespoon of the oil over moderately high heat until very hot. Add the tuna steaks and cook until the outside is brown but the center is still rare, about 1½ minutes per side. Alternatively, cook the tuna on an outdoor grill.

2. Heat a large frying pan over moderate heat. Add the pine nuts and toast, stirring occasionally, until golden, about 3 minutes. Remove and set aside.

3. Heat the remaining 2 tablespoons of the oil in the frying pan. Add the

onion, celery and fennel. Cook, stirring occasionally, until the vegetables are just tender, about 10 minutes.

4. Stir in the vinegar and cook until almost evaporated. Add the tomatoes and juice, sugar, the remaining ¾ teaspoon salt and ¼ teaspoon pepper. Cook the sauce, stirring occasionally, until the fennel is very soft, about 30 minutes.

5. Add the olives and raisins. Cook 15 minutes longer. If the sauce gets too thick, stir in 2 to 3 tablespoons water.

6. Just before serving add the tuna steaks. Warm over moderate heat, breaking the tuna into bite-size pieces, about 2 minutes.

7. In a large pot of boiling, salted water, cook the linguine until just done, about 12 minutes. Drain. Toss the pasta with the sauce and the pine nuts.

Perciatelli with Grilled Tuna, Capers and Marjoram

Marjoram has a sweet, almost flowery aroma. In tomato sauces it makes a nice change from oregano, which can be overpowering. Add the tuna just before serving so that it doesn't overcook.

SERVES 4

¾ pound fresh tuna steak, 1 inch thick
1¾ teaspoons salt
⅛ teaspoon fresh-ground black pepper
1 tablespoon lemon juice
5 tablespoons olive oil
1 onion, chopped
5 anchovy fillets, chopped
 Pinch dried red-pepper flakes
3 cloves garlic, minced
½ cup dry white wine
2½ pounds plum tomatoes, about 12, seeded and chopped (5 cups)
2 tablespoons capers, rinsed
4 sprigs fresh marjoram, leaves chopped, or ¾ teaspoon dried
¾ pound perciatelli, or spaghetti

WINE RECOMMENDATION:
SEEK OUT A CRISP, DRY WHITE WINE WITHOUT TOO MUCH IN THE WAY OF PERSONALITY, WHICH WOULD ONLY INTERFERE WITH THE HEARTY FLAVORS OF THIS DISH. A YOUNG VERDICCHIO FROM THE ITALIAN MARCHES REGION WOULD GO NICELY, AS WOULD A GLASS OF GALESTRO, ALSO FROM ITALY.

1. Season the tuna steak with ¼ teaspoon of the salt, the black pepper and lemon juice. In a medium frying pan, heat 2 tablespoons of the oil over moderately high heat until very hot. Add the tuna and cook until the outside is brown but the center is still rare, about 1½ minutes per side. Remove the tuna from the pan.

2. Reduce the heat to moderately low. Add the remaining 3 tablespoons oil to the pan. Add the onion, anchovies and red-pepper flakes. Cook, stirring occasionally, until the onion is translucent, about 5 minutes.

3. Add the garlic and cook 1 minute longer. Add the wine and cook until almost evaporated. Stir in the tomatoes and remaining 1½ teaspoons salt. Simmer about 15 minutes. If the sauce is

dry, stir in about ¼ cup water.

4. Just before serving add the tuna steak, capers and marjoram. Warm, breaking the tuna into bite-size pieces, about 2 minutes.

5. In a large pot of boiling, salted water, cook the perciatelli until just done, about 14 minutes. Drain. Toss with the tuna sauce.

—Erica De Mane

TO RINSE OR NOT TO RINSE

Capers, the buds of the Capparis spinosa bush, are cured in salt or in vinegar. The salt is usually rinsed off before using capers. The vinegar has a strong caper-infused acidic flavor. While it gives a nice balance to some dishes, it can overpower milder ingredients. When you prefer a more subtle flavor, rinse the capers with water before using.

Pasta and Poultry

Fusilli with Grilled Chicken and Summer Vegetables

This light yet satisfying combination is equally good either warm or at room temperature. To use leftover chicken, substitute about two-and-a-half cups shredded meat for the grilled breasts. You can also oven-roast the vegetables at 450° for about 15 minutes rather than grilling them.

SERVES 6

¼ cup plus 2 tablespoons olive oil, plus more for grilling

¼ cup red-wine vinegar

¼ cup chopped red onion

¾ cup chopped fresh basil

¼ cup chopped fresh parsley

2¾ teaspoons salt
    Fresh-ground black pepper

1 pound tomatoes, about 2, seeded and chopped (2 cups)

2 zucchini (about ½ pound), cut lengthwise into 3 slices

2 yellow summer squash (about ½ pound), cut lengthwise into 3 slices

1 pound boneless, skinless chicken breasts

¾ pound fusilli

WINE RECOMMENDATION:
To complement this dish, choose from any number of light and refreshing young Italian white wines, including trebbiano and Orvieto.

1. Light the grill. In a large bowl, combine the olive oil, vinegar, onion, basil, parsley, 2½ teaspoons of the salt and ¾ teaspoon pepper. Add the tomatoes.

2. Brush both sides of the zucchini and summer squash with oil and sprinkle with ⅛ teaspoon of the salt and a pinch of pepper. Grill 3 to 6 inches from heat, turning occasionally, until brown, 8 to 10 minutes. Chop and add to tomatoes.

3. Brush both sides of chicken with oil and sprinkle with the remaining ⅛ teaspoon salt and a pinch of pepper. Grill until just done, about 5 minutes per side. Let rest 5 minutes. Cut into slices, across the grain, and add to the vegetables.

4. In a large pot of boiling, salted water, cook the pasta until just done, about 13 minutes. Drain and toss with the chicken and vegetables.

—Judith Sutton

Cavatappi with Piquant Tomato and Chicken Sauce

This long-simmered sauce melds mild chicken with the bolder flavors of red wine, rosemary, garlic, pepper and tomatoes. The sauce can be made well ahead of time. Simply reheat and toss with just-cooked pasta right before serving.

SERVES 4

¼ cup olive oil

2 teaspoons chopped fresh rosemary, or ¾ teaspoon dried rosemary, crushed

4 cloves garlic, minced

6 anchovy fillets, chopped

½ teaspoon dried red-pepper flakes, or more to taste

1 3-pound chicken, cut into eight pieces

3½ cups canned tomatoes with their juice (28-ounce can), chopped

½ cup red wine

½ cup Chicken Stock, page 29, or canned low-sodium chicken broth

1 tablespoon red-wine vinegar

1½ teaspoons salt

¾ pound cavatappi
Grated Parmesan cheese, for serving

1. In a large frying pan, heat the oil over moderate heat. Add the rosemary, garlic, anchovies and red-pepper flakes and cook until fragrant, about 2 minutes. Add the chicken and turn to coat.

2. Add the tomatoes, wine, chicken stock, vinegar and salt. Simmer the chicken, stirring occasionally, until the meat is very tender, about 45 minutes. Remove the chicken. Continue simmering the sauce until thickened, about 30 minutes longer.

3. When the chicken is cool enough to handle, pull the meat from the skin and bones and cut it into bite-size pieces. Return the chicken to the sauce.

4. In a large pot of boiling, salted water, cook the cavatappi until just done,

about 13 minutes. Drain. Return the cavatappi to the hot pot. Add the sauce and toss. Serve with Parmesan cheese.

—Erica De Mane

ANCHOVY PASTE

Anchovies are tiny silver fish from the Mediterranean. They're usually sold as flat or rolled fillets, salted and packed in oil. The fillets are great to have on hand as a flavorful addition to a variety of pasta dishes. Even more convenient, however, is anchovy paste because it keeps virtually forever. For recipes that call for anchovy fillets, substitute half a teaspoon of paste for every two fillets.

THE OTHER GRATING CHEESES

Most people automatically reach for Parmesan when they want grated cheese for pasta, and indeed in our recipes that's what we've uniformly called for as a generic name for Italian grating cheese. But don't overlook other possibilities. Pecorino Romano, the pungent sheep's-milk cheese from Southern Italy, is an excellent choice, especially (since it's sharper) with robust tomato sauces and assertive vegetables like broccoli rabe and cauliflower. There are many brands of this cheese available, our favorites being Locatelli and Brunelli. Aged Asiago is another good cheese that has less of a bite than Pecorino Romano and is creamier when melted.

Fettuccine with Chicken, Olives and Roasted Garlic

When slowly roasted, garlic becomes sweet and mellow. Here a whole head is roasted in olive oil; then the flavorful oil is used to cook the chicken. If any of the oil is left over, be sure to save it. Use it in salad dressing or toss it with plain pasta as a side dish.

SERVES 4

1   head garlic
½   cup olive oil
     Egg Pasta Dough (3-egg quantity), page 11, or ¾ pound dry fettuccine
¼   pound green beans, cut into ½-inch pieces
1   pound boneless, skinless chicken breasts
     Salt
     Fresh-ground black pepper
1½   pounds tomatoes, about 3, seeded and chopped (3 cups)
6   tablespoons chopped fresh basil
2   tablespoons chopped fresh flat-leaf parsley
14   black olives, pitted and halved

WINE RECOMMENDATION:
A LIGHT, REFRESHING WHITE WINE WILL PAIR WELL WITH THIS RICH, GARLICKY SAUCE. TRY A CORTESE DI GAVI FROM PIEDMONT IN ITALY OR AN ITALIAN PINOT GRIGIO.

1. Heat the oven to 325°. Separate the garlic cloves but do not peel them. In a small, deep baking dish, combine the garlic cloves and oil. Cover with a lid or aluminum foil and roast in the oven until the garlic cloves are soft but not mushy, 30 to 40 minutes. Drain the garlic, reserving the oil, and let cool slightly. Peel the garlic.

2. Roll the pasta dough, if using, to less than ¹⁄₁₆ inch thick by hand or with a pasta machine. Cut into ¼-inch-wide strips and put on a baking sheet dusted with flour.

3. In a small saucepan of boiling, salted water, cook the green beans until tender, about 7 minutes. Drain.

4. In a medium frying pan, heat 1 tablespoon of the garlic oil over moderately high heat. Season the chicken breasts with ⅛ teaspoon salt and a pinch

of pepper and add it to the pan. Cook the chicken until brown, about 3 minutes. Turn, cover the pan and cook over moderate heat until just done, about 5 minutes longer. Remove the chicken and let rest 5 minutes. Cut crosswise into thin slices.

5. In a large bowl, combine the garlic, green beans, tomatoes, basil, parsley, 1 teaspoon salt and ¼ teaspoon pepper. Add 3 tablespoons of the garlic oil, the chicken and olives and toss.

6. In a large pot of boiling, salted water, cook the fettuccine until just done, about 4 minutes for fresh or 12 minutes for dry. Drain. Toss with the chicken mixture and serve.

—Judith Sutton

ROASTING GARLIC

Roasted garlic is positively addictive. Roasting subdues the strong flavor and softens the crunch to a smooth, spreadable texture. Individual cloves of garlic can be roasted in olive oil, as in this recipe. Alternatively, roast the whole head: Cut off the top third and save it for another use. Rub the cut head of garlic with olive oil and put it on a piece of aluminum foil. Drizzle on a little more oil, sprinkle with a pinch of salt and pepper and top with a thin slice of butter. Add a bit of thyme, if you like, and seal the foil. Roast in a 400° oven until the garlic is soft, about 45 minutes. Often served whole with a small knife for scooping out the flesh and spreading it on bread, roasted garlic also makes a delicious, simple pasta sauce when mashed into olive oil and melted butter.

Chicken and Linguine with Golden Fennel

Shredded cooked chicken breasts are tossed with sautéed fennel and a light white-wine sauce. Fresh tarragon reinforces the anise flavor of the fennel.

SERVES 4

3   tablespoons olive oil
2   fennel bulbs (about 1¾ pounds), diced, feathery tops reserved
     Salt
     Fresh-ground black pepper
1   pound boneless, skinless chicken breasts
¾   cup Chicken Stock, page 29, or canned low-sodium chicken broth
¼   cup dry white wine
3   tablespoons chopped fresh tarragon, or 1 tablespoon dried
2   tablespoons butter, at room temperature
¾   pound linguine

WINE RECOMMENDATION: PAIR THE ANISE FLAVORS OF THIS DISH WITH A BOLD WHITE WINE, SUCH AS A VOUVRAY (CHENIN BLANC) OR A SANCERRE (SAUVIGNON BLANC) FROM THE LOIRE VALLEY IN FRANCE. WHILE THE SANCERRE SHOULD BE A RECENT VINTAGE, VOUVRAY BENEFITS FROM FIVE YEARS OF AGING.

1. In a large frying pan, heat 2 tablespoons of the oil over moderately high heat. Add the fennel, 1 teaspoon salt and ½ teaspoon pepper. Cook, stirring frequently, until the fennel is soft and golden, 8 to 10 minutes.

2. In a medium frying pan, heat the remaining tablespoon oil over moderately high heat. Season the chicken with ⅛ teaspoon salt and a pinch of pepper and add it to the pan. Cook the chicken until brown, about 3 minutes. Turn the chicken, cover the pan and cook over moderate heat until just done, about 5 minutes longer. Remove the chicken, let it rest 5 minutes and then tear the meat into large shreds.

3. Add the stock and wine to the pan, along with the dried tarragon, if using. Boil, scraping the bottom of the pan to

dislodge any brown bits, until reduced to about ½ cup. Remove the pan from the heat and whisk in the butter and fresh tarragon, if using.

4. In a large pot of boiling, salted water, cook the linguine until just done, about 12 minutes. When the pasta is almost done, add the fennel and chicken to the sauce, with any juices that may have accumulated on the plate, and reheat.

5. Drain the linguine and toss it with the chicken mixture. Top with a few fennel sprigs.

PASTA SERVED AT ROOM TEMPERATURE

Many pasta dishes are good served either hot or at room temperature. Served after cooling down, Fettuccine with Chicken, Olives and Roasted Garlic, page 201, or Bow Ties with Salami and Salsa Verde, page 303, for instance, taste great during the warm summer months and work perfectly for entertaining because they don't require last-minute cooking. What they have in common is a "sauce" that is essentially oil, or sometimes oil and vinegar. Don't try this idea on pasta with cream or cheese sauce, on baked pasta or on any pasta with a thick tomato sauce. Delicious when hot, they congeal into an unappetizing mass when cool. Some recipes, such as the one on this page, can be converted. Just replace the butter with olive oil. And remember, room temperature is the key. Since cold deadens flavor, almost nothing is at its best straight out of the refrigerator.

Cat's-Ear Pasta with Chicken and Portobello Mushrooms

Chef Susanna Foo remembers making cat's-ear pasta by hand with her grandmother in Taiwan. She has found that Italian orecchiette is an excellent substitute and uses it in her easy-to-make version of this family heirloom. Freezing the chicken breasts for 20 minutes makes cutting them into matchstick strips easier.

SERVES 4

2	tablespoons soy sauce
3	tablespoons gin
1	egg white, lightly beaten
1	teaspoon cornstarch
½	pound boneless, skinless chicken breasts, cut into ⅛-inch matchstick strips
¾	pound orecchiette
1	cup Chicken Stock, page 29, or canned low-sodium chicken broth
½	cup cooking oil
½	pound portobello mushrooms, stems removed, caps cut in half and then into thin slices
3	shallots, cut into thin slices
½	head green cabbage (about 1 pound), shredded
3	scallions including green tops, cut into 2-inch lengths
1	tomato, seeded and diced (about 1 cup)
1	teaspoon salt
¼	teaspoon fresh-ground black pepper

WINE RECOMMENDATION:
THE MILD FLAVORS OF THIS DISH, WITH ITS CLEAR CHINESE INFLUENCE, WILL PLAY WELL AGAINST A FULL-BODIED BUT RESERVED WHITE WINE, SUCH AS PINOT BLANC FROM ALSACE IN FRANCE OR PINOT BIANCO FROM THE ALTO ADIGE REGION OF ITALY.

1. In a medium bowl, combine the soy sauce, gin, egg white and cornstarch. Add the chicken and toss.

2. In a large pot of boiling, salted water, cook the orecchiette until just done, about 15 minutes. Drain and toss with ½ cup of the chicken stock.

3. In a large nonstick frying pan, heat the oil over moderate heat. Add the chicken mixture and stir-fry for 3 minutes. Add the mushrooms and shallots and stir-fry until the mushrooms are soft, about 5 minutes. Add the pasta and remaining ½ cup stock. Cook until liquid is absorbed, about 3 minutes. Add the cabbage, scallions, tomato, salt and pepper. Cook, stirring, until the cabbage softens slightly, about 2 minutes. Serve at once.

—Susanna Foo
Susanna Foo Chinese Cuisine

Fettuccine with Chicken, Potatoes and Bitter Greens

You may want to try a different leafy vegetable for this recipe—broccoli rabe, kale, mustard greens, Belgian endive and radicchio would all do nicely.

SERVES 4

Egg Pasta Dough (3-egg quantity), page 11, or ¾ pound dry fettuccine

2 pounds chicken breasts on the bone

1 quart Chicken Stock, page 29, or canned low-sodium chicken broth

2 onions, 1 quartered, the other cut into ¼-inch slices

1 bay leaf

6 sprigs parsley

2 teaspoons salt

4 tablespoons butter

½ pound boiling potatoes, peeled and cut into ½-inch dice

¼ teaspoon fresh-ground black pepper

1 large head escarole (about 1½ pounds), cut into thin strips
 Grated Parmesan cheese, for serving

WINE RECOMMENDATION: THIS HEARTY DISH, WITH ITS BITTER EDGE FROM THE ESCAROLE, WILL PAIR WELL WITH A RUSTIC AND ACIDIC WHITE WINE, SUCH AS DRY ANJOU OR SAUMUR. BOTH ARE FROM THE LOIRE VALLEY IN FRANCE AND BOTH ARE MADE FROM THE CHENIN BLANC GRAPE.

1. Roll the pasta dough, if using, to less than ⅟₁₆ inch thick by hand or with a pasta machine. Cut into ¼-inch-wide strips and put on a baking sheet dusted with flour.

2. In a large saucepan over high heat, combine the chicken breasts, stock, the quartered onion, bay leaf, parsley and 1 teaspoon of the salt and bring to a boil. Lower the heat and simmer until the chicken is cooked, about 15 minutes.

3. Remove the chicken and strain the stock. Reserve 2 cups of the stock and save the rest for another use. When the chicken is cool enough to handle, remove the meat from the skin and bones. Tear the meat into large shreds.

4. In a large saucepan, melt the butter over moderately low heat. Add the sliced onion and cook, stirring occasion-

ally, until soft and golden, about 10 minutes. Stir in the potatoes, the 2 cups chicken stock, remaining 1 teaspoon salt and the pepper. Simmer over moderate heat until the potatoes are tender, about 12 minutes. Add the escarole and cook, stirring, until wilted and tender but still green, about 4 minutes.

5. Stir in the reserved chicken and cook until just heated through, 1 to 2 minutes.

6. Meanwhile, in a large pot of boiling, salted water, cook the fettuccine until just done, about 4 minutes for fresh or 12 minutes for dry. Drain and toss with the sauce. Serve with Parmesan cheese.

—Jan Newberry

Linguine with Spicy Thai Chicken

Cilantro, ginger and lime juice give lots of fresh flavor to this pasta dish, an Asian-inspired twist on the popular pesto Genovese.

SERVES 4

2	packed cups chopped fresh cilantro leaves and stems (1 large bunch)
1	large fresh jalapeño pepper, seeded and chopped
2	cloves garlic
1	tablespoon minced fresh ginger
1¾	teaspoons salt
½	cup olive oil
3	tablespoons lime juice, from about 2 limes
1	pound boneless, skinless chicken breasts
¾	pound linguine

WINE RECOMMENDATION:
LOOK FOR A FULL-BODIED GEWÜRZTRAMINER FROM ALSACE IN FRANCE OR A DEMI-SEC (OFF-DRY) VOUVRAY FROM FRANCE'S LOIRE VALLEY TO COMPLEMENT THE FRAGRANT ASIAN FLAVORS OF THIS DISH.

1. In a food processor, combine the cilantro, jalapeño pepper, garlic, ginger, salt, oil and lime juice and process to a smooth puree.

2. Transfer ¼ cup of the puree to a shallow bowl, add the chicken and toss. Broil the chicken about 4 inches from the heat, turning once, until just done, about 8 minutes. Let the chicken rest 5 minutes. Cut it into ¼-inch slices across the grain.

3. In a large pot of boiling, salted water, cook the linguine until just done, about 12 minutes. Drain. Toss the pasta with the chicken and remaining cilantro puree and serve.

—Judith Sutton

Curried Chicken with Carrots on Fried Cellophane Noodles

When fried, cellophane noodles puff up. They make a crisp nest for this medium-hot curry topped off with basil, cilantro, peanuts and a squeeze of lime. The longer the chicken marinates, the stronger the flavor will be.

SERVES 4

2   shallots, minced

2   cloves garlic, minced

3   tablespoons Asian fish sauce (nam pla or nuoc mam)*

1½   tablespoons curry powder

2   teaspoons sugar

½   teaspoon fresh-ground black pepper

4   stalks lemongrass*, bottom ⅓ only, 1 stalk minced and 3 stalks cut into 2-inch lengths, or ½ teaspoon grated lemon zest and three 3-inch strips lemon zest

2   cups plus 2 tablespoons cooking oil

2   pounds boneless chicken breasts, with skin

3   1.8-ounce packages cellophane noodles (bean threads)

1   small red chile pepper, minced, or ¼ teaspoon dried red-pepper flakes

2   carrots, cut into ¼-by-2-inch sticks

1   cup water

½   cup thick unsweetened coconut milk, spooned from the top of a chilled can

¼   cup chopped peanuts

¼   cup chopped fresh cilantro

2   tablespoons chopped fresh basil

1   lime, cut into wedges

* Available in Asian markets

WINE RECOMMENDATION: THIS MILDLY SPICY ASIAN DISH WILL PAIR WELL WITH A GEWÜRZTRAMINER FROM ALSACE IN FRANCE OR WITH A GLASS OF BEER.

1. In a shallow dish, combine the shallots, garlic, fish sauce, curry powder, sugar, black pepper, minced lemongrass and 1 tablespoon of the oil. Add the chicken breasts and turn to coat them. Cover and marinate at least 2 hours. Overnight is not too long.

2. In a deep frying pan, heat 2 cups of the oil over moderately high heat to 375°. Divide the noodles into 6 parts. Cook one part at a time: Carefully drop them in the hot oil. Within 5 seconds they should puff up and turn white. With tongs, turn the noodles over and cook 2

to 3 seconds to puff the second side. Remove the noodles and drain on paper towels.

3. In a large frying pan, heat the remaining 1 tablespoon oil over moderately high heat until very hot. Add the chicken breasts, skin-side down, with the marinade and cook until the chicken is brown, about 3 minutes. Turn the chicken and add the chile, carrots, lemongrass pieces and water. Reduce the heat to low, cover and simmer until the chicken and carrots are cooked, about 10 minutes. Uncover and increase heat to moderate. Stir in the coconut milk and simmer 1 minute. Remove chicken from the pan and cut in half lengthwise and then crosswise into ½-inch slices.

4. Arrange the noodles on plates. Top with the chicken and sauce, the peanuts, cilantro and basil. Garnish with the lime wedges.

—Marcia Kiesel

REGULATING THE HEAT IN CHILE PEPPERS

The heat of fresh and dried chile peppers is concentrated in the ribs and seeds. If you prefer a milder chile flavor, remove them; if your taste is for hot, include them, or at least some of them. Since the hotness varies from one chile to another, even among the same variety, we suggest removing the ribs and seeds and reserving them. If the dish you are seasoning could stand more heat, add the reserved seeds and ribs to taste.

Bow Ties with Turkey and Wild Mushrooms

Quickly made, yet luxurious, this recipe is great for easy weeknight meals and entertaining weekends alike. If you're serving it as a first course for a dinner party, it will serve six.

SERVES 4

2	tablespoons butter
2	tablespoons olive oil
1	pound turkey cutlets, cut into ¼-inch strips
1	teaspoon salt
¼	teaspoon fresh-ground black pepper
½	pound white mushrooms, sliced
½	pound wild mushrooms, such as shiitakes, chanterelles or portobellos, sliced
1	small red bell pepper, cut into thin slices
1	small onion, chopped
2	cloves garlic, minced
1	teaspoon chopped fresh thyme, or ½ teaspoon dried
1	cup Chicken Stock, page 29, or canned low-sodium chicken broth
1	cup heavy cream
¾	pound bow ties
2	tablespoons chopped fresh flat-leaf parsley

WINE RECOMMENDATION:
THE RICH FLAVORS OF THE CREAM SAUCE AND THE MUSHROOMS ARE BEST MATCHED WITH AN EXPANSIVE WHITE WINE, SUCH AS A California chardonnay OR A PINOT GRIS FROM ALSACE IN FRANCE.

1. In a large frying pan, heat 1 tablespoon of the butter and 1 tablespoon of the oil over high heat. Add the turkey and sprinkle with ½ teaspoon of the salt and ⅛ teaspoon of the pepper. Sauté the turkey, about 1 minute per side. Remove to a plate.

2. Add the remaining 1 tablespoon butter and 1 tablespoon oil to the frying pan over high heat. Add the mushrooms, bell pepper, onion, garlic and thyme and cook, stirring occasionally, until the vegetables are brown, about 10 minutes. Add the stock and scrape up any brown bits from the bottom of the pan. Reduce the liquid to ½ cup, about 4 minutes. Stir in the cream, the remaining ½ teaspoon salt and ⅛ teaspoon pepper and simmer until the sauce thickens slightly, about 5 minutes.

3. In a large pot of boiling, salted water, cook the bow ties until just done,

about 15 minutes. Drain.

4. Add the turkey and parsley to the sauce and heat through. Toss with the pasta and serve.

—Grace Parisi

USING HERBS: FRESH VS. DRIED

Happily, herbs are more accessible today than ever and are increasingly sold fresh. While fresh herbs are a delight, dried herbs, which are both convenient and economical, can be a good substitute and in some cases are preferable. As a general rule, use soft-leaved herbs, such as parsley, basil and cilantro, fresh because most of their flavors are lost in drying. Tougher-leaved herbs, such as thyme and oregano, dry well. Remember that drying concentrates flavor; use about one-third as much dried as fresh. The concentrated flavor is precisely what can make dried herbs a better choice. Bay leaves, for instance, have little flavor when fresh, but just one dried leaf is enough to permeate a whole dish.

Pastina with Brined Turkey and Wild Mushrooms

Brined turkey and the tiniest of all pasta, the group of various shapes called pastina, combine with wild mushrooms, garlic, thyme and pancetta to make a superb and unusual dish that resembles risotto in consistency. Brining the turkey by macerating it in a mixture of brown sugar, salt, water and spices before cooking adds flavor and, above all, keeps the meat moist. Chef Michael Chiarello, who learned this technique from famed California chef Jeremiah Tower, uses it for many different cuts of meat and likes to brine whole turkeys for Thanksgiving.

SERVES 4

½   cup dark-brown sugar
½   cup kosher salt
2   cups water
3   juniper berries
1   bay leaf
6   black peppercorns
1   1-pound piece of turkey breast, with the skin
¼   cup olive oil
2½ to 3½ cups Turkey or Chicken Stock, page 29, or canned low-sodium chicken broth
¾   pound acini di pepe, or another pastina
4   tablespoons butter
½   pound wild mushrooms, such as chanterelles or porcini
¼   teaspoon salt
¼   pound pancetta, chopped
4   cloves garlic, minced
1½   tablespoons chopped fresh thyme, or 1½ teaspoons dried

¼   teaspoon fresh-ground black pepper
1   cup grated Parmesan cheese, plus more for serving
1½   cups pea shoots, or 1 bunch watercress (about 6 ounces), thick stems removed, chopped
¼   cup balsamic vinegar

WINE RECOMMENDATION:
THE COMPLEX FLAVORS OF THIS DISH WILL BE DELIGHTFUL WITH A GLASS OF HEARTY RED WINE, SUCH AS A YOUNG ZINFANDEL FROM CALIFORNIA OR A SALICE SALENTINO FROM SOUTHERN ITALY.

1. In a medium saucepan, combine the sugar, kosher salt, water, juniper berries, bay leaf and peppercorns. Bring to a boil, transfer to a medium bowl and cool completely. Add the turkey and let sit for 1 hour. Remove the turkey and pat dry. Discard the brine.

2. Heat the oven to 350°. In a small flameproof casserole, heat 2 tablespoons of the oil over moderate heat. Sear the

turkey, skin-side down, until golden, about 5 minutes. Turn the turkey skin-side up. Add enough of the turkey stock to come halfway up the turkey. Bring to a boil. Cover and cook in the oven until the meat is tender, about 15 minutes. Cool. Cut the meat with the skin into ¼-inch dice. Pour the cooking liquid into a measuring cup. Add enough of the remaining stock to measure 2½ cups and reserve.

3. In a large pot of boiling, salted water, cook the pastina until almost tender, but still slightly underdone, about 4 minutes. Drain, rinse with cold water and drain thoroughly.

4. In a medium saucepan, heat the remaining 2 tablespoons oil and 2 table-spoons of the butter over moderate heat. Add the mushrooms and the salt and cook until dark brown and beginning to crisp, about 8 minutes. Add the pancetta and garlic and cook for 1 minute. Add the turkey, reserved turkey-cooking liquid, the pastina, thyme and pepper. Bring to a boil, reduce the heat and simmer, stirring, until no longer soupy, about 5 minutes. Stir in the remaining 2 tablespoons butter, ¾ cup of the Parmesan and the pea shoots.

5. Put 1 tablespoon of the vinegar in each of 4 shallow bowls and pour the pasta over the vinegar. Top each serving with 1 tablespoon of the remaining Parmesan. Serve with extra Parmesan.

—Michael Chiarello
Tra Vigne

PEA SHOOTS

The current darling of the chef set is the pea shoot, also known as a pea sprout, though it's actually beyond the sprout stage. The green shoots, which are the flavorful young stalks and leaves of snow peas, taste like a cross between snow peas and bean sprouts. Look for pea shoots in Asian markets or specialty stores. Or substitute watercress, which has a different taste but similar texture and strength of flavor.

Fettuccine with Sherried Onions, Chicken Livers and Sage

You'll be surprised how delicious chicken livers can be when combined with caramelized onions, sherry and sage. Just be sure to keep them on the pink side so that they don't dry out.

SERVES 4

Egg Pasta Dough (3-egg quantity), page 11, or ¾ pound dry fettuccine

6   tablespoons butter

2   pounds onions, cut into thin slices

2   teaspoons salt

⅓   cup dry sherry

1   tablespoon chopped fresh sage, or 1 teaspoon dried

1   teaspoon sugar

1   pound chicken livers, cut into 1-inch pieces

1   cup Chicken Stock, page 29, or canned low-sodium chicken broth

WINE RECOMMENDATION:
The assertive flavors of chicken livers and onions are best with a full-bodied, flavorful wine, such as pinot gris from Alsace. An interesting alternative would be a spätlese riesling from Germany.

1. Roll out the pasta dough, if using, to less than 1/16 inch thick by hand or with a pasta machine. Cut into ¼-inch-wide strips and put on a baking sheet dusted with flour.

2. In a large frying pan, melt the butter over moderately low heat. Add the onions and salt and cook, stirring occasionally, until translucent, about 5 minutes. Add the sherry, sage and sugar and cook, stirring occasionally, until the onions are golden brown and are reduced to a jam-like consistency, about 30 minutes.

3. Push the onions to one side of the pan and increase the heat to moderately high. Add the chicken livers and cook until browned but still pink inside, about 3 minutes. Remove the livers and onions and cover to keep warm. ➤

4. Add the chicken stock to the pan. Boil over high heat, scraping the bottom of the pan to dislodge any brown bits, until reduced to about ½ cup.

5. In a large pot of boiling, salted water, cook the fettuccine until just done, about 4 minutes for fresh or 12 minutes for dry. Drain. Toss with the stock, chicken livers and sherried onions.

—Jan Newberry

PASTA WITH MEAT

Pappardelle with Veal and Mushroom Ragù

Pappardelle is traditionally served with a hare sauce, but, wild rabbits being scarce in today's markets, this veal ragù makes a delicious substitute. The full-flavored sauce can be made well ahead of time.

SERVES 4

Egg Pasta Dough (3-egg quantity), page 11, or ¾ pound dry pappardelle

3 tablespoons olive oil

2 ounces salt pork, cut into fine dice

1 onion, chopped fine

1 carrot, chopped fine

1 rib celery, chopped fine

1 pound boneless veal shoulder, cut into ¼-inch cubes

½ cup dry white wine

1 cup Chicken Stock, page 29, or canned low-sodium chicken broth

3½ cups canned tomatoes with their juice (28-ounce can), chopped

1¼ teaspoons salt
Fresh-ground black pepper

1 tablespoon chopped fresh sage or 1 teaspoon dried

3 tablespoons butter

½ pound cremini or other mushrooms, cut into thick slices

2 tablespoons lemon juice

½ cup chopped fresh flat-leaf parsley
Grated Parmesan cheese, for serving

WINE RECOMMENDATION:
THIS HEARTY DISH PAIRS NICELY WITH A HEARTY RED WINE WITH FIVE TO TEN YEARS OF AGE, SUCH AS AGLIANICO DEL VULTURE FROM THE "ARCH" OF ITALY'S BOOT OR GIGONDAS FROM THE RHÔNE VALLEY IN FRANCE.

1. Roll out the pasta dough, if using, to less than ⅟16 inch thick by hand or with a pasta machine. Cut into ¾-inch-wide strips and put on a baking sheet dusted with flour.

2. In a large pot, heat the oil over moderate heat. Add the salt pork, onion, carrot and celery. Cook, stirring occasionally, until the vegetables are soft and starting to brown, about 8 minutes.

3. Increase the heat to moderately high. Add the veal and cook until brown on all sides, about 5 minutes. Add the wine and cook until almost evaporated. Add the chicken stock and tomatoes with their juice, 1 teaspoon of the salt, ¼ teaspoon pepper and the dried sage, if using. Reduce the heat to low. Simmer the ragù, partially covered, until the veal is very tender, about 1½ hours. ➤

4. In a large frying pan, melt the butter over moderately high heat. Add the mushrooms, the remaining ¼ teaspoon salt and ⅛ teaspoon pepper. Cook, stirring occasionally, until brown, about 5 minutes. Add the lemon juice.

5. Stir the fresh sage, if using, the mushrooms and parsley into the ragù.

6. In a large pot of boiling, salted water, cook the pappardelle until just done, about 4 minutes for fresh and 12 minutes for dry. Drain. Return the pasta to the hot pot. Add the veal ragù and toss. Serve with Parmesan.

—Erica De Mane

CREMINI MUSHROOMS

Think of cremini mushrooms, with their subtle earthy taste, slightly dense flesh and dusty brown caps, as white mushrooms that are one step closer to the woods. The texture is a bit meatier and the cost a little higher (but not so elevated as that of other "wild" mushrooms). You can usually substitute white mushrooms.

Rotelle with Grandma's Sunday Meat Sauce

Grace Parisi, one of our favorite cooks, told us: "A Sunday visit with my grandmother in Brooklyn wouldn't have been complete without pasta covered with this rich and hearty sauce. She always sent each of us home with enough leftovers for two more meals."

SERVES 6

¼	cup plus 1 teaspoon olive oil
½	pound boneless pork shoulder, cut into 1-inch cubes
½	pound boneless veal shoulder, cut into 1-inch cubes
½	pound mild Italian sausage
2	onions, minced
4	cloves garlic, minced
3½	cups crushed tomatoes (28-ounce can)
1	cup water
1	tablespoon tomato paste
1½	teaspoons sugar
½	teaspoon dried oregano
1	bay leaf
¾	teaspoon dried thyme
1¼	teaspoons salt
½	teaspoon fresh-ground black pepper
¼	teaspoon dried rosemary, crushed
1	slice firm white bread
1	tablespoon milk
1	egg
1	tablespoon grated Parmesan cheese
2	tablespoons chopped fresh parsley
¼	pound ground beef
¼	pound ground pork
2	tablespoons flour
1	pound rotelle (wagon wheels)

 WINE RECOMMENDATION:
MATCH THIS FULL-FLAVORED, FAMILY-STYLE PASTA WITH A ROBUST, YOUNG RED WINE. LOOK FOR A VERY RECENT VINTAGE OF CHIANTI OR CHIANTI CLASSICO FROM ITALY. AN AMERICAN ALTERNATIVE (WHICH SOME BELIEVE TO HAVE ITALIAN ORIGINS) IS A YOUNG ZINFANDEL FROM CALIFORNIA.

1. In a large saucepan, heat 2 tablespoons of the oil over moderately high heat. Add the pork cubes to the pan and cook until brown on all sides, about 5 minutes. Remove and brown the veal. Remove and brown the sausage. Cut the sausage into 1-inch pieces.

2. Discard all but 1 tablespoon fat from the pan. Reduce the heat to moderately low. Add half the onions and a quarter of the garlic and cook, stirring occasionally, until translucent, about 5 minutes. Return the pork, veal and sausage to the pan. Add the crushed tomatoes, water, tomato paste, sugar, oregano, bay leaf, ¼ teaspoon of the thyme,

¾ teaspoon of the salt and ¼ teaspoon of the pepper. Simmer the sauce, covered, stirring occasionally, 1½ hours.

3. Meanwhile, make the meatballs: In a medium frying pan, heat 1 teaspoon of the oil over moderately low heat. Add the remaining onion and garlic and cook, stirring occasionally, until translucent, about 5 minutes. Add the remaining ½ teaspoon thyme and the rosemary and cook until fragrant, about 1 minute. Transfer to a medium bowl to cool.

4. In a small bowl, soak the bread in the milk until soggy. Mix in the egg, Parmesan, parsley, the remaining ½ teaspoon salt and ¼ teaspoon pepper. Add the bread mixture, ground beef and ground pork to the onions and garlic and mix well.

5. Shape the mixture into 6 meatballs. Dust the meatballs with flour. Heat the remaining 2 tablespoons oil in the frying pan over moderately high heat. Brown the meatballs, about 3 minutes. Add the meatballs to the sauce and cook, partially covered, 30 minutes longer.

6. In a large pot of boiling, salted water, cook the rotelle until just done, about 12 minutes. Drain. Transfer the pasta to a large platter. Arrange all the meats around the edge and pour the sauce on top.

—Grace Parisi

Flavors of India Pasta

Ginger, cumin, turmeric and coriander lend their distinctive flavors to this ground-lamb sauce. The spiciness is set off with a dollop of plain yogurt and a sprinkling of fresh cilantro just before serving.

SERVES 4

2	tablespoons cooking oil
1	onion, chopped
2	cloves garlic, minced
½	pound ground lamb
2	teaspoons grated fresh ginger
1½	teaspoons ground coriander
¾	teaspoon ground cumin
¾	teaspoon ground turmeric
¼	teaspoon dried red-pepper flakes
1	teaspoon salt
¾	cup water
1¾	cups canned tomatoes (14½-ounce can), drained and chopped
¼	cup chopped fresh cilantro
¾	pound spaghetti
¼	cup plain yogurt

WINE RECOMMENDATION:
THE SPICY INDIAN FLAVORS IN THIS DISH WILL GO WELL WITH A VOUVRAY DEMI-SEC FROM THE LOIRE VALLEY IN FRANCE OR, AS A SECOND CHOICE, A CHENIN BLANC (THE VARIETAL USED TO MAKE VOUVRAY) FROM CALIFORNIA.

1. In a large frying pan, heat the oil over moderate heat. Add the onion and cook until it begins to brown, about 5 minutes. Add the garlic and cook 1 minute longer.

2. Stir in the ground lamb, ginger, coriander, cumin, turmeric, red-pepper flakes and salt and cook until the lamb turns brown, about 3 minutes.

3. Add the water and tomatoes. Cover and simmer the sauce 15 minutes. Stir in 2 tablespoons of the cilantro.

4. In a large pot of boiling, salted water, cook the spaghetti until just done, about 12 minutes. Drain. Serve the pasta topped with the sauce, a dollop of yogurt per serving and the remaining 2 tablespoons cilantro.

Green-Curry Beef on Rice Noodles

Making this spicy recipe will prove to you how simple it is to put together a Thai curry paste. The green-curry paste includes hot chile, dried shrimp, lemongrass, ginger, fish sauce and cilantro. It's light-years away from store-bought curry powder.

SERVES 4

¾ pound dried rice noodles, medium width*

1 pound beef round

2 teaspoons Asian sesame oil

2 tablespoons soy sauce

1½ teaspoons fresh-ground black pepper

¼ cup dried shrimp*

2 large green chiles, such as poblano or New Mexico, or 4 fresh jalapeño peppers

6 cloves garlic, minced

4 shallots, minced

2 stalks lemongrass, bottom third only, minced*, or 1 teaspoon grated lemon zest

2 tablespoons minced fresh ginger

2 tablespoons sugar

2 tablespoons Asian fish sauce (nam pla or nuoc mam)*

¼ cup chopped fresh cilantro, plus 2 tablespoons whole cilantro leaves, for garnish

2 tablespoons plus 2 teaspoons cooking oil

⅔ cup Chicken Stock, page 29, or canned low-sodium chicken broth

¼ cup thick unsweetened coconut milk, spooned from the top of a chilled can

¼ cup chopped peanuts

* Available in Asian markets

WINE RECOMMENDATION:
TRY THIS DISH WITH A VERY COLD GLASS OF VOUVRAY DEMI-SEC, AN OFF-DRY WHITE WINE FROM THE LOIRE VALLEY IN FRANCE. GEWÜRZTRAMINER FROM ALSACE WOULD BE ANOTHER GOOD SELECTION.

1. In a large bowl, cover the rice noodles with cold water and leave to soften, 20 to 30 minutes. Drain and set aside.

2. Cut the beef into ¼-inch-thick slices. Stack the slices and cut them into ¼-inch-wide strips about 2 inches long. Put the beef in a medium bowl. Add the sesame oil, soy sauce and ½ teaspoon of the pepper. Toss to coat the meat. Set aside to marinate for about 10 minutes.

3. Put the dried shrimp in a small bowl and cover with hot water. Let soak for 5 minutes. Drain and mince the

shrimp. Put them in a medium bowl.

4. Roast the chiles over an open flame or broil 4 inches from the heat, turning with tongs as each side blisters and blackens, about 10 minutes in all. When cool enough to handle, pull off the charred skin. Remove the stems and most of the seeds. Mince the chiles and add to the shrimp. Add the remaining teaspoon pepper, the garlic, shallots, lemongrass, ginger, sugar, fish sauce, chopped cilantro and 2 teaspoons of the cooking oil.

5. In a wok or large frying pan, heat the remaining 2 tablespoons cooking oil over moderately high heat until very hot. Add the beef and stir-fry until brown, 2 to 3 minutes. Add the green-curry paste and stir-fry until fragrant and beginning to brown, 2 to 3 minutes. Pour in the chicken stock and simmer until the liquid reduces slightly, about 3 minutes. Turn off the heat and stir in the coconut milk.

6. In a large pot of boiling, salted water, cook half of the noodles, stirring constantly, until translucent but still slightly chewy, about 1 minute. Lift the noodles from the water with tongs and drain. Cook the remaining noodles. Top with the beef mixture, the peanuts and cilantro leaves and serve.

—Marcia Kiesel

COCONUT MILK: MAKING YOUR OWN

The only hard part about making coconut milk is peeling the fresh fruit. If you can buy it in already peeled chunks, the rest is a breeze. If not, put the whole coconut in a bowl and crack it all over with a hammer, letting the juice run into the bowl. Strain the juice and reserve. Pry out the meat and peel off the brown skin. Cut the meat in pieces and puree them, along with the reserved liquid and a cup of boiling water, in a food processor or blender. Let the mixture sit for an hour and then strain it through cheesecloth or a fine-mesh sieve. Squeeze the pulp well to get all the milky liquid. Coconut milk keeps in the refrigerator for about two weeks.

Red-Chile, Beef and Shiitake-Mushroom Stroganoff

Chile, shiitakes and fresh herbs give Stroganoff a whole new taste. New Mexican Chimayo chile powder or ancho chile powder, both medium-hot, are good here. You can also use half supermarket chili powder and half paprika.

SERVES 4

1	pound filet mignon or filet mignon tips
1	tablespoon cooking oil
2	tablespoons butter
1	onion, chopped fine
½	pound white mushrooms, cut in half
6	ounces shiitake mushrooms, stems removed, caps cut in half
1	teaspoon salt
1	teaspoon flour
⅔	cup Chicken Stock, page 29, or canned low-sodium chicken broth
½	cup heavy cream
2	teaspoons Dijon mustard
1½	teaspoons Chimayo or ancho chile powder, or another medium-hot chile powder
1	tablespoon paprika
½	pound wide egg noodles
¼	cup sour cream
1	tablespoon chopped fresh dill
1	tablespoon chopped fresh parsley
1	teaspoon fresh thyme, optional
⅛	teaspoon fresh-ground black pepper

WINE RECOMMENDATION: LOOK FOR A REFRESHING RED WINE THAT WILL COMPLEMENT THE MEAT AND MUSHROOMS BUT NOT BE OVERWHELMED BY THE CHILE. A YOUNG CALIFORNIA RHÔNE-STYLE WINE, BASED ON A VARIETAL SUCH AS MOURVEDRE OR GRENACHE, WILL GO NICELY, AS WILL A LIGHT, YOUNG SHIRAZ FROM AUSTRALIA.

1. Cut the filet into ¼-inch-thick slices. Stack the slices and cut them into ½-inch-wide strips. Heat a large nonstick or cast-iron frying pan over high heat. Toss the meat with the oil and sear, in batches if necessary, until medium rare, about 1 minute per side. Remove from the pan.

2. In a medium frying pan, melt the butter over moderately low heat. Add the onion and cook, stirring occasionally, until translucent, about 5 minutes. Increase the heat to moderate, add the mushrooms and ¼ teaspoon of the salt and cook, stirring, until the mushrooms are well browned, about 20 minutes. Reduce the heat, add the flour and cook, stirring, for 1 minute. ➤

3. Add the stock, cream, mustard, chile powder, paprika and meat juices, if any. Simmer over low heat until the sauce thickens, about 5 minutes.

4. In a large pot of boiling, salted water, cook the noodles until just done, about 9 minutes. Drain.

5. Add the meat, sour cream, dill, parsley, thyme, the remaining ¾ teaspoon salt and the pepper to the sauce. Heat but do not boil, or the sauce may curdle. Serve the sauce over the noodles.
—Mike Fennelly
Mike's on the Avenue

MAKING SPECIAL CHILE POWDERS

Although several varieties of dried chiles are now available in supermarkets, equivalents in ground form are not so easy to come by. Rather than mail-ordering ancho chile powder, for example, you can easily grind your own. Roast the dried chiles of your choice in a heavy, dry frying pan over medium heat. A cast-iron pan is ideal. You'll need to turn the rubbery pods occasionally until they are fragrant, brittle and slightly darkened, about five minutes. Watch carefully because the peppers burn easily. They can also be roasted in a 350° oven for about ten minutes. Cool, discard the stems, ribs and seeds and pulverize the pods in a spice grinder, blender or coffee grinder. Strain the chile powder to remove any large bits. Store it in spice jars or tins in a dark cupboard or in the freezer, where it keeps indefinitely.

Ziti with Sausage, Peppers and Ricotta

The combination of sausage and peppers can't be improved upon. Here they join ziti in an easy, always satisfying pasta dish. The addition of ricotta makes the sauce creamy.

SERVES 4

¾ pound mild or hot Italian sausage
1 tablespoon olive oil
2 red bell peppers, cut into thin slices
1 onion, chopped
2 cloves garlic, minced
1¾ cups canned tomatoes with their juice (14½-ounce can), chopped
1 teaspoon dried marjoram
1 teaspoon salt
¼ teaspoon fresh-ground black pepper
¾ pound ziti
1 cup ricotta cheese
2 tablespoons chopped fresh flat-leaf parsley

WINE RECOMMENDATION:
ALONGSIDE THIS DISH, WITH ITS FAMILIAR ITALIAN TASTES, SERVE A LIGHT, FRUITY RED WINE, SUCH AS A DOLCETTO FROM ITALY OR A CORBIÈRES FROM FRANCE.

1. Remove the sausage meat from its casing. In a large frying pan, heat the oil over moderate heat. Cook the sausage, breaking it up, until brown, about 3 minutes. Remove with a slotted spoon and discard all but 1 tablespoon fat.

2. Reduce the heat to moderately low. Add the bell peppers, onion and garlic. Cook, stirring occasionally, until the peppers are soft, about 15 minutes.

3. Add the sausage, tomatoes, marjoram, salt and pepper. Cook the mixture, stirring occasionally, over moderately high heat until thickened, about 10 minutes.

4. In a large pot of boiling, salted water, cook the ziti until just done, about 13 minutes. Drain. Toss with the tomato mixture, ricotta and parsley.

Penne with Roasted Peppers, Tomatoes and Sausage

Again we see the classic combination of sausage, tomatoes and peppers.
As in the preceding recipe, you can choose mild or hot Italian sausage.

SERVES 4

2   red bell peppers
2   tablespoons olive oil
½   pound mild or hot Italian sausage,
      cut into ¼- to ½-inch slices
3   cloves garlic, minced
3½   cups canned tomatoes (28-ounce
      can), drained and chopped
¾   teaspoon salt
¾   pound penne
¼   teaspoon fresh-ground black pepper
      Grated Parmesan cheese, for serving

WINE RECOMMENDATION:
A YOUNG FRUITY RED WINE THAT CAN BE
SERVED SLIGHTLY CHILLED WILL GO BEST
WITH THIS DISH, ESPECIALLY IF HOT SAU-
SAGES ARE USED. TRY A BEAUJOLAIS FROM
FRANCE OR A BARDOLINO FROM ITALY.

1. Roast the peppers over an open flame, or broil 4 inches from the heat, turning with tongs as each side blisters and blackens, about 10 minutes in all. When cool enough to handle, pull off the skin. Remove the stems, seeds and ribs. Cut the peppers into ½-inch dice. Reserve any liquid from the peppers.

2. In a large frying pan, heat the oil over moderate heat. Add the sausage and cook until browned, about 10 minutes. Add the garlic and cook until fragrant, about 30 seconds. Add the tomatoes and salt. Cook over moderately high heat for about 15 minutes. Stir in the roasted peppers with any juice.

3. In a large pot of boiling, salted water, cook the penne until just done, about 13 minutes. Drain. Return the pasta to the hot pot. Add the sausage mixture with the black pepper and toss. Serve with Parmesan.

—Jane Sigal

235

Chinese Egg Noodles with Spicy Ground Pork and Eggplant

Feeling adventurous? This is the hottest recipe in the book. It's the black-bean sauce with chile, available at Asian markets, that does it. If you prefer caution, start with half the amount specified and add more to taste.

SERVES 4

½ pound ground pork
3½ tablespoons soy sauce
1 tablespoon dry sherry
1 small eggplant (about ¾ pound)
¾ cup Chicken Stock, page 29, or canned low-sodium chicken broth
½ teaspoon sugar
1 tablespoon cornstarch
1 tablespoon cooking oil
2 scallions including green tops, chopped
1½ teaspoons minced fresh ginger
2 cloves garlic, minced
1 tablespoon black-bean sauce with chile
½ pound dried Chinese egg noodles
2 tablespoons chopped fresh cilantro

WINE RECOMMENDATION:
THE FIERY MIXTURE OF THESE NOODLES JUST DOESN'T WORK WELL WITH WINE. IF WINE IS A MUST, CHOOSE A GEWÜRZTRAMINER FROM ALSACE IN FRANCE OR THE SAME WINE FROM CALIFORNIA. IT'S UNLIKELY, HOWEVER, THAT ANY WINE WILL BE AS GOOD WITH THIS DISH AS COLD BEER.

1. Heat the oven to 450°. In a medium bowl, combine the pork with 2 tablespoons of the soy sauce and the sherry.

2. Prick the eggplant several times with a fork, put on a baking sheet and bake, turning once, until the eggplant is wrinkled and quite tender, about 30 minutes. When cool enough to handle, cut the eggplant in half, scoop out the flesh and chop it.

3. In a small bowl, combine the remaining 1½ tablespoons soy sauce, the chicken stock, sugar and cornstarch.

4. In a wok or large frying pan, heat the oil over moderately high heat. Add the scallions, ginger, garlic and black-bean sauce. Cook, stirring, 1 minute. Add the pork and cook until it is no

longer pink, about 5 minutes. Add the eggplant. Stir the chicken-stock mixture and then add it to the wok. Simmer until thickened, about 5 minutes.

5. In a large pot of boiling, salted water, cook the noodles until just done, about 7 minutes. Drain. Add the noodles to the wok and toss with the pork mixture. Top with the chopped fresh cilantro and serve.

—Jan Newberry

STIR-FRYING BASICS

◆ Stir-frying, which grew out of a culture where labor was cheap and fuel expensive, demands a cook who's organized and works fast. Chop and prepare all the ingredients before you begin and have everything within arm's reach of the stove.

◆ A large pan is essential for stir-frying. Be sure the pan is big enough to hold all the ingredients without crowding so they fry rather than steam and so there's plenty of room to toss the food about. A round-bottomed pan will not heat evenly on a flat coil, and so, if you cook on an electric stove, use a flat-bottomed wok or frying pan. A gas flame, which reaches up around the sides of the pan, heats round and flat-bottomed pans equally well. Most electric woks heat unevenly and are useless for stir-frying.

◆ The crisp textures and intense flavors associated with stir-frying are a result of the high temperature at which the food cooks. If the oil isn't hot enough, the food steams rather than fries, and essential juices are lost. Regulate the heat to maintain an even sizzle. The pan should be just hot enough to sear the ingredients without scorching or browning.

◆ The small pieces of food used for stir-frying cook quickly, especially at a high temperature. Stir constantly to ensure that they cook evenly without burning.

Vietnamese Vermicelli

If you've never tried cooking a Vietnamese dish, this is the place to start. The recipe is quick and full of flavor.

SERVES 4

½   pound well-trimmed pork shoulder, loin or tenderloin

1   shallot, minced

1   clove garlic, minced

2   teaspoons curry powder

¼   teaspoon ground turmeric

½   teaspoon sugar

2   tablespoons Asian fish sauce (nam pla or nuoc mam)*

¼   teaspoon fresh-ground black pepper

2   tablespoons plus 2 teaspoons cooking oil

10   ounces dried Chinese or Japanese vermicelli, or angel-hair pasta

1   small red chile pepper, minced, or ¼ teaspoon dried red-pepper flakes

1   red bell pepper, cut into thin slices

1   green bell pepper, cut into thin slices

1   medium onion, cut into thin slices

¾   cup Chicken Stock, page 29, or canned low-sodium chicken broth

3   tablespoons chopped peanuts

¼   cup chopped fresh cilantro

1   lime, cut into wedges

    * Available in Asian markets

WINE RECOMMENDATION: A GEWÜRZTRAMINER FROM FRANCE OR CALIFORNIA WILL WORK WELL ALONGSIDE THIS SPICY PORK DISH. A COLD BEER WILL ALSO DO JUST FINE HERE.

1. Cut the meat into ⅛-inch-thick slices. Stack the slices and cut them into ½-inch-wide strips about 2 inches long. In a shallow bowl, combine the shallot, garlic, curry, turmeric, sugar, 1 tablespoon of the fish sauce, the pepper and 2 teaspoons of the oil. Add the pork and toss to coat. Set aside to marinate.

2. In a large pot of boiling, salted water, cook the pasta, stirring constantly, just until pliable, about 2 minutes. Drain. Rinse with cold water. Drain thoroughly.

3. In a wok or large frying pan, heat the remaining 2 tablespoons oil over moderately high heat until very hot. Add the chile, bell peppers and onion. Cook, stirring, until wilted, about 3 minutes. Add the pork with the marinade and cook, stirring, until the pork is cooked through, about 3 minutes. Add the chicken stock and remaining 1 tablespoon fish sauce and when it boils, add the vermicelli. Toss to blend. Serve at once with the peanuts and cilantro on top and the lime wedges on the side.

—Marcia Kiesel

239

Rice Noodles with Pork and Black-Bean Sauce

Fresh scallions and cilantro accent the pungent and spicy sauce in this specialty of China. Cut back on the chile peppers if your tolerance for heat is low.

SERVES 4

¾   pound dried rice noodles, medium width or fine*

1   cup Chicken Stock, page 29, or canned low-sodium chicken broth

4   teaspoons sake or dry white wine

3   tablespoons whole-bean black-bean sauce or 2 tablespoons smooth black-bean sauce*

2   teaspoons oyster sauce

2   teaspoons Asian sesame oil

1   teaspoon cornstarch

1   teaspoon sugar

½   teaspoon fresh-ground black pepper

1   1½-inch piece fresh ginger

4   teaspoons cooking oil

½   pound ground pork

½   pound mushrooms, sliced

4   cloves garlic, minced

2   small red chile peppers, minced, or ½ teaspoon dried red-pepper flakes

4   scallions including green tops, chopped

2   tablespoons torn fresh cilantro leaves

* Available in Asian markets

WINE RECOMMENDATION:
PAIR THIS RICH, COMPLEX DISH WITH A FAIRLY SIMPLE BUT FULL-BODIED WHITE WINE. A GOOD BET IS PINOT BLANC FROM ALSACE IN FRANCE. YOU WANT ONE WITH PLENTY OF BODY. AN EASY ALTERNATIVE HERE IS BEER.

1. In a large bowl, cover the rice noodles with cold water and leave to soften, 20 to 30 minutes. Drain and set aside.

2. In a small bowl, combine the chicken stock, sake, black-bean sauce, oyster sauce, sesame oil, cornstarch, sugar and pepper.

3. Peel the ginger and cut it into the thinnest possible slices. Stack the slices and cut them into shreds. You should have 2 tablespoons shredded ginger.

4. In a wok or large frying pan, heat 2 teaspoons of the cooking oil over moderately high heat. Add the ground pork and cook, breaking up the meat, until the meat firms up and releases fat and moisture, about 1 minute. Scrape into a strainer over a bowl and drain the pork, pressing to remove excess fat.

5. Heat the remaining 2 teaspoons cooking oil in the wok. Add the mushrooms and cook 2 to 3 minutes. Add the ginger, garlic and chiles. Cook, stirring, until fragrant, about 30 seconds. Add the pork and stir-fry until cooked through, 2 to 3 minutes longer. Stir the chicken-stock mixture and pour it into the wok. Cook until the mixture boils and thickens, another minute or two. Remove from the heat and cover to keep warm.

6. In a large pot of boiling, salted water, cook half the noodles, stirring, until translucent but still slightly chewy, about 1 minute. Lift the noodles from the water with tongs and drain. Cook the remaining noodles in the same way.

7. Stir the scallions into the pork and bean sauce. Pour the mixture over the noodles and stir gently. Top with cilantro leaves and serve.

—Marcia Kiesel

HOT CHILE PEPPERS

When a recipe calls for hot chiles, use any sort of hot pepper you like. Asian cooks prefer the Thai, also known as bird chile, but Mexican serrano or jalapeño peppers are fine, too. Keep in mind that the smaller the pepper the hotter it tends to be. (One exception to this rule is the Scotch Bonnet, considered the hottest chile. It's bigger than either serrano or Thai chiles.) Green and red chiles are the same fruit at different stages of ripeness. Though there is a difference in taste, you can use them interchangeably. Green chiles have a sharp, more immediate bite. Ripe, red peppers are sweeter, and their heat comes on more slowly.

Pork and Bok Choy over Fresh Rice Noodles

The mild flavor of bok choy, or Chinese cabbage, blends with a variety of flavors. Here a combination of cumin, chile pepper, lemongrass, coconut milk and lime adds plenty of kick.

SERVES 4

½ pound lean pork shoulder or loin

½ cup Chicken Stock, page 29, or canned low-sodium chicken broth

2 tablespoons soy sauce

1 tablespoon white vinegar

⅛ teaspoon cumin seeds, chopped

⅛ teaspoon ground turmeric

¼ teaspoon fresh-ground black pepper

1 tablespoon Asian fish sauce (nam pla or nuoc mam)*

1 teaspoon Asian sesame oil

2 teaspoons sugar

¾ pound fresh rice-noodle sheets, or fresh Japanese udon, or ¾ pound dried Japanese udon*

1 tablespoon cooking oil

2 large shallots, minced

3 cloves garlic, minced

1 stalk lemongrass, bottom ⅓ only, cut into ½-inch pieces*, or one 3-inch strip lemon zest

1 small red chile pepper, seeded and minced, or ¼ teaspoon dried red-pepper flakes

1 pound bok choy, cut into 2-inch strips (about 4 cups)

⅓ cup unsweetened coconut milk

1 lime, cut into wedges

* Available in Asian markets

WINE RECOMMENDATION:
MOST WINES RISK OBLITERATION BY MORE THAN ONE OF THE VARIOUS PUNGENT INGREDIENTS IN THIS DISH. A LIGHT GEWÜRZTRAMINER FROM ALSACE WOULD WORK, BUT AN ICE-COLD BEER IS THE PERFECT MATCH.

1. Cut the meat into ⅛-inch-thick slices. Stack the slices and cut them into ½-inch-wide strips about 2 inches long. In a medium bowl, combine the pork with the chicken stock, 1 tablespoon of the soy sauce, 1 teaspoon of the vinegar, the cumin, turmeric and pepper.

2. In another medium bowl, combine the remaining 1 tablespoon soy sauce, 2 teaspoons vinegar, the fish sauce, sesame oil and sugar.

3. If using fresh rice-noodle sheets, cut into 1-inch-wide strips. Rinse the noodles under hot water to separate them. Set aside in a colander. If using fresh udon, cook in boiling water until tender but still slightly chewy, about 6

minutes. Drain, rinse with cold water and drain thoroughly. If using dried udon, cook in boiling water until tender but still slightly chewy, about 15 minutes. Drain, rinse with cold water and drain thoroughly.

4. Remove the pork from the marinade. Set the marinade aside. In a wok or large frying pan, heat the cooking oil over moderately high heat. Add the pork and stir-fry until brown, about 3 min-

utes. Add the shallots, garlic, lemongrass and chile and stir-fry until fragrant, about 2 minutes. Stir in the reserved marinade, the other soy-sauce mixture and the bok choy and simmer until the bok choy is tender and the liquid has reduced slightly, about 3 minutes. Add the coconut milk and simmer 1 minute longer. Stir in the noodles and cook until heated through. Serve with the lime wedges.

—Marcia Kiesel

COCONUT MILK: OUR FAVORITE BRANDS

Let's set one thing straight. Coconut milk is not the juice inside fresh coconuts. Rather it is the thick liquid you get from soaking ground coconut in water and squeezing it out. You can make the milk yourself, page 229, but it can be time consuming. For sauces and noodle dishes, a good-quality, canned coconut milk, available in Asian markets and most supermarkets, is an excellent substitute. Of the canned varieties, Taste of Thailand is our favorite. Chef's Choice, Chaokoh and Goya are also good. Coconut milk behaves like cows' milk; if left to sit, coconut "cream" rises to the top. The cream, which is often referred to in recipes as thick coconut milk, can be used separately to enrich and thicken dishes. Refrigerating the milk solidifies the cream so that it's easier to spoon off the top. For most recipes you'll want to blend the milk and cream. Simply shake the can before opening.

Pasta-Wrapped Hot Thai Meatballs

Crisp threads of fresh pasta surround these succulent Thai meatballs. Served on peppery arugula leaves with a tangy dipping sauce, they are perfect with cocktails. Pick up the meatball with its greenery, wrap the leaf around the little pasta package and dunk it in the sauce.

MAKES 48 BITE-SIZED MEATBALLS

5	small dried shiitake mushrooms, or other dried mushrooms
½	pound ground beef
½	pound ground pork
3	tablespoons chopped fresh cilantro
2	tablespoons Asian fish sauce (nam pla or nuoc mam)*
1	scallion including green top, minced
1	egg white, lightly beaten
2	teaspoons minced fresh ginger
2	cloves garlic, minced
1½	teaspoons cornstarch
1	teaspoon minced red chile pepper, or ¼ teaspoon dried red-pepper flakes
1¼	teaspoons salt
½	pound thin fresh Chinese egg noodles*, or fresh angel hair Cooking oil, for frying
1	large bunch arugula, stems removed, or 1 head butter lettuce Tangy Mint and Cilantro Dipping Sauce, page 246

*Available in Asian markets

WINE RECOMMENDATION: CHOOSE A LIGHT WHITE WINE THAT WILL BE HARDLY NOTICED BETWEEN BITES OF THESE MEATBALLS WITH THEIR TANGY SAUCE. PINOT BIANCO FROM ALTO ADIGE OR FRIULI IN ITALY WILL BE FINE, ALTHOUGH BEER OR COCKTAILS WILL LIKELY DO JUST AS WELL.

1. In a small bowl, soak the shiitake mushrooms in hot water until softened, about 20 minutes. Drain and rinse well under running water to remove any sand or grit. Chop the mushrooms and transfer to a large bowl.

2. Add the ground beef, ground pork, cilantro, fish sauce, scallion, egg white, ginger, garlic, cornstarch, chile and salt to the mushrooms. Mix well. Shape into small meatballs, using about 1½ teaspoons of the mixture for each.

3. Wrap 2 or 3 strands of the noodles around each meatball, lightly pressing them into the meat. You needn't be too fussy about this. A few hanging strands add to the charm of these little meatballs. Alternatively, chop the noodles into ½-inch pieces and roll the meatballs in it. ➤

4. Fill a deep, heavy frying pan with enough oil to cover the meatballs, about 2 inches. Heat to 375°. Add the meatballs in batches so that they're not crowded. Fry until golden and crisp, about 3 minutes. Drain on paper towels and serve with arugula leaves and a bowl of the Tangy Mint and Cilantro Dipping Sauce.

—Grace Parisi

TANGY MINT AND CILANTRO DIPPING SAUCE

Mint and cilantro, a classic combination in Southeast Asian cooking, flavor this sweet and tangy dipping sauce from Thailand.

MAKES ABOUT 1¼ CUPS

1	cup rice-wine vinegar
⅓	cup sugar
1	teaspoon minced red chile pepper
½	red bell pepper, chopped
1	teaspoon minced fresh ginger
1½	tablespoons chopped fresh cilantro
1½	tablespoons chopped fresh mint

1. In a small saucepan, combine the vinegar, sugar, chile, bell pepper and ginger. Simmer until reduced to 1¼ cups, about 20 minutes. Let cool.

2. Stir in the cilantro and mint. Serve at room temperature.

Noodles and Hungarian Meatballs with Caraway and Sour Cream

Choose either hot or sweet paprika for this flavorful sauce. It's just as good, or even better, the next day, but don't add the sour cream until shortly before serving.

SERVES 4

¼   cup cooking oil
2   onions, sliced
1   red bell pepper, cut into thin strips
1   teaspoon caraway seeds
¾   pound ground beef
¼   cup milk
3   tablespoons fresh bread crumbs
3   tablespoons chopped fresh parsley
1   clove garlic, minced
2½   teaspoons salt
¼   teaspoon fresh-ground black pepper
2   tablespoons paprika
1   tablespoon tomato paste
1   cup beer
1   cup Chicken Stock, page 29, or canned low-sodium chicken broth
1   cup sour cream
¾   pound wide egg noodles

WINE RECOMMENDATION: MATCH THE HUNGARIAN TASTE OF THIS DISH WITH A HUNGARIAN WINE BASED ON A VARIETAL SUCH AS CABERNET SAUVIGNON OR MERLOT. OR SEEK OUT THE MORE CLASSIC AND UNIQUELY HUNGARIAN RED WINE, EGRI BIKAVÉR (LITERALLY, "BULL'S BLOOD").

1. Heat 2 tablespoons of the oil in a large frying pan over moderately low heat. Add the onions, bell pepper and caraway seeds and cook, stirring occasionally, until the vegetables are soft and golden brown, about 25 minutes.

2. Meanwhile, combine the ground beef, milk, bread crumbs, 2 tablespoons of the parsley, the garlic, ¾ teaspoon of the salt and ⅛ teaspoon of the pepper. Shape into 12 meatballs. In a medium frying pan, heat the remaining 2 tablespoons oil over moderately high heat. Fry the meatballs until brown on all sides, about 3 minutes. Drain on paper towels.

3. Add the paprika, tomato paste, the remaining 1¾ teaspoons salt and ⅛ teaspoon pepper to the onion mixture and cook, stirring, about 30 seconds. Add the beer and chicken stock. Cover and sim-

247

mer 5 minutes. Add the meatballs. Cover and simmer until the meatballs are cooked through, about 10 minutes longer. Just before serving, stir in the sour cream and bring the sauce to a simmer. Do not boil or the cream may separate.

4. In a large pot of boiling, salted water, cook the egg noodles until just done, about 9 minutes. Drain. Serve the egg noodles topped with the meatballs, sauce and remaining 1 tablespoon parsley.

Neapolitan Meatballs with Linguine

Raisins and pine nuts add an element of surprise to these meatballs from Southern Italy. This recipe is adapted from the great classic *Italian Regional Cooking* by Ada Boni.

SERVES 4

½ pound ground beef
½ cup fresh bread crumbs, toasted
¼ cup grated Parmesan cheese, plus more for serving
1 tablespoon milk
1 egg, beaten to mix
½ clove garlic, minced
¼ cup golden raisins
¼ cup pine nuts
2 tablespoons chopped fresh flat-leaf parsley
¾ teaspoon salt
¼ teaspoon fresh-ground black pepper
3 tablespoons olive oil
3 cups Basic Italian Tomato Sauce, page 22, pureed
¾ pound linguine

WINE RECOMMENDATION:
MEATBALLS THAT INCLUDE THE SWEETNESS OF RAISINS WILL GO WELL WITH A YOUNG, FRUITY RED WINE, SUCH AS BARDOLINO FROM NORTHERN ITALY OR BEAUJOLAIS FROM FRANCE.

1. In a medium bowl, combine the ground beef, bread crumbs, Parmesan, milk, egg, garlic, raisins, pine nuts, parsley, salt and pepper. Shape into 24 one-inch meatballs.

2. In a medium frying pan, heat the oil over moderately high heat. Add half of the meatballs and fry until brown on all sides, about 3 minutes. Drain on paper towels. Repeat with the remaining meatballs.

3. In a large saucepan, heat the tomato sauce over moderate heat. Add the meatballs and simmer, covered, until the meatballs are cooked through, about 5 minutes.

4. In a large pot of boiling, salted water, cook the linguine until just done, about 12 minutes. Drain. Serve the meatballs and sauce on top of the pasta and pass the additional Parmesan cheese.

Spaghetti and Meatballs

Combining ground beef and pork with Parmesan, parsley and a touch of lemon zest results in an irresistible rendition of the classic Italian-American meatball. After browning, the meatballs are simmered in the thick tomato sauce, and each improves the other.

SERVES 4

½   pound ground beef

½   pound ground pork

⅓   cup grated Parmesan cheese, plus more for serving

¼   cup fresh bread crumbs

¼   cup chopped fresh flat-leaf parsley

1   egg, beaten to mix

2   cloves garlic, minced

½   teaspoon grated lemon zest

1   teaspoon salt

¼   teaspoon fresh-ground black pepper

¼   cup olive oil

2½   cups Classic American-Style Tomato Sauce, page 23

¾   pound spaghetti

WINE RECOMMENDATION:
TO COMPLEMENT THIS VERSION OF SPA-GHETTI AND MEATBALLS WITH ITS HINT OF LEMON, CHOOSE A LIGHT AND FRUITY GAMAY-BASED RED WINE FROM BEAUJOLAIS OR THE LOIRE VALLEY IN FRANCE.

1. In a medium bowl, combine the ground beef and pork, Parmesan, bread crumbs, parsley, egg, garlic, lemon zest, salt and pepper. Shape the mixture into 12 meatballs. In a medium frying pan, heat the oil over moderately high heat. Fry the meatballs until brown on all sides, about 3 minutes. Drain on paper towels.

2. In a large saucepan, bring the tomato sauce to a simmer. Add the meatballs to the sauce. Cover and simmer until the meatballs are cooked through, about 15 minutes.

3. In a large pot of boiling, salted water, cook the spaghetti until just done, about 12 minutes. Drain. Serve the meatballs and sauce on top of the pasta and pass the additional Parmesan cheese.

PASTA SALADS

Pasta Salad di Palermo

We predict that this easy and perfectly delicious salad will become one of your favorites. Serve it as a welcoming first course or alongside grilled chicken.

SERVES 6

¼ cup pine nuts
1   red bell pepper
¾ pound penne
½ cup black olives, pitted and halved
¼ cup sun-dried tomatoes, chopped
¼ cup chopped fresh flat-leaf parsley
2   tablespoons capers, rinsed
2   tablespoons olive oil
¾ teaspoon salt
⅛ teaspoon fresh-ground black pepper
1   1-ounce piece Parmesan cheese

WINE RECOMMENDATION:
WITH ALL OF THE SALTY, FULL-FLA-VORED INGREDIENTS IN THIS SALAD (OLIVES, SUN-DRIED TOMATOES AND CAPERS), THE BEST CHOICE WILL BE A WHITE WINE THAT COMBINES A SMALL AMOUNT OF SWEETNESS (TO STAND UP TO THE SALTY FLAVORS) AND ACIDITY (TO PROVIDE REFRESHMENT). TWO WINES THAT WOULD WORK HERE ARE A RIES-LING FROM THE MOSEL-SAAR-RUWER IN GERMANY OR AN ALSATIAN PINOT BLANC.

1. Heat the oven to 350°. Put the pine nuts on a baking sheet and bake in the oven, shaking the pan once or twice, until the nuts are fragrant and golden, about 5 minutes. Or toast in a dry frying pan over moderate heat.

2. Roast the bell pepper over an open flame or broil 4 inches from the heat, turning with tongs as each side blisters and blackens, about 10 minutes in all. When the pepper is cool enough to handle, pull off the charred skin. Remove the stem, seeds and ribs. Cut the pepper into thin slices.

3. In a large pot of boiling, salted water, cook the penne until just done, about 13 minutes. Drain. Rinse with cold water and drain thoroughly. ➤

4. In a large bowl, combine the roasted-pepper strips, penne, olives, sun-dried tomatoes, parsley, capers, oil, salt and pepper.

5. With a vegetable peeler, shave thin slices of Parmesan. Top the salad with the Parmesan and toasted pine nuts.

—Grace Parisi

ROASTED PEPPERS

Roasting peppers brings out their sweetness and gives them a more intense, slightly smoky flavor. Peppers can be roasted on a grill over a hot charcoal or gas fire, underneath a broiler or over a gas burner. Turn peppers as they cook so that they roast evenly, and be sure to let their skins blister and blacken completely. This is what separates the skin from the flesh and makes peeling easy.

Pesto and Rigatoni Salad with Summer Tomatoes

When there is pesto in the refrigerator, this pasta salad can be prepared in minutes. It's perfect with a glass of wine after a long day in the sun.

SERVES 4

¾   pound rigatoni
¾   cup Pesto alla Genovese, page 27
1   pound tomatoes, about 2, seeded and chopped (2 cups)

WINE RECOMMENDATION:
A CRISP, YOUNG ITALIAN WHITE WINE WILL GO NICELY WITH THE REFRESHING FLAVOR OF THE PESTO. CONSIDER EITHER A VERDICCHIO FROM THE ITALIAN MARCHES REGION OR AN ORVIETO.

1. In a large pot of boiling, salted water, cook the rigatoni until just done, about 14 minutes. Just before draining, stir about 2 tablespoons of the pasta water into the pesto. Drain the rigatoni, rinse with cold water and drain thoroughly.

2. In a large bowl, combine the rigatoni and pesto. Just before serving, stir in the tomatoes.

Pasta Primavera Salad

A colorful pasta salad with spring vegetables is a perfect addition to the first barbecue of the year. To cut steps, we cook the vegetables right with the pasta, adding them near the end of the cooking time.

SERVES 4

1	red bell pepper
½	pound broccoli
½	pound fusilli
½	pound asparagus, peeled and cut into 1-inch pieces
1	cup fresh or frozen peas, thawed
1	6-ounce jar marinated artichoke hearts, drained and cut into pieces
½	cup black olives, pitted and chopped
3	tablespoons red-wine vinegar
1	clove garlic, minced
½	teaspoon salt
¼	teaspoon fresh-ground black pepper
⅓	cup olive oil
¾	cup grated Parmesan cheese

WINE RECOMMENDATION: PAIR THIS LIGHT DISH WITH THE FRESH FLAVORS IN A YOUNG PINOT GRIGIO OR PINOT BIANCO FROM THE FRIULI REGION OF ITALY.

1. Roast the pepper over an open flame or broil 4 inches from the heat, turning with tongs as each side blisters and blackens, about 10 minutes in all. When cool enough to handle, pull off the charred skin. Remove the stem, seeds and ribs. Cut the roasted pepper into medium dice.

2. Cut off and divide the broccoli florets. Peel the stem and slice it into ¼-inch rounds.

3. In a large pot of boiling, salted water, cook the fusilli until almost done, about 10 minutes. Add the broccoli, asparagus and fresh peas, if using, and cook 4 minutes. Drain. Rinse with cold water and drain thoroughly.

4. In a large bowl, combine the roasted pepper, pasta, cooked vegetables and thawed frozen peas, if using, the artichokes and olives.

5. In a small bowl, whisk the vinegar with the garlic, salt and pepper. Add the

oil slowly, whisking. Stir this vinaigrette into the pasta with the Parmesan cheese. If preparing the salad in advance, do not add the dressing or cheese until just before serving.

BROCCOLI STEMS

Many people think the broccoli florets are the most appealing part of the bunch, but the peeled stalks are just as tasty, and we think the texture is even nicer. They're good sliced and cooked with the florets, or cut into matchstick strips and used as a vegetable in their own right.

BLACK OLIVES

Literally hundreds of olive varieties are grown in Italy, France and Greece. Happily, more and more of them are making their way to specialty shops and ethnic markets in this country, and a growing number of California producers are selling similar types. Some names of black olives to look for are Gaeta, Provençale, Niçoise and Kalamata. They will be more flavorful and pungent than those from California sold in cans, which we can't recommend.

Spanish Orzo Salad

Golden with saffron and studded with shrimp, mussels, chicken and chorizo, this stunning salad resembles paella. It is perfect as a cool main course on a warm summer evening.

SERVES 6

1½ pounds chicken breasts on the bone
1   small yellow onion, chopped
1   carrot, chopped
1   rib celery, chopped
3   sprigs fresh flat-leaf parsley, plus ¼ cup chopped
1   bay leaf
2   teaspoons salt
4   peppercorns
¾   cup plus 2 tablespoons olive oil
1   red onion, chopped fine
1   red bell pepper, chopped
1   green bell pepper, chopped
¼   pound dried chorizo or pepperoni, sliced thin
1   teaspoon ground cumin
¼   teaspoon dried red-pepper flakes
1½ pounds tomatoes, about 3, peeled, seeded and chopped (3 cups)
1   pound mussels, scrubbed and debearded
½   cup dry white wine
1   pound medium shrimp
1   teaspoon saffron threads
¾   pound orzo
½   cup lemon juice, from about 3 lemons
1   clove garlic, minced
½   teaspoon fresh-ground black pepper

WINE RECOMMENDATION:
THIS HEARTY SALAD WILL PAIR NICELY WITH A RICH, YOUNG WHITE WINE FROM THE SOUTH OF FRANCE, SUCH AS A CÔTES DU RHÔNE, OR A FULL-BODIED CHARDONNAY FROM CALIFORNIA.

1. In a medium saucepan, combine the chicken, yellow onion, carrot, celery, parsley sprigs, bay leaf, 1 teaspoon of the salt and the peppercorns. Add enough cold water to cover and bring to a simmer over moderately high heat. Reduce the heat and simmer until the chicken is cooked through, about 15 minutes. Remove the chicken. When it is cool enough to handle, remove the meat from the skin and bones. Cut the meat into thin slices against the grain and put into a large bowl.

2. In a medium frying pan, heat 2 tablespoons of the oil over moderately low heat. Add the red onion, bell peppers and chorizo and cook, stirring occasionally, until the onion is translucent, 5 to 10 minutes. Add the cumin and cook 1 minute. Add the red-pepper flakes and tomatoes and cook for 3 minutes. Add to the chicken.

3. Discard any mussels that are broken or do not clamp shut when tapped.

In a large pot, combine the mussels and wine. Cover and bring to a boil over high heat. Cook, shaking the pan occasionally, until the mussels begin to open, about 3 minutes. Remove the open mussels and continue to cook, uncovering the pot as necessary to remove mussels as soon as their shells open. Discard any mussels that do not open after cooking.

4. Reserve 4 mussels for garnish. Working over the pan to catch the juice, remove the remaining mussels from their shells and add them to the bowl of chicken and vegetables. Strain the liquid through a sieve lined with a paper towel and add to the bowl of chicken and vegetables.

5. In a large saucepan of boiling, salted water, cook the shrimp until just done, about 2 minutes. Drain, shell and add the shrimp to the other ingredients.

6. In a large pot, bring 2 quarts of salted water to a boil. Add the saffron and orzo and boil until just done, about 12 minutes. Drain. Rinse with cold water and drain thoroughly. Add to the salad along with the chopped parsley.

7. In a small bowl, whisk the lemon juice with the garlic, the remaining 1 teaspoon salt and the pepper. Add the remaining ¾ cup oil slowly, whisking. Pour over the salad and toss gently. Top with the reserved mussels and serve at room temperature.

TOMATOES—PEELED AND SEEDED

The tomato skin can be tough and the seeds watery. Get rid of neither, either or both depending on the tomatoes and on the dish you're making. For easy peeling, cut out the core and slash an "X" in the opposite end. Then plunge the tomatoes into boiling water and leave just until the skin begins to curl away from the "X", ten to fifteen seconds. When cool enough to handle, strip away the skin. Cut the tomatoes in half crosswise and squeeze out the seeds, or scoop them out with your fingertips.

Middle-Eastern Orzo Salad

Tabbouleh lovers will appreciate this new take on a familiar favorite. It makes a good accompaniment to grilled lamb, chicken or pork.

SERVES 6

¾	pound orzo
1½	pounds tomatoes, about 3, seeded and chopped (3 cups)
1	large cucumber, seeded and chopped (about 2 cups)
6	scallions including green tops, chopped
1	cup chopped fresh flat-leaf parsley
6	tablespoons chopped fresh mint
5	tablespoons lemon juice, from about 2 lemons
2½	teaspoons salt
½	teaspoon fresh-ground black pepper
¾	cup olive oil

SCALLION TOPS

Many cooks don't use the green tops of scallions. We nearly always include them in recipes for both their bright color and good flavor. Sliced scallion tops are also a good substitute for chives, which can be hard to find.

WINE RECOMMENDATION:
LOOK FOR A YOUNG, CRISP WHITE WINE TO MATCH THE REFRESHING TASTE OF THIS PASTA. ANY NUMBER OF ITALIAN WHITE WINES WILL DO, INCLUDING ORVIETO AND GALESTRO.

1. In a large pot of boiling, salted water, cook the orzo until just done, about 12 minutes. Drain. Rinse with cold water and drain thoroughly.

2. Combine with the tomatoes, cucumber, scallions, parsley and mint.

3. In a small bowl, whisk the lemon juice with the salt and pepper. Add the oil slowly, whisking. Pour the dressing over the salad and toss.

Fusilli Salad with Fresh Tomato Salsa and Avocado

Cubes of smooth avocado balance the lively tomato salsa in this refreshing summertime salad.

SERVES 4

1½ pounds tomatoes, about 3, seeded and chopped (3 cups)
1   small red onion, chopped
1 to 2 fresh jalapeño peppers, seeded and minced
3   tablespoons chopped fresh cilantro
3   tablespoons red-wine vinegar
3   tablespoons olive oil
1½ teaspoons salt
¼   teaspoon fresh-ground black pepper
¾   pound fusilli
1   large avocado, preferably Haas, cut into ¼-inch dice and tossed with a little lemon juice or vinegar to preserve color

WINE RECOMMENDATION: PAIR THIS SALAD WITH EITHER A VERY COLD, CRISP BOTTLE OF YOUNG ITALIAN WINE WITHOUT MUCH PRESENCE, SUCH AS FRASCATI OR ORVIETO, OR WITH AN ICED PITCHER OF SANGRIA.

1. In a large bowl, combine the tomatoes, onion, jalapeño, cilantro, vinegar, oil, salt and pepper.

2. In a large pot of boiling, salted water, cook the fusilli until just done, about 13 minutes. Drain. Rinse with cold water and drain thoroughly.

3. Toss the pasta with the salsa and diced avocado.

 ## THE BEST AVOCADOS

For the buttery rich texture and slightly nutty flavor you expect from an avocado, choose a California variety. The bumpy-skinned Haas is readily available. Large, smooth-skinned Florida-grown avocados are watery and often stringy. They also tend to spoil quickly. Leave them in the produce bin. Often touted for having less fat than Haas, they also have far less flavor.

All-American Macaroni Salad

A favorite side dish at picnics and barbecues, this salad is best when tossed together shortly before serving. Otherwise, the macaroni absorbs the dressing, and you lose the nice creaminess. But you can cook the macaroni and combine all the other ingredients ahead of time.

SERVES 4

½	pound elbow macaroni or ditali
½	cup mayonnaise
½	cup sour cream
1½	tablespoons red-wine vinegar
1	rib celery with leaves, minced
2	scallions including green tops, chopped
⅓	cup green olives, pitted and chopped
2	tablespoons chopped pimientos
1	tablespoon chopped fresh parsley
½	teaspoon Worcestershire sauce
¾	teaspoon salt
¼	teaspoon fresh-ground black pepper

WINE RECOMMENDATION: Uncork a simple, light bottle of red or white wine with an appeal as straightforward as the flavors of this classic. A young and slightly chilled red Beaujolais would be perfect, as would a cool bottle of white zinfandel from California.

1. In a large pot of boiling, salted water, cook the macaroni until just done, about 8 minutes. Drain. Rinse with cold water and drain thoroughly.

2. In a large bowl, combine the remaining ingredients.

3. Add the macaroni and toss.

QUICK DRY FOR PARSLEY

Next time you wash a bunch of curly parsley, try squeezing it dry with your hands. You can practically wring it out without any damage to the leaves. The water runs out, and the tightly curled leaves spring right back into shape. Don't try this with Italian parsley, though. You'll crush the flat leaves, and water will still cling.

Pasta Shells with Scallop Seviche

Seviche, a Latin American dish, is essentially marinated seafood. It often includes hot peppers and onions, too. The acidity of the marinade "cooks" the fish, making it firm and opaque. Treating scallops in this way and tossing them with pasta shells, bell peppers and cilantro produces a delicious and refreshing salad.

SERVES 4

1   pound sea scallops, halved horizontally
      Juice of 4 limes
      Juice of 1 lemon
¾   pound medium pasta shells
1   red onion, chopped fine
4   scallions including green tops, chopped
1   tomato, seeded and diced (about 1 cup)
1   red bell pepper, cut into 1½-inch-long matchstick strips
2   fresh jalapeño peppers, seeded and minced
¼   cup chopped fresh cilantro
2   teaspoons salt
2   tablespoons white-wine vinegar
2   teaspoons Dijon mustard
¼   teaspoon fresh-ground black pepper
⅓   cup olive oil
1   avocado, preferably Haas, sliced

WINE RECOMMENDATION:
LOOK FOR A FRESH WHITE WINE TO MATCH THE LIVELY FLAVORS OF THE SEVICHE. A VINHO VERDE FROM PORTUGAL WOULD BE A GOOD CHOICE. BEER WILL ALSO TASTE GREAT ALONGSIDE THIS DISH.

1. In a stainless-steal or glass bowl, combine the scallops, lime juice and lemon juice. Cover and refrigerate for at least 2 hours.

2. In a large pot of boiling, salted water, cook the shells until just done, about 10 minutes. Drain, rinse with cold water and drain thoroughly.

3. In a large bowl, combine the pasta, onion, scallions, tomato, peppers, cilantro and salt. Add the scallops and 2 tablespoons of the citrus juice. Discard the remaining juice.

4. Whisk the vinegar with the mustard and pepper. Add the oil slowly, whisking. Pour all but 1 tablespoon over the salad and toss. Gently toss the avocado with the remaining dressing and top the salad with the slices.

Shrimp and Bow-Tie Salad with Avocado Dressing

Vibrant green with avocado and cilantro and tangy with lime, this unusual dressing tastes a lot like guacamole. The lime juice not only adds flavor but preserves the avocado color for up to eight hours.

SERVES 4

1	pound medium shrimp
2	very ripe avocados, preferably Haas, chopped
½	cup plain yogurt
½	cup cold water
3	tablespoons lime juice, from about 2 large limes
2	tablespoons olive oil
3	tablespoons chopped fresh cilantro, plus whole leaves for garnish
1	clove garlic, minced
2¼	teaspoons salt
	Pinch fresh-ground black pepper
¾	pound bow ties
½	cup minced red onion, plus thin slices for garnish
6	radishes, cut into thin slices

WINE RECOMMENDATION:
A BOTTLE OF SAUVIGNON BLANC WILL WORK WELL WITH THIS RICH AND TANGY DISH. CHOOSE A RECENT VINTAGE FROM EITHER CALIFORNIA OR NEW ZEALAND.

1. In a large saucepan of boiling, salted water, cook the shrimp until just done, about 2 minutes. Drain and shell. Cut in half horizontally.

2. In a food processor or blender, puree the avocados, yogurt, water, lime juice, oil, chopped cilantro, garlic, salt and pepper.

3. In a large pot of boiling, salted water, cook the bow ties until just done, about 15 minutes. Drain. Rinse with cold water and drain thoroughly.

4. Toss the pasta with the shrimp, avocado dressing, minced onion and radishes. Garnish with the onion slices and cilantro leaves.

Spinach and Smoked-Salmon Pasta Salad with Lemon Cream Dressing

Simple and elegant, this salad requires very little time to prepare. The dressing—lemon juice, cream, salt and pepper—couldn't be easier and is a perfect match for the smoked salmon.

SERVES 4

¾	pound fusilli
1	tablespoon olive oil
½	pound sliced smoked salmon, cut into ½-inch strips
1	pound spinach, stems removed, leaves washed and cut into ½-inch pieces
¼	cup minced red onion
2	tablespoons chopped fresh flat-leaf parsley
2	tablespoons chopped fresh chives
2	tablespoons chopped fresh dill
¼	cup lemon juice, from about 2 lemons
1	cup heavy cream
½	teaspoon salt
⅛	teaspoon fresh-ground black pepper

WINE RECOMMENDATION:
OREGON PINOT GRIS AND SMOKED SALMON SEEMS SUCH A CLASSIC COMBINATION THAT IT'S HARD TO BELIEVE THE WINE HAS ONLY BEEN MADE THERE FOR THE PAST TWENTY-FIVE OR SO YEARS. IN ANY CASE, IT IS THE PERFECT CHOICE HERE WITH THE SALMON AND WITH THE DRESSING. A FRENCH PINOT GRIS FROM ALSACE IS ALSO ACCEPTABLE, BUT THE OREGON VERSION IS WORTH A SEARCH.

1. In a large pot of boiling, salted water, cook the fusilli until just done, about 13 minutes. Drain, rinse with cold water and drain thoroughly.

2. In a large bowl, toss the pasta with the oil. Add the smoked salmon, spinach, onion, parsley, chives and dill.

3. Whisk the lemon juice with the heavy cream, salt and pepper. Pour over the salad and toss.

Seafood Salad with Lemon Vinaigrette

A generous quantity of lemon juice makes this seafood mélange fairly sparkle with fresh flavor. We have chosen mussels, squid and shrimp, but you could prepare the dish with just one of your favorite shellfish or substitute crab, lobster or scallops.

SERVES 4

⅓ cup lemon juice, from about
    2 lemons
⅓ cup chopped fresh flat-leaf parsley
1   clove garlic, minced
1   teaspoon salt
¼ teaspoon fresh-ground black pepper
⅔ cup olive oil
1   pound mussels, scrubbed and
    debearded
½ cup white wine or water
1   pound cleaned squid
1   pound medium shrimp
¾ pound fusilli

WINE RECOMMENDATION:
MATCH THE EXUBERANT FLAVORS IN THIS DISH WITH A MUSCADET FROM THE LOIRE VALLEY IN FRANCE. WITH ITS PÉTILLANCE (A SLIGHT, PRICKLY, BUBBLY SENSATION) AND ACIDITY, IT WILL WORK WELL WITH THE VARIOUS SHELLFISH FLAVORS AND THE LEMON. TRY TO FIND THE MOST RECENT VINTAGE AVAILABLE SINCE THIS IS A WINE IN WHICH FRESHNESS IS PRIZED.

1. In a large bowl, whisk the lemon juice with the parsley, garlic, salt and pepper. Add the oil slowly, whisking.

2. Discard any mussels that are broken or do not clamp shut when tapped. In a large pot, combine the mussels and wine. Cover and bring to a boil over high heat. Cook, shaking the pan occasionally, just until the mussels begin to open, about 3 minutes. Remove the open mussels and continue to cook, uncovering the pot as necessary to remove the mussels as soon as their shells open. Discard any mussels that do not open. Remove the mussels from their shells and add them to the dressing.

3. Cut the squid bodies into ¼-inch rings. Cut the tentacles into halves or

quarters, depending on their size.

4. Bring a large pot of salted water to a boil. Add the squid and cook just until it turns opaque, about 1 minute. Remove the squid with a slotted spoon and add it to the dressing.

5. In the same pot of boiling water, cook the shrimp until just done, about 2 minutes. Drain and shell. Cut each shrimp into 2 or 3 pieces and add to the dressing.

6. In a large pot of boiling, salted water, cook the fusilli until just done, about 13 minutes. Drain, rinse with cold water and drain thoroughly. Toss with the seafood.

SHRIMP AND THEIR FLAVORFUL SHELLS

Shrimp shells are loaded with flavor that the flesh absorbs when the shrimp are cooked unpeeled. Shrimp cooked in their shells also stay moist because the shell protects the meat from drying out. If, for practical reasons, shrimp must be peeled before cooking, reserve the shells and use them, if possible, to add flavor to the sauce, as in Penne with Garlicky Shrimp and Chorizo, page 166, and Noodle Cakes with Shrimp and Roasted-Chile Sauce, page 169.

Rice-Noodle Salad with Pork, Sizzled Leeks and Crisp Sweet-Potato Strips

Rice flour is used to make these fine white noodles, available in Asian markets and the Asian-food section of most large supermarkets.

SERVES 4

½ pound dried rice noodles, medium width or fine*

½ pound lean pork shoulder or loin

1 shallot, minced

2 cloves garlic, minced

¼ cup Asian fish sauce (nam pla or nuoc mam)*

1 tablespoon sugar

2 cups plus 1 tablespoon cooking oil

¼ teaspoon fresh-ground black pepper

1 small red chile pepper, minced, or ¼ teaspoon dried red-pepper flakes

½ teaspoon grated lime zest

¼ cup lime juice, from about 3 limes

2 teaspoons minced fresh ginger

3 tablespoons water

4 leeks, white and light-green parts only, cut into matchstick strips, washed and dried well

1 sweet potato, cut into matchstick strips

¼ cup chopped fresh mint

¼ cup chopped fresh cilantro

¼ cup chopped peanuts

* Available in Asian markets

WINE RECOMMENDATION:
A SIMPLE, REFRESHING WHITE WINE WILL GO BEST WITH THE COMPLEX FLAVORS OF THIS SALAD. TWO VERY DIFFERENT CHOICES ARE A YOUNG FRASCATI FROM ITALY OR A HALBTROCKEN RIESLING FROM THE MOSEL-SAAR-RUWER IN GERMANY.

1. In a large bowl, cover the rice noodles with cold water and leave until softened, 20 to 30 minutes. Drain and set aside.

2. Cut the pork into ⅛-inch-wide slices. Stack the slices and cut them into ½-inch-wide strips about 2 inches long. In a medium bowl, combine the shallot, half the garlic, 1 tablespoon of the fish sauce, 1 teaspoon of the sugar, 1 teaspoon of the oil and the pepper. Add the pork and toss to coat. Set aside to marinate.

3. In a small bowl, combine the remaining garlic, 3 tablespoons fish sauce, 2 teaspoons sugar, the chile, lime zest, lime juice, ginger and water. Set aside.

4. In a medium saucepan, heat 2 cups of the oil to 325°. Fry the leeks, a handful at a time, until lightly browned

271

and crisp, 2 to 3 minutes. Remove with a slotted spoon and drain on paper towels. Next, fry the sweet-potato strips in two or three batches until browned and crisp, about 4 minutes. Remove with a slotted spoon and drain on paper towels.

5. In a large pot of boiling, salted water, cook the rice noodles until just done, 1½ to 2 minutes. Drain. Rinse with cold water and drain thoroughly.

6. In a wok or large frying pan, heat the remaining 2 teaspoons oil over moderately high heat until very hot. Add the pork and marinade and cook, stirring, until lightly browned and cooked though, 2 to 3 minutes. Transfer to a large bowl.

7. Add the noodles and lime mixture to the pork and toss. Just before serving, add the leeks, sweet potato and chopped herbs and toss again. Top with the peanuts and serve.

—Marcia Kiesel

ASIAN FISH SAUCE

Called variously *nam pla* in Thailand, *nuoc mam* in Vietnam, *patis* in the Philippines, *petis* in Indonesia, *tuk trey* in Cambodia and *ngan-pya-ye* in Burma, fish sauces differ only slightly from country to country, and you can use them interchangeably. Made from fermented fish, the sauce is often a critical flavoring in an Asian dish. Because the cooking times in Far Eastern cuisines are generally short, fish sauce adds the depth of flavor that Western cuisines achieve with long, slow simmering. Although the smell of fish sauce is a strong one to Westerners, it dissipates with cooking. On its own the sauce tastes pungent, but when mixed into a dish, it lends mellowness. If you can't find fish sauce, soy sauce is another ingredient that rounds out the flavor of a dish, and, if necessary, you can substitute it in equal amounts.

Grilled-Chicken Pasta Salad with Tarragon and Shallot Dressing

An ideal summertime dish, this is also good in winter made with broiled chicken, rather than grilled, and cherry tomatoes, the only kind that seem to be any good during the cold months.

SERVES 4

6	tablespoons white-wine vinegar
1	teaspoon Dijon mustard
1¾	teaspoons salt
	Fresh-ground black pepper
⅔	cup olive oil
2	shallots, minced
3	tablespoons chopped fresh tarragon
1½	pounds boneless, skinless chicken breasts
¾	pound bow ties
1	pound tomatoes, about 2, seeded and diced (2 cups), or 1 pound cherry tomatoes, halved

WINE RECOMMENDATION: LOOK FOR A YOUNG SAUVIGNON BLANC FROM SANCERRE OR POUILLY FUMÉ IN THE LOIRE VALLEY OF FRANCE. WHATEVER YOU CHOOSE SHOULD HAVE PLENTY OF ACIDITY TO STAND UP TO THE DRESSING.

1. In a large bowl, whisk the vinegar with the mustard, 1½ teaspoons of the salt and ¼ teaspoon pepper. Add the oil slowly, whisking. Add the shallots and 2 tablespoons of the tarragon.

2. Light the grill. Season the chicken breasts with the remaining ¼ teaspoon salt and a pinch of pepper. Grill 3 to 6 inches from the heat until just done, about 5 minutes per side. Alternatively, broil the chicken. Cut into thin slices across the grain. Add the warm chicken to the dressing.

3. In a large pot of boiling, salted water, cook the pasta until just done, about 15 minutes. Drain, rinse with cold water and drain thoroughly. Toss with the chicken. Just before serving, add the tomatoes and the remaining 1 tablespoon tarragon.

273

Asian Noodle Salad with Chicken

Chicken, snow peas, cilantro and peanuts, tossed together with a spicy Asian dressing, make a colorful salad that tastes as lively and refreshing as it looks.

SERVES 4

1   pound chicken breasts on the bone

4   quarter-size slices of fresh ginger and 1½ teaspoons minced fresh ginger

4   scallions including green tops, 2 whole, 2 minced

¾   teaspoon salt

½   pound snow peas, each cut diagonally into 3 pieces

¼   cup cooking oil

¼   cup rice-wine vinegar* or white-wine vinegar

2   tablespoons soy sauce

1   tablespoon Asian sesame oil

¼   cup chopped fresh cilantro, plus whole leaves for garnish

1   clove garlic, minced

1   teaspoon sugar

¼   teaspoon dried red-pepper flakes

½   pound dried Chinese egg noodles*

½   cup peanuts, chopped

1   lime, cut into wedges

*Available in Asian markets

1. In a medium saucepan, combine the chicken, ginger slices, whole scallions and ½ teaspoon of the salt. Add enough cold water to cover and bring to a simmer over moderately high heat. Reduce the heat and simmer until the chicken is cooked through, about 15 minutes. Remove the chicken. When it is cool enough to handle, remove the meat from the skin and bones. Cut the meat into thin slices across the grain.

2. Bring a pan of salted water to a boil and add the snow peas. Return just to a boil and drain. Rinse with cold water and drain thoroughly.

3. In a small bowl, combine the minced ginger and scallions, the cooking oil, vinegar, soy sauce, sesame oil, chopped cilantro, garlic, sugar, red-pepper flakes and remaining ¼ teaspoon salt.

4. In a large pot of boiling, salted water, cook the noodles until just done, about 7 minutes. Drain. Rinse with cold water and drain thoroughly.

5. In a large bowl, toss the chicken, snow peas, dressing, noodles and ¼ cup of the peanuts. Top with remaining ¼ cup peanuts and garnish with the cilantro leaves. Serve with the lime wedges.

BETTER THAN STORE-BOUGHT

The salads in refrigerated deli cases look beautiful but can taste beastly. You can make much better ones at home by adding the dressing at the last minute and avoiding refrigeration as much as possible. Pasta salads are not quite as delicate as mixed green salads, but the sooner they're served after dressing, the better. When tossed ahead of time, they tend to dry out because the pasta absorbs the dressing. And refrigeration changes the pasta's texture—not for the better. If you need to prepare a pasta salad ahead, combine everything but the dressing and mix in a spoonful of oil to prevent the pasta from sticking together. Remove from the refrigerator half an hour before serving and toss with the dressing at the last minute.

Slivered-Pork and Radicchio Salad

A mustard and caper dressing highlights this simple mixture of pork, pasta and radicchio. The combination makes an extraordinary salad.

SERVES 4

⅔ cup plus 2 tablespoons olive oil
2 tablespoons plus 1 teaspoon Dijon mustard
1¼ teaspoons salt
Fresh-ground black pepper
1 pound pork loin
¾ pound bow ties
1 head radicchio, about ¾ pound
¼ cup red-wine vinegar
1 shallot, chopped
1 tablespoon drained capers

WINE RECOMMENDATION: PAIR THE TANGY AND BITTER FLAVORS OF THIS SALAD WITH THE ASSERTIVE TASTE OF A YOUNG SAUVIGNON BLANC. LOOK FOR MEDIUM-BODIED VERSIONS FROM EITHER CALIFORNIA OR NEW ZEALAND.

1. Heat the oven to 450°. In a small bowl, combine 2 tablespoons of the oil, 1 tablespoon of the mustard, ¼ teaspoon of the salt and a pinch of pepper. Coat the pork loin with this mixture. Put in a baking pan and roast until just done, about 35 minutes. Cut into thin slices. Stack and cut the slices into thin slivers.

2. In a large pot of boiling, salted water, cook the bow ties until just done, about 15 minutes. Drain. Rinse with cold water and drain thoroughly.

3. Halve the radicchio and cut out the core. Cut the leaves into bite-size pieces.

4. In a food processor, puree the remaining 4 teaspoons mustard, 1 teaspoon salt and ½ teaspoon pepper, the vinegar, shallot and capers. With the machine running, gradually pour in the remaining ⅔ cup oil.

5. Toss all ingredients in a large bowl.

Spicy Vegetarian Buckwheat-Noodle Salad

The soy-orange dressing and crisp vegetables are a perfect match for the nutty flavor of soba noodles. If you use a shrink-wrapped English cucumber, or any other unwaxed variety, leave the peel on. If the skin feels waxy and you can scrape a ribbon of wax off with your thumbnail, better remove the peel.

SERVES 4

½   pound soba (dried Japanese buckwheat noodles)*
2   tablespoons sesame seeds
¼   cup fresh orange juice, from about 1 large orange
½   teaspoon grated orange zest
2   tablespoons soy sauce
1   teaspoon grated fresh ginger
2   teaspoons white vinegar
1½   teaspoons Asian sesame oil
½ to 2 teaspoons chili oil*
½   teaspoon sugar
½   teaspoon salt
¼   teaspoon fresh-ground black pepper
½   pound green cabbage, or Chinese cabbage, shredded (about 2 cups)
1   medium cucumber, seeded and cut into matchstick strips (about 1½ cups)
5   radishes, cut into matchstick strips (about ½ cup)

*Available in Asian markets

WINE RECOMMENDATION:
THE RUSTIC BUCKWHEAT NOODLES AND ASIAN FLAVORS OF THIS SALAD WILL BE GOOD WITH AN ACIDIC, SLIGHTLY SWEET WHITE WINE FROM GERMANY, SUCH AS A SPÄTLESE RIESLING OR GEWÜRZTRAMINER. THE FRENCH VERSION OF GEWÜRZTRAMINER FROM ALSACE IS ANOTHER POSSIBILITY.

1. In a large pot of boiling, salted water, cook the noodles until just done, about 5 minutes. Drain. Rinse with cold water and drain thoroughly.

2. In a small frying pan over moderate heat, toast the sesame seeds until golden brown, 3 to 4 minutes. Remove and let cool.

3. In a large bowl, combine the orange juice, orange zest, soy sauce, ginger, vinegar, sesame oil, chili oil, sugar, salt and pepper. Add the noodles, cabbage, cucumber and radishes and toss. Serve topped with the sesame seeds.

—Marcia Kiesel

20-Minute Pasta

Also see:

Vermicelli with Scallion Cream

This rich pasta makes an elegant first course or a delicious side dish with chicken or veal. The flavor of scallion comes through clearly yet is delicate.

SERVES 6 AS A FIRST COURSE

2	tablespoons butter
½	cup minced scallions (1 large bunch), white and light-green parts only
½	teaspoon salt
½	cup Chicken Stock, page 29, or canned low-sodium chicken broth
1	cup heavy cream
¼	teaspoon fresh-ground black pepper
¾	pound vermicelli or angel hair

WINE RECOMMENDATION:
A RICH, FULL-BODIED CHARDONNAY FROM EITHER CALIFORNIA OR AUSTRALIA WILL WORK NICELY ALONGSIDE THIS CREAMY DISH.

1. In a small frying pan, melt the butter over moderately low heat. Add the scallions and salt. Cook, stirring occasionally, until the scallions are very soft, about 5 minutes.

2. Add the stock, increase the heat to moderately high and simmer until the stock is reduced to almost a glaze, 3 to 5 minutes. Stir in the cream and bring to a simmer. Cook until slightly thickened, 2 to 3 minutes. Add the pepper.

3. In a large pot of boiling, salted water, cook the pasta until just done, about 9 minutes for vermicelli or 3 minutes for angel hair. Drain.

4. Toss the pasta with the sauce and serve.

—Judith Sutton

Spaghettini with Garlic and Oil

The great things about this simple classic are that it's quick and easy and that the variations are limitless. Try our versions, below, or come up with your own. You might toss in different herbs or any number of possible ingredients such as diced mozzarella or sun-dried tomatoes.

SERVES 4

¾   pound spaghettini
5   tablespoons olive oil
2   large cloves garlic, minced
⅛   teaspoon dried red-pepper flakes
     (optional)
2   tablespoons chopped fresh flat-leaf
     parsley
½   teaspoon salt
⅛   teaspoon fresh-ground black pepper

WINE RECOMMENDATION: Look for a full-bodied, fruity Italian white wine, such as Vernaccia di San Gimignano from Tuscany or Arneis from the Piedmont region.

1. In a large pot of boiling, salted water, cook the spaghettini until just done, about 9 minutes.

2. Meanwhile, heat the oil in a small pan over moderately low heat. Add the garlic and pepper flakes and cook, stirring, until the garlic softens, about 1 minute. Drain the pasta. Toss with the garlic and oil, parsley, salt and pepper.

VARIATIONS ON THE THEME

Add any of the following (or a combination) to the basic recipe above.

◆ ¼ cup grated Parmesan cheese and 1 extra tablespoon olive oil (also good in combination with any of the other variations)
◆ 6 tablespoons chopped fresh basil
◆ 2 teaspoons chopped fresh rosemary
◆ 1 tablespoon dried sage

◆ ½ ounce dried porcini mushrooms, soaked in ½ cup hot water, drained, rinsed and chopped (reserve the soaking water, strain it and add it to the pasta as well)
◆ 6 anchovy fillets, minced, or 1½ teaspoons anchovy paste (excellent combined with the porcini mushrooms)

Fettuccine Alfredo

Simple and delicious, this classic pasta has a creamy sauce flavored with Parmesan cheese and just a pinch of grated nutmeg. Add a salad and you have a perfect supper.

SERVES 4

¾   pound fettuccine
3   tablespoons butter
1   cup heavy cream
    Pinch grated nutmeg
¼   teaspoon salt
⅛   teaspoon fresh-ground black pepper
½   cup grated Parmesan cheese, plus more for serving

 WINE RECOMMENDATION: LOOK FOR A LUSH, FULL CHARDONNAY FROM EITHER CALIFORNIA OR AUSTRALIA TO PAIR WITH THIS RICH DISH.

1. In a large pot of boiling, salted water, cook the fettuccine until just done, about 12 minutes.

2. Meanwhile, heat the butter and cream in a small saucepan. Add the nutmeg, salt and pepper.

3. Drain the fettuccine. Toss with the cream sauce and Parmesan. Serve immediately with extra Parmesan cheese.

Orecchiette with Radicchio and Arugula

The thick, ear-shaped pasta called *orecchiette* (literally, *little ears*) remains chewy even when completely cooked. The fresh arugula is added last to this colorful dish so that it holds its piquant flavor and bright emerald hue.

SERVES 4

¾ pound orecchiette
1 head radicchio (about ¾ pound)
⅓ cup olive oil
4 cloves garlic, minced
¼ cup balsamic vinegar
¾ teaspoon salt
¼ teaspoon fresh-ground black pepper
¾ pound arugula, stems removed and leaves cut into ½-inch strips
Grated Parmesan cheese, for serving

FIRST, BOIL THE WATER

A chef once told us that the first thing he does when he walks into the kitchen is put on a pot of water to boil. "You always need it eventually, and it saves time later on." That advice goes double with pasta. The recipes in this chapter are so quick to put together that you can prepare the sauce in the time it takes the water to boil and the pasta to cook.

WINE RECOMMENDATION:
THE LEAFY VEGETABLES WILL PAIR WELL WITH AN ASSERTIVE, HIGH-ACID WHITE WINE. TRY A YOUNG RIESLING FROM THE ALTO ADIGE REGION OF ITALY OR FROM THE ALSACE REGION OF FRANCE.

1. In a large pot of boiling, salted water, cook the orecchiette until just done, about 15 minutes.

2. Meanwhile, cut the radicchio in half and cut out the core. Cut the leaves into bite-size pieces.

3. In a large frying pan, heat the oil over moderately high heat. Add the radicchio and garlic. Cover and cook, stirring occasionally, until the radicchio wilts, about 2 minutes. Add the balsamic vinegar, salt and pepper and cook, uncovered, until the vinegar is syrupy, about 1 minute. Remove the pan from the heat.

4. Drain the orecchiette. Toss the orecchiette, radicchio and arugula just until the arugula wilts. Serve with Parmesan.

Pappardelle with Porcini and Garlic

You can hardly miss with this classic blend of sautéed mushrooms, garlic, parsley and Parmesan. It's good on almost any kind of pasta.

SERVES 4

¾   pound pappardelle

¼   cup olive oil

1   pound porcini or other wild mushrooms, trimmed and sliced

4   cloves garlic, lightly crushed

1   teaspoon salt

¼   teaspoon fresh-ground black pepper

¾   cup Chicken Stock, page 29, or canned low-sodium chicken broth

2   tablespoons butter

3   tablespoons chopped fresh flat-leaf parsley

¼   cup grated Parmesan cheese, plus more for serving

WINE RECOMMENDATION:
LOOK FOR A RUSTIC, FULL-BODIED RED WINE TO MIRROR THE EARTHY FLAVORS OF THIS DISH. TRY AN AGED (FIVE TO TEN YEARS OLD) BARBARESCO FROM ITALY'S PIEDMONT REGION OR A CHÂTEAUNEUF-DU-PAPE FROM THE SOUTHERN RHÔNE IN FRANCE.

1. In a large pot of boiling, salted water, cook the pappardelle until just done, about 12 minutes.

2. Meanwhile, heat 2 tablespoons of the oil in a large frying pan over moderately high heat. Add half the porcini, 2 cloves garlic, ½ teaspoon salt and ⅛ teaspoon of the pepper. Cook, stirring occasionally, until lightly browned, 3 to 5 minutes. Remove the porcini and discard the garlic. Repeat with the remaining oil, porcini, garlic, ½ teaspoon salt and ⅛ teaspoon pepper. Return all the porcini to the pan and add the stock, butter and parsley. Simmer over moderate heat for 1 minute.

3. Drain the pasta. Toss with the mushroom sauce and the Parmesan. Serve with additional grated cheese.

—Lidia Bastianich
Felidia

Fettuccine with Shiitakes in a Saffron Cream Sauce

Golden saffron sauce and full-flavored mushrooms make this pasta deliciously luxurious. Serve it for an elegant first course, in which case it's enough for six, or with a salad for a fast dinner. The dish is also good without the saffron.

SERVES 4

¾	pound fettuccine
1½	cups dry white wine
1	teaspoon saffron threads, lightly packed
2	tablespoons olive oil
4	tablespoons butter
4	shallots, chopped
1½	pounds shiitake mushrooms, stems removed, caps sliced
1	teaspoon salt
¼	teaspoon fresh-ground black pepper
2	cups heavy cream
¼	cup grated Parmesan cheese
¼	cup chopped fresh flat-leaf parsley

WINE RECOMMENDATION:
THE SUMPTUOUS FLAVORS OF THIS DISH WILL GO WELL WITH AN EXPANSIVE WHITE WINE WITH SOME OAK, SUCH AS A CALIFORNIA OR AUSTRALIAN CHARDONNAY.

1. In a large pot of boiling, salted water, cook the pasta until just done, about 12 minutes.

2. Meanwhile, bring the wine to a boil in a small saucepan and add the saffron. Remove from the heat and let infuse for 5 minutes.

3. In a large frying pan, heat the oil and butter over moderate heat. Add the shallots, mushrooms, salt and pepper and cook until very lightly browned, about 5 minutes. Add the wine and saffron and boil for 2 minutes. Add the cream, bring to a boil, reduce the heat and simmer until slightly thickened, about 2 minutes.

4. Drain the pasta. Toss it with the sauce, Parmesan and parsley.

Spaghetti with Fresh Tomatoes, Basil and Mozzarella

Refreshing and light, this is a perfect pasta for a hot summer day. Serve it warm or at room temperature.

SERVES 4

¾   pound spaghetti
1½ pounds tomatoes, about 3, seeded and cut into ½-inch dice (3 cups)
½   pound fresh mozzarella at room temperature, cut into ¼-inch dice
¾   cup chopped fresh basil, plus whole leaves for garnish
6   tablespoons olive oil
2   teaspoons red-wine vinegar
1   clove garlic, minced
1   teaspoon salt
½   teaspoon fresh-ground black pepper
3   tablespoons grated Parmesan cheese

1. In a large pot of boiling, salted water, cook the spaghetti until just done, about 12 minutes.

2. Meanwhile, combine the tomatoes, mozzarella, basil, oil, vinegar, garlic, salt and pepper in a large bowl.

3. Drain the pasta and toss with the tomato and cheese mixture. The heat of the spaghetti will soften the cheese slightly.

4. Sprinkle with the Parmesan and garnish with the basil leaves.

Fettuccine with Basil and Almonds

Try this Sicilian specialty in the summer when both basil and tomatoes are plentiful.

SERVES 4

¾   pound fettuccine
5   tablespoons olive oil
4   cloves garlic, minced
2   tablespoons fresh bread crumbs
¼   cup finely chopped almonds
1½   pounds tomatoes, about 3, peeled, seeded and cut into ¼-inch strips (3 cups)
½   cup chopped fresh basil
1   teaspoon salt
¼   teaspoon fresh-ground black pepper

WINE RECOMMENDATION: CHOOSE A LIGHT, CRISP AND ADAPTABLE WHITE WINE TO STAY OUT OF THE WAY OF THIS COMBINATION OF TOMATOES, BASIL AND ALMONDS. TRY A RECENT VINTAGE OF SOAVE OR ORVIETO, BOTH FROM ITALY.

1. In a large pot of boiling, salted water, cook the fettuccine until just done, about 12 minutes.

2. Meanwhile, in a medium frying pan, heat 3 tablespoons of the oil over moderate heat. Add the garlic and cook, stirring, for 1 minute. Add the bread crumbs and almonds and cook until the mixture is golden, about 3 minutes.

3. Stir in the remaining 2 tablespoons oil, the tomatoes, basil, salt and pepper and cook for 1 minute.

4. Drain the pasta. Toss it with the sauce.

—Odette Fada
Rex Il Ristorante

Fettuccine with Toasted Pine Nuts

Toasting pine nuts enhances their flavor, and here the strong herbal taste of parsley complements their richness. Serve the fettuccine as a light main course or as an attractive accompaniment to roast chicken.

SERVES 4

¾ pound fettuccine
6 tablespoons butter
⅓ cup pine nuts
3 tablespoons chopped scallions, including green tops
3 tablespoons chopped fresh flat-leaf parsley
1½ teaspoons salt
¼ teaspoon fresh-ground black pepper

WINE RECOMMENDATION: JUST ABOUT ANY CHARDONNAY FROM CALIFORNIA OR AUSTRALIA WILL BE A DELIGHTFUL ACCOMPANIMENT TO THE RICH BUT SUBTLE FLAVOR OF THE PINE NUTS IN THIS DISH.

1. In a large pot of boiling, salted water, cook the fettuccine until just done, about 12 minutes.

2. Meanwhile, melt the butter in a medium frying pan over moderate heat. Add the pine nuts and cook, stirring occasionally, until lightly browned, about 5 minutes.

3. Add the scallions, parsley, salt and pepper and cook 1 minute longer.

4. Drain the fettuccine. Toss it with the pine-nut mixture.

—Jamie Davies
Schramsberg Vineyards

Pasta about Nuts

We're nuts about this unusual recipe contributed by Chef Bob Williamson from Carmel, California. Almond butter, available at health-food stores, lends an intense, nutty taste to the pasta while the pistachios and pine nuts add their own flavors and a pleasant crunch.

SERVES 4

2   tablespoons almond butter*
½   cup hot water
2   tablespoons butter
1   shallot, minced
1   clove garlic, minced
⅓   cup shelled pistachio nuts
⅓   cup pine nuts
1½   teaspoons salt
¼   teaspoon fresh-ground black pepper
¾   pound angel hair
⅓   cup grated Asiago cheese, plus more
     for serving

* Available in health-food stores

WINE RECOMMENDATION: THE RICHNESS OF THE NUTS AND BUTTER WILL BE BEST SERVED BY A FULL-BODIED WHITE WINE. TRY A NOT OVERLY OAKY CALIFORNIA CHARDONNAY OR, FOR A SPLURGE, A VILLAGE-LEVEL WHITE BURGUNDY.

1. In a small bowl, combine the almond butter and hot water.

2. In a medium frying pan, melt the butter over low heat. Add the shallot and garlic and cook, stirring occasionally, until soft, about 2 minutes. Raise the heat to medium, add the pistachios and pine nuts and cook until the nuts brown, about 5 minutes longer. Stir in the salt and pepper.

3. In a large pot of boiling, salted water, cook the pasta until just done, about 3 minutes. Reserve about ½ cup of the cooking water. Drain the pasta. Toss with the almond-butter mixture, the nuts and grated cheese. If the pasta seems dry, add some of the hot pasta water. Serve at once with additional grated cheese.

—Bob Williamson
The Covey

Penne with Tuna and Fennel

Delicious with fennel, this dish is also excellent without it—great for when you come home late and want to make something out of just what's in the cupboard. You can substitute another type of macaroni for the penne rigate.

SERVES 4

¾	pound penne rigate
3	tablespoons olive oil
3	garlic cloves, sliced thin
2	medium fennel bulbs, sliced crosswise
¾	teaspoon salt
¼	teaspoon fresh-ground black pepper
2	6-ounce cans tuna packed in olive oil
¼	cup chopped fresh flat-leaf parsley

WINE RECOMMENDATION: Drink a light and easygoing white wine with this dish, such as a Verdicchio from Italy or a Vinho Verde from Portugal.

1. In a large pot of boiling, salted water, cook the penne until just done, about 13 minutes.

2. Meanwhile, heat the oil in a medium saucepan over moderate heat. Add the garlic, fennel, salt and pepper and cook, stirring occasionally, until the fennel is softened and slightly golden, about 10 minutes. Reduce the heat to low and stir in the tuna with its oil, breaking it into small pieces.

3. Reserve ¼ cup of the pasta water. Drain the penne. Toss with the tuna sauce and parsley. If the pasta seems dry, stir in some of the reserved pasta water.

—Judith Sutton

Spaghettini with Pine Nuts and Spicy Scallops

Here's a special dish with just one trick: Don't overcook the scallops, or you'll have little rubber balls. Use angel hair, spaghetti or linguine in place of the spaghettini if you like.

SERVES 4

¼	cup pine nuts
¾	pound spaghettini
5	tablespoons olive oil
1	pound sea scallops
6	cloves garlic, minced
4	scallions, cut into thin slices, white and green portions kept separate
2	tablespoons chopped fresh flat-leaf parsley, plus ½ cup whole leaves
½	teaspoon dried red-pepper flakes, or more to taste
1	teaspoon salt

SCALLOPS HAVE TOUGH MUSCLES

Attached to each scallop is a small but powerful crescent-shaped muscle. It's often left on, which is why some people think scallops are chewy. Remove this tough little customer. It peels right off.

WINE RECOMMENDATION:
A SIMPLE BUT RICH WHITE, SUCH AS PINOT BLANC FROM ALSACE IN FRANCE, WILL WORK WELL WITH THE SWEETNESS OF THE SCALLOPS YET STAND UP TO THE HEAT OF THE RED-PEPPER FLAKES.

1. In a small frying pan, toast the pine nuts over moderate heat, stirring, until lightly browned, about 5 minutes. Remove.

2. In a large pot of boiling, salted water, cook the spaghettini until just done, about 9 minutes. Drain.

3. While the pasta cooks, heat 1 tablespoon of the oil in a large nonstick frying pan over moderately high heat. Add the scallops and sear until brown on the bottom, 1 to 2 minutes. Turn the scallops and sear until brown on the other side, another minute or two. Remove the scallops from the pan and cut them into quarters.

4. Reduce the heat to moderate. Heat the remaining 4 tablespoons oil in the pan used to toast the pine nuts. Add the garlic, white scallion slices, chopped parsley, red-pepper flakes and salt. Cook,

stirring, until the scallions soften, about 2 minutes.

5. Drain the spaghettini. Toss the pasta with the toasted pine nuts, scallops, scallion mixture, scallion greens and parsley leaves.

—Diana Sturgis

THREE KINDS OF PINE NUTS

While there are numerous varieties of pine nuts, the three most commonly available in North America are the European pignoli from Italy, Spain and Portugal, the Chinese pine nut and the piñon grown in Colorado. The long, narrow European pignoli have the most delicate flavor. They are also the most expensive of the three, running even higher in price than macadamia nuts. Shorter, darker Chinese pine nuts, often sold as "pine kernels," have a distinctive pine flavor. The price is about half to two-thirds that of pignoli. Colorado piñon are often sold as "Indian nuts," usually in the shell. Their color, shape and flavor are similar to those of the Chinese. The price falls between that of the European and the Chinese. Be forewarned that the shell is hard to crack; people use their teeth since the nuts are too small for most nutcrackers. For cooking, we recommend the Chinese nuts because they're reasonably priced and easy to work with. Splurge on pignoli when you want to be absolutely true to a recipe or when making a dish so delicate in flavor that the difference might be noticeable. Piñons are good for snacking.

Broccoli, Garlic and Anchovy Pasta

Excellent fresh broccoli is now available year round. Here it makes a simple chunky sauce that catches between the spokes of the wagon-wheel pasta so that you get just the right amount in each bite.

SERVES 4

¾ pound wagon wheels

1½ pounds broccoli

½ cup olive oil

3 cloves garlic, minced

1 teaspoon anchovy paste

¼ teaspoon dried red-pepper flakes, or more to taste

1 teaspoon salt

½ cup grated Parmesan cheese, plus more for serving

WINE RECOMMENDATION:
LOOK FOR AN ASSERTIVE WHITE WINE TO STAND UP TO THE ANCHOVY, GARLIC AND HOT PEPPERS HERE. A GOOD CHOICE WOULD BE A YOUNG GEWÜRZTRAMINER FROM ALSACE OR A CHENIN BLANC FROM CALIFORNIA.

1. In a large pot of boiling, salted water, cook the pasta until just done, about 12 minutes.

2. Meanwhile, trim off the dry ends of the broccoli stalks. Peel the stems. Cut the stems and florets into ½-inch pieces. Cook the broccoli in a large saucepan of boiling, salted water until just tender, about 4 minutes. Drain.

3. In a large frying pan, heat the oil over moderate heat. Add the garlic and cook until it softens, about 1 minute. Stir in the anchovy paste and red-pepper flakes and cook 1 minute longer. Add the broccoli and salt and cook 4 minutes longer, mashing until half the broccoli is reduced to a thick puree and the rest is left in small chunks. A potato masher works well for this.

4. Toss the pasta with the broccoli and cheese. Serve with extra Parmesan.

Pepperoni Penne

Pizza isn't the only thing that benefits from the hot and salty tang of pepperoni. Brought together by a tomato-flecked cream sauce, penne and pepperoni prove to be perfect partners.

SERVES 4

¾   pound penne rigate
½   pound pepperoni
2   cloves garlic, minced
1   pound tomatoes, about 2, peeled, seeded and chopped (2 cups)
1   cup light cream
½   teaspoon salt
¼   teaspoon fresh-ground black pepper
3   tablespoons chopped fresh flat-leaf parsley
     Grated Parmesan cheese, for serving

WINE RECOMMENDATION:
DRINK A YOUNG, LIGHTHEARTED RED WINE WITH THIS DISH, SUCH AS A CHIANTI FROM ITALY OR A BEAUJOLAIS FROM FRANCE.

1. In a large pot of boiling, salted water, cook the penne until just done, about 13 minutes.

2. Meanwhile, cut the pepperoni lengthwise into quarters and then crosswise into slices about ⅛-inch thick. In a medium frying pan, sauté the pepperoni over moderately high heat until golden, about 2 minutes. Discard all but 3 tablespoons of the fat.

3. Stir the garlic into the pan and cook 30 seconds. Add the tomatoes and cook for 5 minutes. Reduce the heat to low. Stir in the cream, salt and pepper and simmer 1 minute.

4. Drain the pasta. Toss with the pepperoni sauce and parsley. Serve with Parmesan cheese.

Spaghettini with Fresh Tomatoes, Prosciutto and Fried Scallions

Fried scallions and the buttery, salty taste of prosciutto lend depth to this fresh-tasting sauce of barely cooked tomatoes.

SERVES 4

	Cooking oil, for frying
8	scallions including green tops, 4 cut into 2-inch-long matchstick strips and 4 chopped
¾	pound spaghettini
3	tablespoons olive oil
1	tablespoon butter
1½	pounds tomatoes, about 3, peeled, seeded and cut into ½-inch dice (3 cups)
1	teaspoon salt
2½	ounces thin-sliced prosciutto, cut into ½-inch strips
⅛	teaspoon fresh-ground black pepper

WINE RECOMMENDATION: A YOUNG, FRUITY, ACIDIC RED WINE, SUCH AS A BEAUJOLAIS FROM FRANCE OR A DOLCETTO FROM ITALY, WILL COMPLEMENT THE FLAVORS OF THE MAIN INGREDIENTS OF THIS DISH.

1. In a small saucepan, heat ½ inch of cooking oil until very hot, about 350°. Add half of the scallion strips to the oil and fry until tinged with brown, about 1 minute. Drain on paper towels. Repeat with remaining scallion strips.

2. In a large pot of boiling, salted water, cook the spaghettini until just done, about 9 minutes.

3. Meanwhile, in a medium saucepan, heat the olive oil and butter over moderate heat. Add the chopped scallions and cook, stirring, until softened, about 2 minutes. Add the tomatoes and the salt and heat, stirring, just until warm.

4. Drain the spaghettini. Toss the pasta with the tomato mixture, prosciutto and pepper. Serve topped with the fried scallions.

—Jane Sigal

WHAT'S "COOKING OIL"?

When we call for cooking oil in recipes, we mean readily available, reasonably priced nut, seed or vegetable oil with a high smoking point, such as peanut, sunflower, canola, safflower or corn oil. These oils can be heated to about 400° before they begin to smoke, break down and develop an unpleasant flavor. Olive oil has a lower smoking point than the above mentioned oils. While it can certainly be used to sauté over moderate heat, it's not the ideal all-purpose cooking oil.

THE BEST PROSCIUTTO

Prosciutto from Parma, Italy, is generally considered the best, and it's the only imported type commonly available in North America. Prosciutto di Parma, raw, air-dried ham cured with salt and seasonings, has a full, sweet flavor and boasts the highly desired D.O.C. (Denominazione di Origine Controllata), the official Italian stamp of authenticity. Domestic prosciutto is produced by a number of companies in the United States and Canada, but, as good as these products are, the difference between them and imported Italian prosciutto is noticeable. Italian prosciutto usually has superior flavor and texture. This is due partially to ideal air-drying conditions, especially in the hills around Parma. The lengthy Italian finishing process, which lets the hogs mature longer before butchering, also affects flavor and texture. The Italian ham is a little more expensive, but it's worth the price if you're serving prosciutto on its own. For cooking, domestic is fine.

Bow Ties with Prosciutto and Sage Sauce

Fresh sage leaves combine with toasted walnuts and sautéed prosciutto in a garlic-scented olive oil—so simple, yet so good. If you can't get fresh sage, sauté one teaspoon dried sage with the garlic.

SERVES 4

¾ pound bow ties
3 tablespoons butter
1 tablespoon chopped fresh sage, or 1 teaspoon dried
3 tablespoons olive oil
3 cloves garlic, lightly crushed
5 ounces thin-sliced prosciutto, cut into fine strips
½ cup chopped walnuts
¾ cup grated Parmesan cheese
½ teaspoon fresh-ground black pepper

WINE RECOMMENDATION: IT'S BEST TO DRINK A SIMPLE BUT FULL-BODIED WHITE WINE ALONGSIDE THIS RUSTIC DISH. LOOK FOR A PINOT BIANCO FROM THE ALTO ADIGE OR FRIULI REGION OF ITALY OR SEEK OUT ITS FRENCH COUNTERPART, PINOT BLANC FROM ALSACE.

1. In a large pot of boiling, salted water, cook the bow ties until just done, about 15 minutes.

2. Meanwhile, melt the butter with the sage in a small saucepan.

3. In a large frying pan, heat the oil over low heat. Add the garlic cloves and cook until golden, about 7 minutes. Remove and discard the garlic.

4. Add the prosciutto and walnuts and cook, stirring occasionally, until the walnuts are lightly toasted and the prosciutto begins to brown, 6 to 8 minutes. Remove from the heat.

5. Drain the pasta. Toss with the sage butter, prosciutto mixture, cheese and pepper.

—Nancy Verde Barr

Bow Ties with Salami and Salsa Verde

Pungent with the flavors of capers, anchovies, garlic and salami, this pasta is a satisfying main dish or a perfect accompaniment to grilled meats. It's equally good hot, warm or room temperature.

SERVES 4

1	cup fresh flat-leaf-parsley leaves
2	tablespoons capers, rinsed
6	anchovy fillets
2	cloves garlic, chopped
½	cup olive oil
1½	teaspoons red-wine vinegar
¼	teaspoon fresh-ground black pepper
¾	pound bow ties
¼	pound salami, cut into ¼-inch cubes

WINE RECOMMENDATION: A LIGHT, CRISP WHITE WINE WILL PAIR WELL WITH THIS HIGHLY SEASONED PASTA. LOOK FOR A PINOT GRIGIO FROM ITALY OR A CÔTES DE GASCOGNE FROM SOUTHWESTERN FRANCE.

1. In a food processor or blender, puree the parsley, capers, anchovies and garlic with the oil, vinegar and pepper.

2. In a large pot of boiling, salted water, cook the pasta until just done, about 15 minutes. Drain. Toss with the parsley mixture and salami.

—Jan Newberry

SALAMI

Salami from Italy is not allowed in the United States. Many domestic brands, though, are close approximations. Common Italian-style salami types are: Genoa—garlicky, soft; Milano—mild, hard; Sicilian—peppery, hard; and Toscano (closest to Italian-made)—somewhat peppery, full flavored, hard, coarse grind. According to Carmine Dellaporta of Dean & DeLuca, the famed New York food shop, although domestic salami can be delicious, those produced in Italy are often superior, especially because of their wonderful aroma. He attributes their fragrance to Italian drying conditions—most notably the special combination of sea breezes and mountain air found in the Emilia-Romagna region.

Penne with Broccoli Rabe and Sausage

The somewhat bitter flavor of broccoli rabe is mellowed with mild Italian sausage, chicken stock and a pat of butter.

SERVES 4

¾   pound penne
3   tablespoons olive oil
6   ounces mild Italian sausage, casings removed
2   cloves garlic, minced
1   pound broccoli rabe, florets and tender stems and leaves only, washed
¼   teaspoon dried red-pepper flakes
¾   teaspoon salt
¾   cup Chicken Stock, page 29, or canned low-sodium chicken broth
2   teaspoons butter
6   tablespoons grated Parmesan cheese

WINE RECOMMENDATION:
AN ACIDIC AND SLIGHTLY FRUITY WHITE WINE IS MOST LIKELY TO WORK WELL WITH THE BITTER TASTE OF THE BROCCOLI RABE. TRY A YOUNG RIESLING FROM ITALY'S FRIULI REGION OR A YOUNG CHENIN BLANC FROM ONE OF A NUMBER OF APPELLATIONS IN THE LOIRE VALLEY IN FRANCE.

1. In a large pot of boiling, salted water, cook the penne until just done, about 13 minutes.

2. Meanwhile, heat 1 tablespoon of the oil in a large frying pan over moderately high heat. Add the sausage and cook, breaking up the meat, until brown, about 3 minutes. With a slotted spoon, remove the sausage. Discard all but 1 tablespoon fat.

3. Reduce the heat to moderate. Add the remaining 2 tablespoons oil to the pan. Add the garlic and cook, stirring, until it softens, about 1 minute. Add the broccoli rabe with any water that clings to the leaves after washing, the red-pepper flakes and salt. Cover and cook for 5 minutes, stirring occasionally. Stir in the sausage, stock and butter and cook over high heat until the sauce reduces slightly, about 3 minutes. ➤

4. Drain the pasta. Toss with the broccoli-rabe mixture and 3 tablespoons of the Parmesan. Serve topped with the remaining 3 tablespoons Parmesan.

—Lidia Bastianich
Felidia

BROCCOLI RABE

While broccoli rabe (also called broccoli rape) may look like it's a part of the common broccoli plant, it's actually a separate, slightly bitter vegetable related to the turnip. Rappini, another variety of the same family, is less bitter. Broccoli rabe has long been used in Italian cuisine and was introduced to the American market in the '80s. Buy it in winter, the height of its season.

GIVE EGGS A BREAK

The chance of finding an egg infected with salmonella bacteria is variously estimated at fewer than one in 10,000 to fewer than one in 14,000 for the Northeast and Mid-Atlantic regions. (For all other regions, the statistics are far better.) Moreover, the chance of actually getting sick is estimated at one in a million. Almost all the cases of food poisoning reported to the Centers for Disease Control involving eggs result from improper handling of eggs at restaurants and institutions. In most incidents large batches of raw eggs have been held for hours in a warm kitchen. Bacteria can run rampant in such conditions. Cases attributed to egg dishes made at home are rare.

Of course the very safest way to eat eggs is cooked. Salmonella bacteria is killed when food is kept at 140° for three-and-a-half minutes. Thus any method of cooking eggs that sets the white and begins to thicken the yolk will do the trick. Risk of infection increases with raw or lightly cooked eggs, but only slightly. They should be either made into something with a high acid content, such as mayonnaise, or eaten within an hour of preparation. You needn't give up eating dishes such as Spaghetti alla Carbonara, opposite page, made at home, unless you are very young or old, ill or in another group that has trouble fighting infection, or if you're pregnant. Otherwise, the truth is that you're more likely to be kicked by a donkey than to get sick from an egg.

Spaghetti alla Carbonara

This classic Italian dish is a flavorful mixture of pancetta (the Italian version of bacon), Parmesan cheese, eggs and parsley. The heat of the pasta cooks the eggs slightly, producing a creamy sauce.

Serves 4

- ¾ pound spaghetti
- 2 tablespoons olive oil
- 2 tablespoons butter
- ¼ pound pancetta or bacon, cut into ¼-inch squares
- 2 cloves garlic, lightly crushed
- ⅓ cup dry white wine
- 2 eggs
- ½ cup grated Parmesan cheese
- ½ teaspoon salt
- ½ teaspoon fresh-ground black pepper
- 2 tablespoons chopped flat-leaf parsley

PANCETTA

Usually sold rolled up like a jelly roll, pancetta should be about half-and-half meat and fat. It comes from the belly of the pig, as does bacon, but pancetta isn't smoked. It's cured in a mixture of salt, pepper and cloves. You can use bacon in place of pancetta. If you want to remove the bacon's smoky flavor, blanch it in boiling water for three minutes and then drain.

WINE RECOMMENDATION:
Either a white or red wine will work with this simple, soothing pasta. Look for young vintages of either the white Orvieto or the red Dolcetto d'Alba, both from Italy.

1. In a large pot of boiling, salted water, cook the spaghetti until just done, about 12 minutes.

2. Meanwhile, heat the oil and butter in a small frying pan over moderate heat. Add the pancetta and garlic and cook until the pancetta is brown but not crisp, about 4 minutes. Add the wine and simmer until reduced to about 3 tablespoons. Remove the pan from the heat and discard the garlic.

3. In a large bowl, whisk together the eggs, cheese, salt and pepper.

4. Drain the pasta. Add it to the egg-and-cheese mixture and toss quickly. Pour the pancetta mixture over the spaghetti. Add the parsley and toss just until mixed. Serve immediately.

Tortellini with Prosciutto and Snow Peas

Snow peas are a refreshing addition to this prosciutto cream sauce. We call for frozen tortellini, but any shape of stuffed pasta you like will make a good backdrop to the flavorful sauce.

SERVES 4

1	tablespoon butter
2	cloves garlic, minced
1	cup heavy cream
¼	teaspoon salt
¼	teaspoon fresh-ground black pepper
¼	pound snow peas, cut into ¼-inch diagonal slices
2	ounces thin-sliced prosciutto, cut into fine strips
2	tablespoons chopped fresh flat-leaf parsley
¾	pound frozen cheese tortellini Grated Parmesan cheese, for serving

WINE RECOMMENDATION: LOOK FOR A RICH WHITE WINE TO MATCH THE CREAMY SAUCE. A GOOD CHOICE WOULD BE A WHITE CÔTES DU RHÔNE FROM FRANCE OR A CHARDONNAY FROM CALIFORNIA.

1. In a large frying pan, melt the butter over moderately low heat. Add the garlic and cook, stirring, until softened, about 1 minute. Add the cream, salt and pepper. Bring to a simmer and cook until slightly thickened, 2 to 3 minutes.

2. Add the snow peas and cook, stirring, until the peas are just tender, about 2 minutes. Add the prosciutto and parsley and cook over low heat, 1 to 2 minutes longer. Set aside.

3. In a large pot of boiling, salted water, cook the tortellini until just done, about 8 minutes. Reserve ¼ cup of the pasta water. Drain. Return the sauce to low heat. Add the tortellini and cook 1 to 2 minutes to allow the tortellini to absorb some of the sauce. If the sauce seems too thick, stir in some of the reserved pasta water. Serve with Parmesan cheese.

—Judith Sutton

"BLT" Pasta

We like this dish in the spring when piquant arugula (the lettuce of this BLT) is abundant. Cherry tomatoes work well here because they're good all year.

Serves 4

¾   pound fusilli
½   pound bacon, cut crosswise into
    ½-inch-wide pieces
24 cherry tomatoes, halved
1   teaspoon salt
¾   teaspoon fresh-ground black pepper
2   large bunches arugula (about ½
    pound), stems removed, and leaves cut
    crosswise into ¼-inch strips
2   tablespoons butter
2   tablespoons olive oil
1   scallion including green top, cut into
    thin slices
    Grated Parmesan cheese, for serving

WINE RECOMMENDATION: Try to find a straightforward white wine with some body to stand up to the acidity of the tomatoes and the saltiness of the bacon in this dish. A good choice from Alsace in France is pinot blanc; from America, look for a California chenin blanc.

1. In a large pot of boiling, salted water, cook the fusilli until just done, about 13 minutes. Meanwhile, cook the bacon in a large frying pan, stirring occasionally, until golden brown and just crisp, about 5 minutes. Remove and drain on paper towels. Pour off all but 1 teaspoon of the bacon fat.

2. Add the tomatoes, salt and pepper to the pan. Cook over moderate heat, stirring, until the tomatoes soften slightly, about 3 minutes. Add the arugula and cook until just wilted, about 1 minute.

3. Reserve ½ cup of the pasta water. Drain the pasta. Over moderate heat, stir the bacon, pasta and the reserved pasta water into the tomato mixture. Stir together until warmed through, about 1 minute. Stir in the butter and olive oil. Top with the sliced scallions. Serve with Parmesan cheese.

—Judith Sutton

Index

Page numbers in **boldface** indicate photographs

D

E

F

G

H

T

THANKS TO

Cardel, 621 Madison Avenue, New York, NY 10022 for:
"Vence" goblet by Baccarat, page 56; "Acorn" fork by Georg Jensen, page 149; "Imperiatrice Eugenie" dinner plates by Haviland, page 230; "Nacre" dinner plate and "Variations" salad plate by Puiforcat, page 280; "Chalice" wine glass by Dartington, page 290

The L•S Collection, 765 Madison Avenue, New York, NY 10021 for:
"Wind Over Water" platter by Izabel Lam, page 110; "Lily" soup plate by R. Wilhite, and napkin, page 162; "Alexandria" dinner plates by R. Wilhite and flatware by Robert Venturi, page 178

CONTRIBUTORS

Jody Adams is the executive chef at Michela's in Cambridge, Massachusetts.

Nancy Verde Barr is a food writer and cooking teacher and is the author of *We Called It Macaroni* (Knopf).

Paul Bartolotta is the executive chef at Spiaggia in Chicago.

Lidia Bastianich is chef/owner of Felidia and co-owner of Becco, both in New York City.

Richard Benz is the executive chef at Gautreau's in New Orleans.

Ida Bobrow is a home cook with over fifty years cooking experience.

Michael Chiarello is chef/owner of Tra Vigne in St. Helena, California, and is Culinary Director of Napa Valley Kitchens, also in St. Helena.

Scott Cohen is the executive chef at Tatou in New York City.

Jamie Davies is the co-owner and vice president of Schramsberg Vineyards in Calistoga, California.

Erica De Mane is a food writer and chef in New York City who specializes in Italian cooking.

Odette Fada is the executive chef at Rex Il Ristorante in Los Angeles.

Mike Fennelly is the executive chef and co-owner of Mike's on the Avenue in New Orleans. He is the author of *East Meets Southwest* (Chronicle Books) and is working on his second book.

Carol Field is a food writer and the author of *The Italian Baker* (HarperCollins), *Celebrating Italy* (Morrow), *Italy in Small Bites* (Morrow) and the forthcoming *Focaccia* (Chronicle Books).

Jim Flint is an avid home cook specializing in Italian cuisine.

Susanna Foo is chef/owner of Susanna Foo Chinese Cuisine in Philadelphia and is the author of a forthcoming cookbook tentatively titled *Susanna Foo Chinese Cuisine* (Chapters).

Susan R. Friedland is a senior editor at HarperCollins. She wrote the recipes for *The Jewish-American Kitchen* by Raymond Sokolov (Stewart, Tabori and Chang), and is the author of *Ribs* (Harmony), *Caviar* (Scribners) and *The Passover Table* (HarperCollins).

James Galileo is the executive chef and co-owner of Oceana in New York City.

George Germon and **Johanne Killeen** are chefs/owners of Al Forno in Providence, Rhode Island, and the authors of *Cucina Simpatica* (HarperCollins).

Joan Husman and **Catherine Whims** are chefs/owners of Genoa in Portland, Oregon.

Susan Shapiro Jaslove is a food writer and recipe developer in New York City.

Marcia Kiesel is the associate director of *Food & Wine* magazine's test kitchen and co-author of *Simple Art of Vietnamese Cooking* (Prentice Hall).

Jan Newberry is a food writer and a senior editor of *The Great Taste Low Fat* cookbook series for Time-Life Books.

Charles Palmer is chef/owner of two restaurants, Aureole and Chefs Cuisiniers Club, both in New York City. He writes a quarterly newsletter called *C. C. Club News* and is the author of the forthcoming *Great American Food: Cooking with Charles Palmer* (Random House). He is co-owner with Jonathan White of Egg Farm Dairy in Peekskill, New York.

Grace Parisi is a chef, food writer and food stylist in New York City.

Alfred Portale is chef/owner of Gotham Bar and Grill in New York City.

Jimmy Schmidt is chef/owner of The Rattlesnake Club and co-owner of Stelline and other restaurants, all in the vicinity of Detroit, Michigan.

Jane Sigal is a cookbook editor and the author of *Normandy Gastronomique* (Abbeville) and the forthcoming *Backroad Bistros*, *Farmhouse Fare* (Doubleday).

Diana Sturgis is the test-kitchen director of *Food & Wine* magazine.

Judith Sutton is a food writer and freelance chef in New York City.

Bob Williamson is the executive chef of The Covey at Quail Lodge, Carmel, California.